The Athenian Sun in an African Sky

To my family
Kevin and Eleanor Wetmore,
Lisa, John, and Sean Fitzgerald,
Tom and Eileen Wetmore,
Forest Wetmore,
and my partner and soulmate
Maura Chwastyk,
without whose support
(in all senses of the word)
none of this would
have been possible.

The Athenian Sun in an African Sky

*Modern African Adaptations
of Classical Greek Tragedy*

by KEVIN J. WETMORE, JR.

McFarland & Company, Inc., Publishers
Jefferson, North Carolina, and London

Library of Congress Cataloguing-in-Publication Data

Wetmore, Kevin J., Jr., 1969–
    The Athenian sun in an African sky : modern African adaptations
of classical Greek tragedy / by Kevin J. Wetmore, Jr.
      p.   cm.
    Includes bibliographic references (p.) and index.
    ISBN 0-7864-1093-0 (softcover : 50# alkaline paper) ∞
    1. African drama (English)—History and criticism.
2. Greek drama (Tragedy)—Adaptations—History and criticism.
3. Greek drama (Tragedy)—Appreciation—Africa.   4. African
drama (English)—Greek influences.   I. Title.
PR9343.W48   2002
822'.91409896—dc21   2001042564

British Library cataloguing data are available

Manufactured in the United States of America

On the cover: *The Song of Jacob Zulu* by Tug Yourgrau
(Photograph © Jack Mitchell)

McFarland & Company, Inc., Publishers
  Box 611, Jefferson, North Carolina 28640
   www.mcfarlandpub.com

ACKNOWLEDGMENTS

Much hard work and assistance by many fine people helped to make this project what it is. I owe a debt of gratitude to a veritable nation of individuals and groups who gave time, thought, ideas and effort. Any errors in this book are, alas, my own.

Thanks to my teachers: Richard Boon, Amanda Price, Denis Brutus, J. Thomas Rimer, Attilio "Buck" Favorini, Keiko McDonald, and most of all Martin Banham, who introduced me to the study of African theatre and served as inspiration, and Kiki Gounaridou, whose advice, guidance, feedback and insights served only to strengthen myself and the project.

Thanks to my colleagues and friends, whose input and support were invaluable: Christina Petrillo, Neil Bose, Ashley Wells, Javon Johnson, Derrick L. Sanders, Mark Southers, Jon Farris, Peter Pauze, Cynthia Turnbull, Brian Graves, Marilyn Sundin, Rob Ganders, Brian and Marjorie Gill, and Maxine. Support for this study was also provided by *Each One Tell One* and Denison University and I am duly grateful to the powers that be in both organizations.

Thanks to the National English Literary Museum in Grahamstown, South Africa. Curators Paulette Coetzee and Debbie Landman provided much material and information, and gave me time and support for my research. Curator Anne Torlesse was extremely helpful in securing photographs and permissions. The NELM and its wonderful curators do excellent and valuable work and I encourage the support of this fine institution.

Thanks to Femi Osofisan for the use of the unpublished version of *Tegonni* and his insights. Thanks as well to Athol Fugard for his communication during a very busy time. I am grateful to Danny Moleko, formerly of Northwest Arts, for his time and insights.

Many fine people also assisted in securing photographs to accompany the text. I am grateful to Jack Mitchell, Ashley Wells, Pat Miller, Theater Emory, the Market Theatre, Genevieve Cutts, Ruphin Coudyzer, and Christie Kasson and Keith Boone of Denison University.

CONTENTS

INTRODUCTION

The Library Doors of Classical Africa

Let me play with the white man's ways,
Let me work with the white man's brains,
Let my affairs themselves sort out,
Then in sweet rebirth
I'll rise a better man,
Not ashamed to face the world.

Young Africa's Plea
Chief Dennis Osadebay

On library doors
I'll knock aloud and gain entrance
To the strength
Of nations past and present and will read.
I'll brush the dust from ancient scrolls
And drinking deep of the Pyrrhean stream,
Will go forward and do and dare.

Young Africa's Resolve
Chief Dennis Osadebay

The five dozen or so countries that comprise Africa are artificial constructs created by the European partition of Africa, occasionally linking together very different (and sometimes violently oppositional) ethnic groups into single nation-units. Colonialism and its lasting legacy are perhaps the single greatest factor in the development of modern African culture in general and African theatre in particular. Written drama as

1

recognized by the West did not exist in Africa before colonization. Indeed, the Yoruba people of West Africa did not have a written language until the early 19th century, when one was developed in conjunction with the invading Europeans. However, there were (and still are) a variety of traditional performance forms, all of which contain elements common to Western ideas of theatre. Festival, rites of passage, masquerades, storytelling, music, narrative, dance, the use of puppets, dolls, masks and costumes, and other social and celebratory rituals all inform the contemporary (postcolonial) theatre of Africa. Yet Western models of dramaturgy as well, especially Shakespeare, Brecht, and the naturalist/realist playwrights now also inform this theatre. The pervasive influence of Western literature is one of the major issues in contemporary African literary and theatrical criticism, including debates on language ("Can truly 'African' literature be written in a colonial language such as English or French?"), audience ("Is the writer aiming to be 'universal,' thereby appealing to European and American audiences, or writing for a specifically African audience?"), influences (for example, Biodun Jeyifo has accused Wole Soyinka of being too influenced by European models), and resistance to colonialism and neocolonialism.

A trend that has grown since the independence of many African countries in the early 1960s, however, is the use of Greek tragedy as model, influence, and inspiration by African theatre artists. It is a movement that has spawned a number of productions and adaptations in the past four decades. The reasons for the apparent connection between contemporary Africa and ancient Athens are many and varied. Martin Banham, writing in the introduction to *The Cambridge Guide to African and Caribbean Theatre*, states, "The roots of theatre in Africa are ancient and complex and lie in the areas of community festival, seasonal rhythms, and religious ritual..." (3). As with Greek tragedy, African theatre is community-based with a strong connection to ritual origins. The similarity of function and form between the theatres of Africa and Athens becomes more apparent when one considers the political, social, and religious aspects and contexts of those theatres. Greek tragedy is also a less stigmatized model, as it is both ancient and, although imported with colonialism, not originally part of the imperial cultures which colonized Africa.

These answers, however, do not account for the rich and complex cross-cultural exchanges occurring not only between cultures but also between historic periods. The debate is further complicated and compounded by the complex history of the study of the relations between Greece and Africa. In books such as Martin Bernal's *Black Athena*, Afrocentric theories of the origins of Western civilization in general and Greek culture in particular are proposed. A number of scholars have challenged these theories, such as Mary Lefkowitz in *Not Out of Africa* and *Black Athena Revisited*. Afrocentric classicism implies that African adaptation of Greek tragedy is, in fact, reappropriation of Afro-Greek culture by Africans; but this opinion remains hotly contested.

The question then is what role Afrocentric classicism plays in the adaptation of Greek texts to African contexts. Furthermore, even if it does play a role, does that matter to the indigenous audiences? *The Cambridge Guide to African and Caribbean Theatre* claims that in regard to adaptations, "their audiences neither know nor care about the originals..." (72). This fact would seem to imply that the adaptations do not generate any meaning for the indigenous audience by contrasting the text of the original with the new text, but rather generate meaning solely on their own terms.

One can also claim that the Greek material serves as an outside matrix of interpretation, a frame upon which the indigenous experience can be explored from without, yet not necessarily from an imperialist European point of view. Thus, Greek adaptations become plays of self-exploration and colonial resistance. They generate meaning by rejecting Eurocentrist interpretation and indigenous explanation, and rather explore the modern African experience through a hybrid of classical Europe and contemporary Africa. Such plays are not only cross-cultural, but also cross-temporal, using material two and a half millennia old to comment on contemporary political and social situations in an entirely different culture from the source culture and an entirely different historical period from the original.

The first two chapters of this book engage these theories and the history of Greece and Africa. The first chapter, "Africa's Classical Legacy — Athens' African Legacy," briefly explores the cross-cultural currents between Greece and Africa in classical times and the manner in which that history has been constructed, deconstructed, and reconstructed by classicists, both Afrocentric and Eurocentric since that period.

The second chapter, "Attic Tragedy — Afric Tragedy," examines the cultural similarities between ancient Athens and colonial Africa which predispose Greek theatre as a model for adaptation by African playwrights. Adaptation, cross-cultural, intercultural, and postcolonial theories are mined for their use in understanding the phenomenon. Tragic theory is then explored as a methodology for understanding African tragedy, initially focusing on Aristotle and the idea of *hamartia* and then subsequent Western theories of tragedy, finally examining African theories of tragedy.

The remaining chapters are organized along thematic lines, formalistic lines, and, in the case of *Antigone* and *The Oresteia*, surveys of individual plays. Although attention is paid to the place of these plays within their historic contexts, chronology is less important for the purposes of this study. The plays' initial Athenian contexts are considered, followed usually by an inquiry into the African cultural context into which the Greek tragedy is transculturated. Often, as will be seen, the result is a conceptually different understanding of human action or cultural values being highlighted by the different contexts: justice in *The Oresteia*, ritual sacrifice in *The Bacchae*, funerals and burial in *Antigone*, or fate in *Oedipus Rex*.

"Ritual, Roots, and Tragic Form," the third chapter, continues to explore the theories of the first two chapters within the specific contexts of plays which consciously experiment with ritual and tragic form. Wole Soyinka's *The Bacchae of Euripides* and John Pepper Clark's *Song of a Goat* by their very titles acknowledge a kinship with Greek antecedents.[1] Soyinka's theories of Yoruba tragedy are further considered in this chapter as well.

The fourth chapter, "The Voice of the Polis," focuses on adaptations which emphasize the political meaning of the play over the ritual elements. Ola Rotimi's *The Gods Are Not to Blame* (a Nigerian *Oedipus Rex*), Efua Sutherland's *Edufa* (a Ghanan *Alcestis*), and Guy Butler's *Demea* (a South African *Medea*) all use Greek originals to comment on political and social conditions in contemporary African society. The dramas do not so much play on form and ritual, as do those in the third chapter, but rather use the theme and message of the original to warn their audiences of political and social dangers.

"Orestes in South Africa," the fifth chapter, engages two plays which use the various versions of the story of Orestes in order to explore specific violent events in South African history. Athol Fugard's *Orestes* uses Euripides' play to dissect the psychology of action behind the John Harris bombing of 1964. Over two decades later, Tug Yourgrau and Ladysmith Black Mambazo dramatized the trial and execution of Andrew Zondo, an ANC guerrilla who bombed a shopping mall, through the lens of *The Oresteia* in *The Song of Jacob Zulu*. Both plays use the themes of justice, revenge, kinship, and the place of the law to illuminate the social, political, and cultural issues behind the violent resistance to apartheid in South Africa.

"African Antigones," the final chapter, explores the most popular Greek tragedy to be adapted in Africa. With more adaptations and productions of the original by university groups, touring companies, professional and community theatres than any other Greek tragedy (and quite possibly than all other Greek tragedies combined), *Antigone* is the tragedy

---

[1]Clark's title plays on the Greek word tragodoi, *which literally means "goat song."*

at the center of the Afro-Greek world. The play's themes of obedience to the gods, the power of the state, the rule of law, the struggle for power, and the damage done to individuals and society by political strife and unjust laws resonate powerfully within the modern African experience. Four different adaptations of *Antigone* are considered: *Odale's Choice* by Caribbean author Edward Kamau Brathwaite, writing in Ghana; *Tegonni*, Femi Osofisan's dialectical retelling of the story in which Greek Antigone meets her African "descendant" in late 19th-century Nigeria, originally performed in the United States; *The Island* by John Kani, Winston Ntshona, and Athol Fugard, in which two prisoners in South Africa act out the story of Antigone for their fellow inmates; and Congolese playwright Sylvan Bemba's *Black Wedding Candles for Blessed Antigone*, in which an African actress playing Antigone becomes a figurehead for revolution when her politician husband is assassinated.

For the purposes of this study I have embraced a variety of methodologies of analysis. As my intent is to examine the relationship between African adaptation, Greek original, and the cultural contexts of each, I have attempted to suit the methodology to the play. The overall goal is not to examine all of these plays using only a single theory or line of approach, but rather study the rich tapestry of thought, theory, and cultural contact which informs all of them. In other words, the theoretical net has been cast wide to hold the variety of adaptations contained herein.

This study attempts to engage many different cultures simultaneously. As Abiola Irele writes in *The African Experience in Literature and Ideology*, African literature is "a phenomenon which, by its nature, is irreducible to any sort of common measure" (23), which certainly makes the task of the scholar out to explore the manner in which African literature has engaged historic European literature significantly difficult. While this book is a survey of the different ways in which African playwrights have adapted Greek texts into African contexts, I have tried to avoid "pigeonholing," reductivism, or generalizing about African literature, theatre, or drama. Furthermore, Africa is the name of the continent; "Africa" actually refers to some 55 countries, hundreds of cultures, thousands of languages and dialects, and hundreds of millions of people. To say anything about "Africa" is to generalize about a very diverse body. Care has been taken to identify the very specific contexts of individual plays as well as the implications these specifics may have for the general. I have attempted to follow through on Irele's suggestion not to dissect the works of African literature and drama, but rather to "apprehend it in its complex resonances" (24).

The study of these adaptations is made more difficult by both the scope and size of the continent and the sheer amount of drama being written and theatre being performed on it, as well as the access and availability of material both inside and outside the individual nations. The drama that is published and available in Africa (let alone in the U.S. and Europe) is only a small fraction of the theatre actually occurring in Africa. It is impossible for any one person to locate, observe, investigate, and analyze all the connections between African theatre and Greek tragedy in all the productions in Africa. The plays considered in this volume represent some of the better-known examples, are written by some of the most significant dramatists, and, with one exception, have all been published. I make no claim for either comprehensive coverage of the phenomenon, or for having the last word on the subject. Please consider this work as a beginning, rather than a culmination of inquiry.

Unless otherwise indicated, all quotations from the original Greek tragedies are taken from *The Complete Greek Tragedies*, edited and translated by David Grene and Richmond Lattimore. Quotations from Greek tragedies are cited by line number, not page number.

Finally, to borrow a page from David Kerr, whose *African Popular Theatre* remains one of the best books on African drama to date, I must also call attention to the occasional "absence of strict orthographic accuracy" in the quoting of titles, character names, passages, and so on in languages such as Yoruba, isiZulu, Gikuyu, kwaSwahili, and Akan (x). The absence of particular diacriticals is dictated by the limitations of the author's word processor and in no way should be interpreted as an attempt to denigrate or anglicize these languages.

AFRICA'S CLASSICAL LEGACY—
ATHENS' AFRICAN LEGACY

And knowledge was scant,
Men called me Dark Africa.
Dark Africa?
I, who raised the regal pyramids
And held the fortunes of Conquering Caesars
In my tempting grasp.
Dark Africa?
Who nursed the doubtful child
Of civilization
On the wand'ring banks
Of the life-giving Nile,
And gave to the teeming nations
Of the West a Grecian gift.

— *My Africa*
Michael Dei-Anang

The Mediterranean world in the classical era was a sphere of active cultural exchange between Greece, Asia Minor, and North Africa. Many cultures intermixed and influenced each other. In the West, ancient Greece in general and Athens in particular are regarded as a crux in the history of Western civilization. The culture of cultural appropriation in this era, however, allows for many groups to claim the Greek heritage, or to claim the heritage is not Greek at all, having been appropriated from Egypt, or Asia, or Africa. The claims primarily can be divided into Eurocentric, or traditional, classicism and Afrocentric classicism.

Many groups want to claim the legacy of Greece. For example, Sierra

Leone refers to its capital, Freetown, as "the Athens of West Africa" (Maja-Pearce, 11). Classical Athens is the ideal. Classical Athens stands for excellence in politics, philosophy, art, and science. Classical Athens stands for cultural sophistication and true democratic freedom.

According to traditional classicists, over the course of two brief centuries one small geographic area in Southern Europe produced the beginnings of theatre, literature, political science, scientific inquiry, and philosophical thought which many consider to be the basis of Western culture and civilization. From the rise of the Romans to the present day the West has looked to the era of classical Greece as a "Golden Time," a period during which art, science, and philosophy were valued and developed. The Greeks provide a model to emulate: warriors, scientists, artists, and philosophers, their society was and is regarded as a milestone in the evolution of culture and civilization. As George Steiner notes in his study on *Antigone*, little is left for us to think about in terms of the human condition that did not originate with the Greeks (129).

Yet the "Golden Age" was golden for but a few. The reality of the Greek world was that only property-owning male citizens actually had any rights or power, had access to the culture that is so admired. Noble Athens was actually an imperial power that abused the trust put in it by the other members of the Delian League. Admittedly, however, as a model for "civilization," most Western cultures up to and including present day ones would find the reality to be an equally satisfactory model. Yet the myth of Athens as the first true democracy is one of the cornerstones of Western civilization. Athens and Greece are the origin point of who and what we citizens of the 20th and 21st centuries are, or, more accurately, who and what we claim to be.

The reality differs from the ideal. Much scholarly ink has been spilled about the interaction between cultures of the ancient Mediterranean and whether or not Greek culture originated with the Greeks or was appropriated from the Orient or Africa. In this chapter I will briefly explore the issues surrounding the historic interactions of Greece and Africa. I will then examine the history of that history, in other words, the different interpretations given to that interaction, Afrocentric and Eurocentric. Lastly, I will establish what impact, if any, the Afrocentric classicism has had on African adaptation of Greek tragedy.

Greek Colonization and the Greek Construction of Africa

Despite its democratic image, Athens was the first European colonial power. From the eighth to the sixth centuries B.C.E. a "great wave of colonization" moved from Greece to sites in Italy and Sicily (Starr, 216). Chester G. Starr claims that the primary reasons for Greek colonization were the economic advantages that colonies provided, the need for the migration of surplus population when the polis became overcrowded, and expanded agricultural needs resulting therefrom: places where much food could be grown to support the population of the polis, although "military and naval considerations also played a part" (217–18). Thus, Greek colonies were founded for very similar reasons as the later European ones: to increase the economic, military, and political power of the homeland.

In their histories and personal accounts of the colonial venture, the Greeks used linguistic and narrative strategies to describe their actions which were similar to those of the modern colonizers of Africa and the "New World." Carol Dougherty sees "many of the themes and narrative conventions prominent in European accounts of American settlement" in the Greek literature (4). Chief among these is the idea that the territory being settled is somehow "virgin." The expansion of the colonists, according to both ancient and modern narrative, is into empty, not occupied space. Dougherty writes of the "tendency to describe the colonial site as … an unoccupied territorial expanse waiting for the Greek settlers to bring order and civilization" (4). As the second half of the preceding quotation shows, the colonial mind must believe not only that it is moving into unoccupied space, but also that colonization brings civilization.

Examples of this mindset abound in European accounts of the colonization of Africa in the 19th century. Basil Davidson reports that Sir Charles Eliot, Britain's first High Commissioner to East Africa, "believed that the African continent was a tabula rasa for the European to deal with as he pleased" (*Genius*, 39). In other words, the Greek attitudes towards the land, peoples, and cultures which they were colonizing and whose space they were appropriating was very similar to the attitudes of the later European colonizers of Africa: they were bringing civilization to an unoccupied land.

However, we must also note that significant differences between the colonial activities exist as well. The manner in which the Greeks created a colony differs from the later imperial model, as the Greeks always followed the organizing principle of the polis. Starr notes that "each colony was founded as a polis," and the colony "usually was entirely independent of the home state" (218). While political and economic ties, as well as literally kinship ties, continued to exist between colony polis and home polis, both would work for mutual benefit, rather than the colony existing to serve and enrich the home state. Initially, at least, Greek colonial practice was less imperialism than expansionism.

During the second wave of colonization, however, in the era of Athenian imperialism, Greece grew to resemble 19th century Europe in practice and philosophy. The Athenian Empire, as an outgrowth of the Delian League, expanded to encompass colonies in Asia Minor, around the Black Sea, and surrounding the Aegean in the sixth and fifth centuries B.C.E. Unlike the alliances between home polis and colony polis of the previous era of Greek colonization, "Athens boldly and openly exploited its imperial position" (Starr, 311). Athens benefited from its imperial policies at the expense of its colonies. Money, raw materials, and allegiance flowed back to Athens, while the colonies received little material benefit in return.

Furthermore, unlike the earlier wave, this colonization also involved the deliberate imposition of Athenian cultural values. Frantz Fanon, author of the seminal *The Wretched of the Earth*, considers the Greeks the first European imperialists in that volume: "Europe ... had hellenized the Asians; she had created a new breed, the Greco-Latin Negroes" (8). Fanon further cites the historical irony of the European ideal of humanism, as first espoused by the Greeks, in the reality of colonial capitalism, which destroys humans and their culture (13–14). Fanon sees Athens as the first European colonial power.

Herein lies our first example of Afrocentric classicism: the dismissal of claims of Greek cultural superiority in the face of Athenian imperialism. Fanon is essentially correct in his supposition that the Greeks are the first European colonizers, but he invokes the comparison not to claim the legacy of Greece, but to demonstrate that the Europeans have always been exploiters of "the wretched of the earth." Fanon rejects Greece and its cultural heritage. He compares them to the Europeans who imposed their culture and values on Africa 2,000 years later.

Such comparisons are useful for contextualizing the historic relationship between Greece and Africa. In particular, the issue of language demonstrates the similarity between Athenian imperialism and later European imperialism. Many African writers tell stories of not being allowed to use their indigenous languages at school, of being beaten for speaking "tribal languages," of having to write in the colonial language in order to be understood by the various peoples in their own country because of the manner in which Africa was partitioned. Until recently, only Tanzania had an indigenous language as its official language. Almost all African countries use English, French, or Portuguese as the "official" language. Similarly, the ancient Greeks imposed their language on conquered lands. The Greeks referred to non–Greeks as "Barbarians," as they speak *bar bar*, nonsense. In other words, the ancient Greeks based people's identities and value on whether or not they spoke Greek; to not speak Greek was to be

different and inferior. Therefore, as Dougherty reports, Greek colonization "includes supplanting native speech as well" (159). The speakers of
bar bar were required to learn Greek in order to participate within the culture and society: "For language, that is the language of the colonist, is the
sign of culture and civilization. Confrontation with foreign peoples who
speak a different tongue demands strategies for dealing with such linguistic and cultural conflicts" (159). So writes Dougherty of the Greeks, but
the statement just as easily applies to the European attitudes towards Africa.
Ngugi wa Thiongo, Ola Rotimi, and Wole Soyinka, among others, have
written about the imposition of colonial language and the suppression of
indigenous tongues. The Greeks, in other words, behaved just as the Europeans did two millennia later: they imposed their language and its attendant culture and values on the peoples of the colonized lands while
simultaneously discouraging indigenous language and its attendant culture and values.

The arts became sites for representing the colonizers, the colonized,
and the positive side of the colonial process. Pindar's odes mention Africa
as a place in which the Greeks have taken the land as a man takes a wife.
Pindar was an aristocratic citizen of Thebes, and his odes celebrate athletic victory through colonial narrative. In *Pythia 9* Apollo goes to Africa,
forcibly takes a wife, and they produce a son who is a great hero. In line
8 Africa is referred to as "the third branch of the mainland earth," Europe
being the first and the second Asia. Apollo, a metaphor for Greece, forcibly
marries Africa and the result of this union is the good of all. Pindar closes:
"Therefore, be a citizen friend or opponent, let him not darken the thing
labored well for the good of all" (lines 93–4). This ode, while celebrating
athletic victory, compares that victory with successful colonization, celebrating colonialism, and observing that the consequences are "for the good
of all." Pindar's ode clearly demonstrates the attitude that colonization
brings civilization and is therefore of benefit to the colonized.

The theatre, as well, became a site in which colonized people could
be represented and constructed. Many of the Greek poleis have origin
myths, narratives that explain how and why the polis happened to come
into existence. Many of these narratives involve an ancestral figure that
came from somewhere else and created the city: witness Cadmus who first
"settled" Thebes. Dougherty observes that Greek theatre was "a suitable
context for exploring a city's colonial origins" (91). The ramification of
dramatizing a city's colonial origins (real or mythic) is to construct a positive view of colonialism. By dramatizing its colonial origin on the tragic
stage, a polis asserts that its own identity developed from the colonial
experience. Colonies are thus demonstrated to be the infant stage of a

civilization's development. This belief creates an evolutionary model of the development of cultures, a model very much in keeping with later European cultural attitudes. One need only look at *The Golden Bough*, or any of the early anthropological works, Cambridge school or otherwise, in order to see a belief in the evolution of cultures which, accordingly, implies that 19th century Africa was similar to Europe of 3,000 years earlier.

Africa was first represented on the Greek stage in the early tragedies. The Greeks were the first to "invent Africa" as V.Y. Mudimbe puts it in *The Idea of Africa* (xv). According to Mudimbe, the West "has been 'inventing' Africa for centuries" (xv). In their theatre the Greeks presented and represented Africa and Africans on stage. Neither the playwrights nor the actors were African. To the best of our knowledge, none of the tragedians had been to Africa. Yet in plays such as *The Suppliants* of Aeschylus and Sophocles' *The Aithiopes*, Africa was used as a setting and characters of African origin are represented. According to Afrocentic classicists, thus begins the representation of Africa as Other, of not allowing Africa and Africans to represent themselves.

The Greeks called Africa "Libya," and its denizens are Aithiopes or Aethiopes. This name is derived from "the proper name of Vulcan's son in Greek mythology," and "is the generic qualification of any dark-skinned person," claims Mudimbe (25). He cites "the power of the Greek paradigm" in the historic Western view of Africa, in which all non–Greeks (read "non–Europeans") were *agrioi* (savages) or *barbaroi* (non–Greek-speaking barbarians (71). If, as Mudimbe claims, the Greeks were the first to "invent Africa," they were not the last to invent an Africa inferior to themselves.

We should note that the Greek paradigm sees Africans as remote and foreign, exotic beings from Pindar's "third part of the earth." Yet, as with later European accounts of Africa, this paradigm is based solely on ignorance. Grace Beardsley in her seminal study of Africans in classical society admits that the "mythical Ethiopians" are "really Greek ... a product of the Greek imagination and a tradition of Greek literature" (9). Thus, the Greeks made up or assumed much about Africa due to a lack of real knowledge. Beardsley notes, "The absence of exact geographic knowledge really confused Greek writers" (1). Much of what was learned about Africa was either from encounters with Africans in Greece or secondhand accounts from those few who went to Africa. This fact bears out Mudimbe's contention that in the absence of true knowledge of Africa, the Greeks simply invented it.

For example, Hanno, a Carthaginian admiral, voyaged down the coast of Africa in 470 B.C.E., just ten years after the Athenians defeated the

Carthaginians at Himera in Sicily. His journey is recorded in *The Periplus*. He and his crew passed the Pillars of Heracles, and up an altar to Poseidon. They then journeyed "to the Horn of the South," a peninsula on the Western coast of Africa in present-day Sierra Leone (6). While there, they encountered "gorillae," which they killed and flayed, bringing the skins back to Carthage.

The journey took place in the fifth century B.C.E. and provided much information for Greek and Carthaginian historians who had not gone on the voyage themselves. It does not appear, however, that any Athenians or other Greeks voyaged significantly into sub–Saharan Africa, only into North Africa. By default, then, most information about Africa came through Africans living in Greek polis, who were, as Frank M. Snowden, Jr., observes in *Blacks in Antiquity*, not a significant number within the population (184).

In this same work Snowden argues that the Greek word "Aethiopian" specifically designates dark-skinned persons of African origin (vii), as opposed to persons of color from Asia Minor or the present day Middle East. Yet, in *Before Color Prejudice*, Snowden argues that "Aethiopia" specifically refers to the region of the Nile Valley South of the first cataract, which the Greeks also referred to as "Lower Nubia" (3). Thus, as noted above, the Greeks were uncertain about the geography and ethnicity of indigenous Africans. The Greeks do, however, distinguish between dark-skinned people from below Egypt and all other North African and Middle Eastern peoples, demonstrating an awareness of them as a separate group.

Aethiopians first appear in Homer, but historically are not encountered in large groups until 480 B.C.E. when Ethiopian mercenaries served in Xerxes' army. Then, during the rise of the Athenian empire, an increase in the number of Africans encountered occurred, both in Africa and in Greece. A fascination with things African by the Athenians was the end result of these meetings, and, as Snowden reports, the Athenian dramatists made use of the interest in distant peoples and events, bringing them closer to home by presenting them on stage (*Before*, 48). On stage, in art, and in literature a veritable plethora of Africans were represented to the Greeks by the Greeks. While the plays concerning "Aethiopians" have been mostly lost, the admittedly fragmentary evidence indicates a perception of African as wholly Other: "as black, as speaking a different tongue, and as living in Africa," claims Snowden (*Blacks*, 156). Thus, many Athenians encountered their first (and possibly only) Africans through the theatre, and those Africans were represented as different, foreign, and distant.

Snowden and Bearsley both conclude that the Greeks were not racist, at least not in the modern sense, and that skin color was not a factor in ascribing any attributes to a people. Color is "not an issue," even in plays concerned with African settings or Aethiopians (Snowden, *Before*, 48). Careful examination of the extant plays, such as *The Suppliants* of Aeschylus, confirms this fact. The Greeks, the Athenians in particular, were rather objective in their portrayal of Africa, "Aethiopians," and things African. Errors and misrepresentations were the result of ignorance, rather than of a malicious desire to misrepresent another ethnic group. The historians Herodotus and Diodorus admired Ethiopian justice and the reputation of Africans for skill in battle and resistance to outside domination. Nowhere in the material record is there any evidence of Greek racism or prejudice based upon a person's skin color or African origin.

Once the idea of people whose skin was dark became commonplace, Africans were accepted into the Athenian Empire under the same qualifications as everyone else. To the ancient Athenians, citizenship was the primary (and largely only) distinguisher between men. Any black-skinned person whose parents were citizens of Athens was also a citizen, with all rights and privileges. In short, the Greeks had no prejudice against Africans qua Africans, and Athenian imperialism notwithstanding, the Greek attitude towards Africans as people was significantly different from that of the Europeans who colonized Africa 2,000 years later. The ironic paradox of Greek theatre is that it both supported colonization but presented Africans objectively and without prejudice.

In an interesting reversal, Martin Bernal cites the Greek theatre as proof that the poleis of Greece were originally colonies of the Egyptians and Phoenicians. Bernal writes in the first volume of *Black Athena* that the city-states of the Peloponnesus were colonized people themselves, descended from the Egyptians and Afro-Asiatic peoples and cultures. This belief, that Greek culture is actually African in origin, is the central tenet of Afrocentric classicism. As proof, Bernal offers Aeschylus's *The Suppliants*, the very play which Snowden claims demonstrates the lack of racism in Athenians, as "the drama in which settlement on the Greek mainland is a central theme" (88). The play describes the arrival in Argos of the 50 daughters of Danaos, the titular suppliants fleeing Egypt. Bernal uses the play, among other evidence, to prove the existence of large waves of Egyptian colonization that the Greeks attempted to portray in inversion, with the Egyptians arriving as weak suppliants, rather than as powerful, invading conquerors (89). Yet, as noted above, the Greeks never tried to hide the colonial past of their cities. Rather they used their colonial pasts to justify their own colonial practice. The Greeks believed, however, that their colonial forebears were from other parts of Greece, not Africa or Egypt.

Hence, Bernal's contention that Aeschylus's play was part of a larger "cover up" of the African origins of Greek culture. It is the role of the Afrocentric classicist to dispute how much influence Africa had on the development of Greek culture.

Afrocentric Classicism

At the heart of Afrocentric classicism lie two beliefs: that the culture of ancient Greece (primarily Athens) is Egyptian in origin, and that the Egyptians were "Black Africans." The next step of the syllogism concludes that Western civilization, tracing its origins to Greece, is therefore actually African in origin. Martin Bernal, author of the three-volume *Black Athena: The Afroasiatic Roots of Classical Civilization,* is perhaps the best-known and most controversial theorist to explore these ideas, though he is by no means alone in his beliefs. In the first volume, subtitled *The Fabrication of Ancient Greece 1785–1985,* Bernal claims that Europeans rewrote classical history in order to deny a cultural connection between Greece and Africa. He proposes two models of Greek history: the "Aryan Model," which sees Greece as "essentially European or Aryan," and the "Ancient Model," which posits Greece "on the periphery of the Egyptian and Semitic cultural area," i.e., Africa and the Middle East (I:1). Bernal's very terminology demonstrates his ideology: "Aryan," suggesting a white-supremacist origin, and "Ancient," suggesting an older, more accurate view, which is in keeping with Bernal's claim of the reason for the shift in understanding. He claims the Aryan model was created to keep black slaves in Europe and America subjugated: "Another way of looking at these changes is to assume that *after the rise of black slavery and racism, European thinkers were concerned to keep black Africans as far as possible from European civilization*" (italics in original) (I: 30). In other words, Europeans began to rewrite the history of Greece when the slave trade began. Bernal attempts to reestablish the "Ancient Model," returning Greek culture to its true Afroasiatic origins and "lessen[ing] European cultural arrogance" (I: 73).

Bernal uses the festival of Dionysus in Athens, the origin of Greek tragedy, to prove a cultural link between Greece and Egypt. He cites the parallels between the Abydos Passion Play, an acting out of the death of Osiris in Egypt, and the festival of Dionysus (I: 65). Bernal puts great stock in the parallels between Osiris and Dionysus, claiming that "oracular ram/goat cults" in Egypt in the 20th century B.C.E. are associated with Amon and Osiris, whose "Greek equivalents" are Zeus and Dionysus (I: 64). Observing that "tragedy" comes from *tragos*, "goat," Bernal concludes that Greek tragedy must derive from the goat sacrifice rituals of Osiris of

Egypt (I: 65). If one believes Bernal, then the African continent is the motherland of drama as well, a fact that some African playwrights and theatre artists might seize upon, as we shall examine below.

In the second volume of *Black Athena*, subtitled *The Archeological and Documentary Evidence*, Bernal explains how the cult of Dionysus was "derived" from the cult of Osiris (II: 244). In the 12th dynasty of Egypt, the pharaoh Senwosre I (also called Sesostris) conquered much of the Egyptian world circa 1991 B.C.E., and served as model for Osiris in Egypt and Dionysus in Asia Minor and Greece (II: 238). Thus, claims Bernal, Dionysus is the mythologized version of Sesostris, a preservation of a cultural memory of the real, historic conquests of an Egyptian pharaoh that occurred more than a dozen centuries before the rise of Athens.

Bernal continues his hypothesis of Egyptian colonization, stating that "Kekrops" founded the city of Athens, and that the story of that founding is the narrative hidden within *The Suppliants* (II: 32). Bernal concludes that the Egyptians, who are "Black Africans" (whatever that may mean), founded colonies in Greece, and that Greek culture, including the drama, developed out of Egyptian culture, and the proof of all this is in linguistic, historic, and religious parallels between ancient Greece and ancient Egypt that European historians have tried to hide or disguise for the past three centuries.

Cheikh Anta Diop, of Senegal, argues the same case along both similar and different lines. In *Civilization or Barbarism?* he argues that three factors define cultural identity: historical ("cultural cement" which connects the past to the present, and requires knowledge of that past), linguistic (connection to a mother tongue, such as French, Spanish and Italian all developing from Latin), and psychological (what Diop calls "national temperament") (211–218). These three factors determine the identity of a culture and can establish unity or connections with other, related cultures.

Diop reasons that cultural identity proves African origins of Greek civilization. He asserts that "the Egyptians were Blacks," and, as this is "a conscious, historical fact," it cannot be disputed (2). He further posits that "Egypt was the quasi-exclusive teacher of Greece in all periods on the road to civilization," citing a definitive link between Dionysus and Osiris as an example (152). Lastly, in a chapter entitled "Greek Vocabulary of Black African Origin," Diop maintains that many religious, civic, and everyday words from ancient Greek have Egyptian etymologies. Having proven historic, linguistic, and "psychological" connections between Greece and Egypt, Diop claims ancient Greece as the cultural child of "Black Africa."

Difficulty arises in substantiating the claims of Diop and Bernal. Both would have Greece seen as the stepchild of African parents whom later

(European) historians claimed was self-generating, born fully formed like Athena from the head of Zeus, and not of African origin. Both offer circumstantial evidence and conspiracy theories to support their claims. Both also exhibit faulty logic and "fuzzy thinking," which argue against their claims.

Afrocentric classicists have at the center of their concern the issues of race and color. In *Black Zeus: African Mythology*, Edward L. Jones asserts three premises behind his study of Greece: "that Egypt was Africa; that the origins of the gods was Africa; and that since the gods were started by Africans and named by them, then the gods were surely black like them" (5). Ignoring that historical evidence indicates the Greeks did not regard their gods as black, Jones's premises are rooted in a modern understanding of color and race, which is precisely the problem which many classicists (Eurocentric or otherwise) have with them.

At the forefront of the backlash against Afrocentric classicism is Mary Lefkowitz, whose *Not Out of Africa* and *Black Athena Revisited* (which she edited with Guy MacLean Rogers) criticize writers such as Bernal, Diop, and Jones for writing out of context, selectively using facts, and for failing to distinguish between contemporary and ancient perceptions of race and ethnicity. Lefkowitz finds a methodological flaw with Afrocentric classicism, as well: its practitioners' motivations are predetermined by ethnicity ("my skin speaks for me," she calls it), which is her chief objection to Diop's approach: "... it requires its adherents to confine their thinking to rigid ethnic categories that have little demonstrable connection with practical reality" (159). According to Lefkowitz, historians must distinguish between what is "foreign" to the ancient Athenians and how they perceived race, ethnicity, and skin color, and 20th-century perceptions of same. As noted above, in regard to Frank M. Snowden, Jr.'s, research into race in the ancient world, the Athenians did not have what would be recognized as racism or color prejudice. They simply distinguished between citizen, resident noncitizen, and foreigner. An African foreigner was no different because of his skin color than an Asian foreigner or foreigner from another polis.

Snowden, in his essay in *Black Athena Revisited*, objects to the interchangeable use of "black," "Egyptian," "African," and "Black African" in Afrocentrist writings, in particular when these are also believed to be synonymous with the modern use of "black," "Negro," or "African-American" (Bernal, 127). Much like ours, the classical world was multicultural. The peoples of that time, however, neither necessarily fitted into nor identified themselves with our contemporary definitions of race, ethnicity, or personal and collective identity.

The question then is why the classical legacy of Greece must be ascribed to Africa. As Basil Davidson indicates, African achievements equal and perhaps exceed those of the Greeks (36–7). Davidson also maintains that many of the Egyptian/African cultural modes supposedly appropriated by the Greeks were also found in Sumerian and Babylonian cultures, as well as in sub–Saharan cultures such as the Dogon and Bambara peoples (38). It may be that some of these modes are common across many different cultures and the relationship between them should be regarded as corresponding, rather than causal. Rather than engaging the ancient world on contemporary political and ethnic terms, perhaps a more useful approach would be to engage it using contemporary cultural terms.

The Hellenic, Hellenistic, and Roman eras were periods of remarkable cross-cultural exchange. Not until the 20th century did the world again seen a "global village" such as the one around the Mediterranean, in which languages, religions, arts, customs, cultures, and practices commingled and influenced and informed one another. The cultures of the Afro-Greek era were remarkably intercultural; Dionysus himself provides an example of acculturation, having emerged out of Asia Minor as an agricultural/fertility deity and entered Greek culture as the god of wine and theatre.

The similarity of our era and the multicultural classical period may provide insight into the occurrence of African-Greek tragedy: the beginning of the 21st century is a period of interculturalism; one in which language, belief systems, art, performance, and cultural forms are widely shared across national and ethnic borders, an issue which I shall explore in more detail in the next chapter. Africa was an integral part of the classical world, and the cultures of Africa, Asia Minor, and Europe freely intermixed. A number of important classical philosophers and theologians were African: Origen, Tertullian, Augustine, Clemens, Alexandinus, and Cyril, to name but a few. As V.Y. Mundimbe in *The Idea of Africa* observes, the earliest African literature consists of African writers writing in Greek, and then Latin, among them the playwright Terence (176). Few would consider Terence an "African author," as part of a cultural grouping, but this point serves to prove that the cultural boundaries of the 21st century do not apply to the cultures of the classical era, and that the geographic boundaries do not always coincide with the cultural boundaries, as contemporary Africa demonstrates.

Edward Said acknowledges one of Bernal's most important subjects in a manner which Bernal does not: all culture is hybrid and ancient Greek culture in particular made no attempt to hide its hybridic nature. The Europeans of the 19th century were the first people to ignore the Greeks' acknowledgment of their hybrid past (*Culture*, 15–16). On this point, the Afrocentrists are correct: the modern Western tradition was to disregard (and even work to obscure) the hybrid origins of Greek culture, origins which the Greeks themselves never denied.

Similarly, ancient Greek culture then became part of the hybrid origins of European culture, appropriated for the use of Western humanists during the restoration. Just as the Greeks represented the Africans on stage without actual interactions with Africans, the Europeans appropriated and constructed the Greek world "without the troublesome interposition of actual Greeks," to steal Said's phrase (*Culture*, 195). Likewise, Greek tragedies now serve African playwrights without the "troublesome interposition" of those same Greeks. In short, much of the cultural continuum of the classical world has been appropriation and representation without true knowledge of the actual, original cultures. The classical heritage, in short, is a history of hybrids developed out of hybrids. In this sense, Afrocentric classicism is just as one-sided as Eurocentric classicism as it discounts part of the hybrid: all origins must be accounted for to understand the culture in its context.

In his seminal work *Orientalism*, Said provides another possible model for African-Greek cultural interaction: Egypt. Egypt, according to Said, "was the focal point of the relationships between Africa and Asia, between Europe and the East, between memory and actuality" (84). In short, Egypt was a hybrid culture that influenced and was influenced by all of the surrounding cultures. One might argue that Egypt was far more of a melting pot than the United States ever was. Whereas Egypt's geographic location assured its intercultural and multicultural nature, Greece's maritime conquests and economic imperialism brought it into contact with a wide variety of cultures, ensuring its hybrid nature. The polis system also ensured that Greek culture would be hybrid: the "nation" consisted of smaller subcultures with a common language. Athens, however, was as different from Sparta in its values and traditions as it was from the cultures of Asia Minor.

In other words, the Greeks did not merely owe "a cultural debt to the ancient Near East," as Guy MacLean Rogers claims (449), nor is Greek culture solely derived from Egyptian, as Diop and Bernal would have it. Mary Lefkowitz rightly claims that "to show influence is not to show origin" ("Introduction," 6), disproving their main contentions. Rather, the classical world, remarkably similar in many ways to our own, was a world in which culture flowed freely. The Greeks in general and Athens in particular were influenced by the cultures of Egypt, Africa, and Asia, and the Greeks, conversely, influenced those cultures. The complexity of this intercultural flow finds its reflection in the 21st century when, once again, ancient Greek culture is appropriated and absorbed by Africans. To put it another way, the culture of ancient Greece is the product of Africa and Europe, though classicists of both persuasions claim its legacy as their sole property.

The Impact of Afrocentric Classicism on Greco-African Adaptations

The history of Greek colonization and Afrocentric classicism results in three different ways to view the connection between Greece and Africa. The first point of view sees Greece as the original European imperialist power. Many of the Greek poleis, including Athens, had colonies in Africa and Asia Minor. The Greeks tended to regard the colonized areas as unsettled wilderness to which they brought civilization, ignoring any indigenous populations already present, much as later European imperialists did. The Greeks were also among the first to construct Africa in art, in literature, and on stage, viewing it as a remote, foreign, "dark" continent, categorizing Africans as wholly Other. Frantz Fanon regards the Athenians as the first colonial power, forcing Africans to assimilate Greek culture, placing Africans under European social, economic, cultural, and psychological domination. Africans were represented on the Greek stage, which, by representing them, robbed Africans of their own voice, thereby controlling the image of Africa and Africans. Tragedy is thus a tool of colonization and colonial domination used by the Europeans; the Greeks' legacy is that of African oppression.

The second view of the relationship between Greece and Africa takes as fact the Egyptian colonial origins of the Greek polis. In this scenario, Greece developed out of African colonies on the Peloponnesian peninsula; therefore Greek mythology, language, philosophy, and culture largely derives from Afro-Egyptian culture. (Interestingly, the proponents of this argument do not see African imperialism in the same negative light as European imperialism.) The African origins of Greek culture have been obscured and hidden by Western historians for racist reasons, but Greek culture and all the cultures derived from Greek culture are actually the descendants of an African legacy.

The third view sees a complex, symbiotic relationship in which all the cultures of the ancient Near East influence one another. Athens and the other *poleis* were certainly influenced by African culture, but this statement in no way implies that Greek culture is African in origin. The Greeks had a much different concept of race, ethnicity, and citizenship than we denizens of the present era. Africans were not perceived as inferior nor were the Greeks prejudiced against them because of skin color. "Aithiopians" were considered different, but were respected for their qualities. The Greeks did not view African origin as problematic.

All three possible interpretations result in complex and challenging possibilities for the playwrights and theatre artists who wish to connect ancient Greece and modern Africa. None of the playwrights and theatre artists considered in this work have cited a belief in Afrocentric classicism as a reason for using Greek material. More often than not, African-American playwrights, not African playwrights, lay claim to the Greek heritage as being African in origin. Perhaps this can be explained by the fact that with the glaring exception of Cheikh Anta Diop who is from Senegal, most of those involved in the Afrocentric classicism movement are American, not African. In other words, Afrocentric classicism, the claiming of Greek culture for Africa, is largely an American undertaking. Most of the African writers considered here are less interested in claiming an ancient heritage for Africa than in writing drama that will engage and please their audiences.

Absence of evidence is not evidence of absence, but not a single African playwright claims to be reappropriating Greek tragedy for Africa. Greek tragedy was introduced into Africa during the colonial era, and was used as a model for indigenous African playwriting and playmaking. For a number of reasons, not least of which are many cultural similarities between ancient Greece and contemporary Africa, Greek tragedy was perhaps the most suitable model for African playwrights to build a hybrid modern drama.

Interestingly, Fanon aside, most African scholars do not condemn the Greeks for their colonial history, nor is Greece considered an imperialist nation. After many African nations achieved independence literary and cultural movements began that rejected all European (read: colonial/imperialist) arts, literatures, and cultures. African writers such as Ngugi rejected European writers and European languages. Theatres and companies stopped performing Molière, Shakespeare, Racine, Shaw, and even Ibsen and Chekhov as all were part of a colonial culture and mind-set that the African artists were attempting to purge in order to establish an independent, postcolonial identity. The ancient Greeks, however, were not considered part of the European culture that was being rejected. Greek tragedy, for a variety of reasons (explored in the next chapter), appealed to African playwrights and could be utilized without the taint of imperialist Europe and the national literatures of the colonial powers. Thus, ironically, Greek tragedy, possibly a means of colonial domination and false representation of Africans, possibly the product of the first European imperial power, was and is considered by African theatre artists to be free from colonial stigma and therefore was and is acceptable material for adaptation and performance.

ATTIC TRAGEDY—
AFRIC TRAGEDY

In *Ancient Sun, Modern Light*, her book on contemporary adaptations and productions of Greek tragedy, Marianne McDonald observes that "Aeschylus shows god questioning god, Sophocles shows man questioning god, and finally Euripides shows man questioning himself. Modern reworkings of classics question the present in terms of the past..." (13). She later notes that the "historic framework and setting" of Greek tragedy "provides its own commentary" (202). In both cases, McDonald claims that the mere act of transposing a Greek tragedy into another setting will generate meaning, linking past to present and using that past as a metaphor for the present.

McDonald notes that there are three requirements for a successful adaptation: the new tragedy must ask questions of its audience, must show conflict, and must connect with issues vital to its (contemporary) audience, otherwise adaptation becomes a mere academic exercise (13). "Successful adaptation," then, as defined by these standards, involves the creation of a new play that generates meaning and message for its target audience and also succeeds qua play and qua theatrical production. It is not enough to simply place a Greek narrative in an African setting. The adaptation must succeed as a play on its own merits, performed in front of an audience who both understand and appreciate the meaning generated by the adaptation. The audience need not understand or be familiar with the original tragedy, but must understand what concerns, themes, and points the adaptation is engaging and how such things are relevant to the audience. In short, adaptation across cultural and historic boundaries can be tricky business.

In order to understand the practice and purpose of African adaptation, I will first examine the relevant issues within myth, epic, and tragedy that predispose Greek tragedy to be ideal for adaptation into African cultural contexts, and then I shall explore the introduction of Greek tragedy to Africa. Next, I will examine tragic theory, beginning with Aristotle and continuing through theatre history to contemporary African theories of tragedy, as well as intercultural and postcolonial theories of theatre, in order to understand better how and why adaptations of Greek tragedy work in Africa. Lastly, after exploring specific issues in form, theme, and content of Greek tragedy as embraced by African cultures I will briefly consider adaptations of Aristophanes's plays and Greek comedy in Africa, in order to determine whether or not all forms of Greek drama are utilized by African artists, or if tragedy is a unique source.

Tragedy, Myth, and Orality: Athens and Africa

At the height of its power and glory in the fifth century B.C.E., Athens had a population of approximately 300,000. Of those, 40,000 were citizens (i.e., adult males of Athenian parentage), 110,000 were members of the households of citizens (i.e., wives, daughters, males not yet of age, and other relatives), 110,000 were slaves, and the remaining people were Greeks of non–Athenian descent (noncitizens/nonslaves) (Baldry, 60). These were the people for whom the Festival of Dionysus was created and they comprised the original audience for Greek tragedy.

The festival was held annually in middle to late March, when sailing was again possible after winter, which meant that foreigners and non–Athenians could attend the festival as well. Rush Rehm believes this period of time also marked a transitional state in Greek agricultural cycles, not yet time to plant the summer crops, or to harvest the winter, therefore the best time for war or conquest by the citizen farmers of the polis (16). Thus, the festival marked the beginning of a period of action by the city and citizens. In the weeks following the festival, the generals for any upcoming campaign would be chosen and plans and goals of both the polis and the military would be argued and decided in the assembly (Rehm, 16). Tragedies, therefore, were presented there at a time when they would have strong political impact, capable of influencing the views and opinions of the citizens who would be making those decisions and plans.

The Festival of Dionysus was state-sponsored and played before an audience of approximately 14,000 spectators, drawn from the different groups noted above. Thus, slightly less than one twentieth of the population of the city of Athens was in attendance at the theatre for any given performance on festival days. The Festival of Dionysus, in addition to being a state-sponsored civic event, was also a religious festival and an artistic competition. As Rehm observes, "production" of tragedy was "participation" in democracy (20). Civic authorities were heavily involved in the organization and execution of the festival and worked very closely with the writers, actors, dancers, and other artists and craftsmen to develop the festival productions. The wealthy citizens who sponsored the individual productions were seen as doing their civic duty and were honored for their patriotic contribution to the community.

The first three days of the seven-day festival were taken up with processions and civic and religious events and ceremonies. Before the tragic competition began the tribute to Athens from the other members of the Delian League would be paraded through the theatre, war orphans and veterans would be presented to the gathered audience, and the awards to citizens for outstanding service to the polis were given out. In short, the Festival of Dionysus was a religious, artistic, civic, social, and political event that glorified the city of Athens and its citizens. It was a celebration of Athenian past and present made possible by the economic growth and prosperity of the city.

Eric A. Havelock argues that the festival also celebrates the cultural advances made by the Greeks moving from a tribal-based oral society to a polis-based literate one. He claims "the literate Athens of 400 B.C. was the child of protoliterate Athens of 500 B.C.," and cites the chorus in Greek tragedy as an example of a relic cultural form which survives an oral society, manifesting itself in written drama (312). This transition is one of the important reasons why Greek tragedy can and does serve as a model for African drama. Many African societies underwent a transition from an orally based culture to a culture with writing during the colonial period. For example, the Yoruba of West Africa had no written language until the advent of the Europeans. One could, following Havelock, argue that literate Africa of the independent era is the child of protoliterate Africa of the pre- and early colonial period, as demonstrated by the use of a griot figure in many contemporary plays.

The griot is a storyteller whose function in an oral society is not merely to tell stories but to serve as that society's historian, lawgiver, teacher, entertainer, and repository for the community's knowledge. Many contemporary African plays use a griot or a griot-like figure to both narrate and comment upon the action, such as the praise singer in Soyinka's *Death and the King's Horseman*. The similar cultural development of ancient Greek tragedy and modern African drama provides common ground by which African artists may see similarities with historical Athens.

Havelock further cites the Greek tragedians' use of Homer as a demonstration of the "continuity in the partnership between oral and written to the close of the fifth century…" (16). Homer's epics were originally oral works, then written works, derived from the oral tradition, finally serving as source material for written plays. Oral epic is the grandfather of written/spoken drama, a hybrid of written culture and oral culture. The shift from orality to literacy transforms the myths that are the original source for epics.

Writing is a private act, as is reading. "Orature," spoken texts, require a communal context for the dissemination of information and ideas. Havelock argues that oral memory deals with the present, not the past (23). An oral culture is a culture whose information is limited to what the living members of that culture have literally heard from those who are older than they. The shift to literacy is about a shift in temporal orientation: writing allows for communication through time, preserving the past for the present, independent of living beings, and preserving the past and present for the future, even after the death of the writer. Thus, the act of writing down epic and myth transforms the activity of sharing them from a public, communal activity focused on the present, to a private, individual activity, which could also focus on the past or the future. Such an action distances myth and epic, which are no longer present, but past; no longer living, but written. Such an action therefore opens myth up to criticism and interpretation.

Charles Segal asserts that "the myths told by tragedy are no longer the myths of an oral society" (*Greek*, 65). Instead the myths are created and generated and transformed by a playwright who uses past myth to comment on present situations. Segal terms them "self-conscious interpreters of myth" (*Greek*, 67). The role of a playwright is not that of Homer or a griot. The playwright does not preserve culture, but rather critiques a culture that, through writing, has already been preserved. In that sense, African adapters of Greek tragedy are doing the exact same thing Greek tragedians did: using the material of the past to comment on the present.

In fact, many African playwrights write in response to the myths and stories of their own cultures. Femi Osofisan, one of the playwrights studied in this survey, claims that he uses the myths of the people in Nigeria both in order to comment on the contemporary political and social situation in Nigeria, but also in order to demonstrate how those myths have been used as political tools by those in power: "I borrow from the ancient forms specifically to unmask them" (qtd. in Bamikunle, 126). Osofisan himself is a Marxist who dramatizes myths in order to "expose the class relations upon which the myths are built" (qtd. in Bamikunle, 127). Similar to the Greek playwrights, Osofisan is a "self-conscious interpreter of myth," writing plays which use mythology recognizable to his intended audience, and yet simultaneously commenting on the myth and the society which created it. Like Euripides, Osofisan hopes to instruct his audience to improve its society by seeing his critique of it. Both ancient Athenian and contemporary African playwrights use the myths of their community not only as source material for drama but also in order to call into question the very things those myths represent. Simon Goldhill calls tragedy a "radical critique" of the discourse of Athens (78). This term could be as easily applied to African adaptation of Greek tragedy that uses Greek tragedy as a "radical critique" of political and social hegemony in Africa.

In *Drama of the Gods*, Martin Owusu notes that in the colonial and postcolonial periods in Africa a number of playwrights have dramatized myth. He categorizes four types of plays that do so. First is what might be termed a straightforward dramatization "with little or no reinterpretation by the dramatist," citing J.P. Clark's *Ozidi* as an example (16). It can be argued that the very act of dramatizing a myth is, in and of itself, a reinterpretation of the myth — the playwright must choose what to present, how to present and represent it, the manner in which the story is framed, and, if more than one version of a myth exists, which version is to be dramatized; in addition, there is the difficulty of having human actors subjectively playing superhuman beings. Nevertheless, we can accept Owusu's category to mean that there is no attempt by the playwright to add ascribed meaning.

Owusu's second category is the presentation of myth as metaphor of social or cultural issues that concern modern African society. To exemplify it, he uses Obotunde Ijimere's *The Imprisonment of Obatala* (16). While on the surface of the drama the narrative tells the story of a traditional myth, the subtext of the play refers to a contemporary problem to which the playwright wishes to draw attention. The original Greek tragedies fit primarily within this category: dramatists as interpreters of myth who use that myth to critique society.

Owusu's third category is the use of myth or ritual as a plot device (16). He uses the examples of Soyinka's *The Strong Breed* and *The Swamp Dwellers*, neither of which has myth for a focus, but employ myth-derived rituals as part of their action.

Lastly, Owusu categorizes plays that transform Western myths and rituals into the African experience. He singles out plays that adapt Greek tragedy into African contexts as an example of this category. Interestingly, while Greek tragedies themselves fit into Owusu's second category of this typology, the African adaptations of those tragedies can fit into any and all of the last three. Adaptations can combine Greek plot with indigenous history as metaphor (*Demea*, *The Gods Are Not to Blame*); they can use Greek tragedy as plot device (*Tegonni*, *Black Wedding Candles for Blessed Antigone*, *The Island*); and all African adaptations of Greek tragedy by their nature transform the original play into a product of the African experience.

Owusu, a playwright himself, compares African playwrights to Greek tragedians, claiming both groups are "modernists" in their respective cultures (128). Like their Greek forbears, African theatre artists rework traditional material in order to make social and political commentary.

To utilize Owusu's conclusions for the purposes of this study, then, we might argue that in the traditional, myth-based cultures of ancient Athens and colonial Africa, the transition from an oral to a literate society, the transformation and critique of myth and society that such a transition allows, and the subsequent dramatization of those myths for the purpose of critique, give rise to similar circumstances for the creation of theatre. African playwrights, seeing similar cultural developments between Greece and African cultures might draw upon the Greek paradigm. This paradigm allows African playwrights to view Greek tragedy as model and source material. This paradigm also causes the Greek material to be more accessible to African artists and audiences than the drama of the Renaissance or modern Western bourgeois drama. Throughout the rest of this chapter I will argue that the perceived cultural similarities between ancient Athens and colonial Africa qualify Greek tragedy as the most appropriate and acceptable literary model of the West both for use as a model to develop a modern African literary drama and for adaptation to African contexts.

Homer and Indigenous African Epic

The narratives of Greek epic, *The Iliad* and *The Odyssey*, are the source for much of Greek tragedy, and the connection between source material and the drama produced from it is significant. J. Michael Walton claims in *Living Greek Theatre* that in addition to dances for Dionysus, Greek tragedy finds part of its origins in the "noncompetitive recitation" of Homer (18). Although, as Walton indicates, *Rhesus* and *Cyclops* are the only extant plays to dramatize incidents fully narrated in Homer, many of the plays rely upon the audience's familiarity with the Homeric poems and this knowledge is taken for granted by the playwrights (97). Ironically, Dionysus appears in neither epic: the god of theatre is absent from the theatre's greatest sources. Nonetheless, if we accept Walton's claims, epic provides tragedy with source, form, and common ground for meeting an audience. The dramatization of Homer's narratives during the festival links "epic Athens" with "literate Athens," as determined from Havelock, above. Epic is a primary root from which drama grows.

Ruth Finnegan in her seminal study *Oral Literature in Africa* does not acknowledge the presence of epic in Africa. Based primarily on formal criteria she concludes African epic does not exist. The works of various African cultures that some call epic, Finnegan claims, do not share the epic form of the European tradition. However, many, such as John William Johnson, Thomas Hale, and Stephen Belcher, who have all written extensively on African epic, disagree with Finnegan. They note that there are common elements between African traditions and the Homeric epic tradition. Johnson, Hale, and Belcher argue that epic is a poetic narrative, of substantial length, with a heroic theme, multigenerational and multifunctional, which is "transmitted by culturally 'traditional' means" (xviii). For the traditional transmission of African epic, Johnson and Hale Belcher acknowledge the griot, known by a variety of local names, "gewel, gawlo, jali, jeli, mabo, gesere, jesere, etc.," as being the indigenous equivalent to Homer (xvii), transmitting African epics among the Soninke, Mande, Songhay, Zarma, Fulbe, and Wolof, among others. Among the Yoruba people, whose playwrights have produced several of the plays examined in this study, the *ijala* or "heroic hunting chants" are performed by singing bards (Okpewho, 133). Much as the Greek bards who developed the Homeric epics were ostensibly inspired by the muses, *ijala* artists claim to be the "mouthpiece of Ogun," singing out of divine inspiration (Okpewho, 47). In both Greek and African cultures, epic is the product of divinely inspired bards, singing lengthy poetic narratives.

Epics from Africa, such as the oral epic of Sun-Jata Keyta, the founder of the Mali empire 900 years ago, whose epic is still sung among of the Mandekan language group, are of equal length to European epics, have heroic themes (such as the founding of the Mali empire), and frequently concern a series of (often prehistoric) events over several generations. In his essay "Yes, Virginia, There Is an Epic in Africa," John William Johnson concludes that epic occurs in Africa in many (if not most) cultures in a wide variety of social, economic, religious, political, and historical contexts.

While the existence of an epic tradition in Africa is of secondary importance to this study, two significant facts emerge which further predispose African use of the Greek paradigm. First, the indigenous experience of epic is very similar to the Greek experience: mythic tales are performed as orature. Second, the form and content of epic is easily adapted into drama: stories of kings, heroes, and ancestors perform impossible tasks, fight against monsters or impossible situations, and eventually succeed at their tasks and found or join the community in which the epic is told. J.P. Clark's *Odizi* is a dramatized epic, as is Obotunde Ijimere's *The Imprisonment of Obatala*. *The Palm Wine Drinkard*, itself a novel by Amos Tutuola based on folklore, has been adapted into one of the most successful and popular plays in Nigeria.

Thus, in both Athens and Africa, epic is the stepping stone between myth and drama, between orature and a work written to be performed. Epic turns myth and folklore into a national literature, a history, which playwrights then use as source material to create drama. African playwrights and audiences can recognize in Greek epic and drama similar patterns of progression as their own dramatized epics.

It is therefore ironic that Greek epic is the form which first indicates the acknowledgment of the "Othering" of Africa from European Greece. As Said writes, "the demarcation between Orient and West ... already seems bold by the time of *The Iliad*" (*Orientalism*, 56). It is in Greek epic that the distinction between Greece and the rest of the world begins to appear. But it is this acknowledgment of difference that makes epic into a self-identifying type of orature, defining the self by what it is not. Similarly, African epic distinguishes between the audience of the epic and everyone else. The development of the epic form marks the beginning of the development of a group identity in narrative: us and everybody else.

The Introduction of Greek Tragedy to Africa

The introduction of the original Greek tragedies to sub–Saharan Africa took place during the colonial era. The two main ways in which the tragedies were introduced were through reading in the colonial educational system and through viewing the dramatic presentation of the plays by either touring European groups or (less often) indigenous school, university, or church drama groups.

In *The Development of African Drama*, Michael Etherton links the incredible significance of theatre and drama to colonial education in Africa, noting that plays were read and performed throughout primary and secondary education, as well as at the university level (63). Drama was a significant tool in the colonial education system.

Of equal importance to colonial pedagogy was classical culture. As educational systems in Africa were modeled by colonial authorities on the educational systems "back home," with their emphasis on Greek, Latin, and classical texts, it is no surprise, as Etherton suggests, that Aristotle's influence was pervasive, and Greek tragedy was on every African syllabus (64–5). Thus, African students from primary to graduate school translated Aristotle, studied Greek mythology, read Greek tragedies, and became as well versed in the classics as any English or French student.

However, as Etherton notes, there is a crucial difference between European use of classical culture in the classroom and African use of these same texts, and that difference is one of historical development: "The Europeans were not being *colonized* by the Greeks or the Romans when they came upon their culture" [emphasis in original] (65). The Europeans consciously chose to use these cultures as part of their educational system, whereas the use of classical culture in the African classroom was part of an imposed colonial culture.

The two crucial differences between classical culture and colonial culture lie in the fact that Greek humanism was radically different than the rest of the colonial culture imparted by the educational system and the forms of mythology behind much of Greek literature was much more familiar to African students than the culture which informs Shakespeare, Molière, and other works of Western literature. Mark Mathabane, in his autobiography about growing up under apartheid in the 1970s, *Kaffir Boy*, tells of reading Tsonga translations of Greek and Roman mythology: "I was drawn to the stories of Atalanta, Philemon and Bacchus, Odysseus and the Trojan War, Jason and the quest for the Golden Fleece. Admittedly they resembled much of African folklore, but they had a freshness that appealed to my imagination" (197). Mathabane admits the similarity between Greek tales and those of his own culture; it is important to note, however, that the Greek myths had been translated into an indigenous African language for the school children. Of equal importance is the fact that the Greek stories, being "new," had an appeal which, as is so often the case, the already familiar or traditional did not. Paradoxically, the similarity between Greek and African mythology allows the African reader to relate to and understand the Greek stories, but their freshness, as Mathabane's statement shows, gave them a novelty the familiar stories lacked. It is this paradox which makes Greek stories appealing.

Similarly, Wole Soyinka encountered the Greeks in school, learning to read the classics in the original languages as he reports in the acknowledgments to his version of *The Bacchae*. His "acquaintanceship with classical Greek" had "a twenty year rust" when he went to write that play (xiii). Yet, this statement indicates that he had read the plays in Greek some 20 years before. As a repercussion of this educational strategy, future African playwrights (and audiences for that matter) were introduced to and familiarized with classical culture very quickly.

Classical culture thus occupied a tension-filled site in the African cultural landscape. As part of the colonial education system it was forced upon the colonized people along with other literatures and philosophies which were touted to be superior to indigenous forms. Classical texts were frequently (though not always) read or taught in the language of the colonizers (English and French) in addition to classical languages, which were also mandatory learning. Yet classical culture, while part and parcel of colonial education, was not in and of itself generally regarded as colonial culture. The Greeks seemed to be separated from the British and French as a culture; the colonizers themselves had borrowed and appropriated the Greeks, but had not created them. Even while things European were rejected, Greek culture was and is still acceptable to many postcolonial education systems. The plays of Shakespeare and Molière might be rejected as imperialist, but Sophocles and Euripides are considered noncolonial literature. In his book *Decolonizing the Mind*, Kenyan author, playwright, and theorist Ngugi wa Thiongo cites Aeschylus, Sophocles, and Aristotle for their "unEnglishness" and establishes that these authors are different, their humanism distinguishing them from the imperialist literatures of Europe (90). The Greeks are acceptable postcolonial reading, from primary through university educations.

The theatrical production divisions of schools and universities, whether in a separate drama and theatre department or as a division of the English or French departments, also played a role in introducing Greek tragedy as works for the theatre. In South Africa alone the archives of the National English Literary Museum are full of reviews of university productions of *Antigone, Oedipus Rex, The Oresteia*, so on, for the past several decades, as well as production reviews for amateur dramatic groups and touring shows. Fugard's Serpent Players performed *Antigone*. Soyinka writes of directing university students in productions of Greek plays. Not a nation in Africa exists that has not seen several university-mounted productions of classical plays. The absence of indigenous playwrights initially also caused amateur groups, church groups, and professional companies that were forming to look to the classical canon for plays to perform in public that would be of interest to an educated indigenous audience.

Tours of professional companies from Europe also brought Greek tragedy to Africa. Initially, during the colonial period, companies from England and France would tour their respective country's colonies with productions of the classics. Then, after independence, especially in the

Francophone colonies, companies toured as part of "cultural diplomacy." As Janet Beik affirms in her study of Hausa theatre, French troupes frequently toured Francophone Africa as a way of maintaining ties between former colony and former imperial power (31). Both Anouilh's adaptation of *Antigone* and a straightforward French translation of the Sophoclean original toured Niger and the other former French colonies within the span of a few years following the Second World War.

In Francophone Africa several playwrights have used the form of Greek tragedy to develop indigenous plays which celebrate local myth and history. Charles Nokan in the Ivory Coast adapted a regional myth in *Abraha Pokou une grande africaine*, in which Queen Pokou secures passage for her people by "sacrificing her child, Agamemnon-like, to a river god," as Conteh-Morgan reports in his study of Francophone drama in Africa (26). Similarly, Debo Adejumo reports the adaptation of Yoruba myth into French in Greek tragic style in Ola Balogun's *Shango*, written in 1968 (65). Adejumo attributes the Francophone African penchant for the model of Greek tragedy to "the 20th century classical tradition," writers such as Sartre, Cocteau, Giradoux, and Gide, all of whom mined classical literature and drama for material through which to explore the contemporary human condition (65–6). In keeping with the intellectual traditions inherited through the French colonial experience, Francophone African nations initially saw much drama based on the classical tradition. However, in the anti–European intellectual backlash following independence in many countries, the result of both Negritude and nationalist movements, this close association between French culture and Greek appropriation seems to have resulted in a decrease in both specific play adaptation and use of the Greeks as a model.

In Anglophone Africa such difficulty did not exist. Whereas in French colonies the colonial education system introduced African playwrights to French playwrights who incorporated classical culture into French culture, such as Racine, Corneille, and Labiche, in British colonies Shakespeare held sway, and therefore became the symbol of British culture and, by extension, imperial culture. As noted above, the Greeks remained "safe" for postcolonial Anglophone Africa.

The other reason why Greek tragedy held such appeal to African theatre artists is its portrayal of archetypal struggles. Setting aside issues of "universality," Greek tragedy does show very paradigmatic conflicts: sibling against sibling, parents against children, citizen against the state. Greek tragedy could therefore be used as a vehicle for social commentary under oppressive regimes, whether in the colonial or postcolonial periods. Just as Anouilh's *Antigone* was produced under Nazi occupation, classical plays could be presented publicly without fear of seeming subversive. But just as Anouilh's adaptation, the play could be as subversive as the artists wanted it to be. Greek tragedy in South Africa during the apartheid era serves as the perfect example.

The censorship laws in South Africa during the apartheid era were extremely restrictive on the nonwhite populations: scripts and performances critical of the government, society, or culture of the R.S.A. were prohibited and actively prevented. Productions of classical plays, however, were deemed acceptable and even commendable and worthwhile, as they were considered to be positive examples of European culture and civilization. Greek tragedies therefore were used by those opposed to apartheid to resist it.

The Theatre Council of Natal (TECON) was founded in 1969 in Durban by members of a student theatre group. Among their first productions was an adaptation of Jean Anouilh's *Antigone* (itself an adaptation of the Sophoclean original) entitled *Antigone in '71*. The production opened with the hanging of a black man and featured a chorus of black women who both supported yet feared Antigone. Instead of using a set, the production projected a film of slum housing, drawing a visual reminder for the audience of the similarities between the injustices of Creon in the play and the economic and political injustice forced upon them by apartheid (Larlham, *Black*, 76). The title alone, *Antigone in '71*, suggests that the play is set in the (then) present day, and that the issues in the play are still relevant to (then) contemporary South Africa. Furthermore, the play was also regarded as safe enough to get the permission of the censor, even if the production would have been seen as controversial and subversive.

TECON was followed by the Imitha Players, founded in 1970 in East London by Skhala Xinwa, who is black, and Rob Amato, who is white. One of Imitha's most important productions was a mixed-race cast performance of the *Oedipus the King* of Sophocles. Similarly, Don Maclennan, a white lecturer at Rhodes University in Grahamstown, recruited black actors in 1974 to form the Inkhwezi Players for the Grahamstown National Arts Festival. They read Euripides's *Alcestis* and several plays by Molière (Larlham, *Black*, 77). The very act of forming a mixed race theatre company was dangerous in apartheid South Africa, and by reading European classics they managed to allay governmental concerns while still resisting apartheid by reading the plays with mixed-race casts.

Barney Simon adapted *Antigone* for performance at the Market Theatre.[1] While the script, at only 36 pages, reads more like a simple transla-

---

[1]The original typescript is in the Barney Simon collection at the National English Literary Museum in Grahamstown, South Africa. I am in their debt for being given access to it.

tion exercise than an adaptation, Simon's main focus is on the concept of "The Law," a term which is bandied about by the characters with great frequency. As in the Sophoclean original, Antigone and Creon debate the correct course of action under the law, but in Simon's adaptation, written to be performed in the historic Market Theatre, itself a symbol of the theatre's resistance to apartheid, the play takes on antiapartheid connotations. Even a straightforward production of *Antigone* can become an act of resistance through the common knowledge of the actors and audience of the social situation in which all live their daily lives.

In South Africa, staging Greek tragedy became a "safe" way to present resistance to apartheid and to subvert the seemingly harmless European cultural origin of the plays. The very act of performing *Antigone* became an act of defiance and resistance. Similarly, Greek tragedy has been staged in a number of other African countries in which "political" drama is forbidden, but European classics may be staged with official permission. The Greek tragedy becomes the vector by which the message of resistance to oppression is delivered to an audience. In some cases, a translation of the tragedy would be staged with a *mise en scène* that suggests a meaning deeper than that found in the text, such as in the productions of TECON and the Imitha Players noted above. In other cases, adapting the narrative or characters of the Greek original to an African context would generate the play's message. While the former provide some very interesting examples of direction and design in Greek tragedy, this study takes the latter type of drama as its subject. In order to understand better the nature of African adaptation of Greek tragedy, it becomes necessary to examine several theories of theatre and adaptation.

Postcolonial Theatre, Transculturation, Hybridity, and the Art of Adaptation — or, Why Children Do Not Always Look Like Their Parents

Even more than as a deceptive tool of resistance within specific political contexts, the adaptation of Greek tragedy by African playwrights can be seen as part of a greater cultural struggle against colonialism and Eurocentric thought. In the colonial era the culture taught in African classrooms was also designed to carry out the objectives of colonial discourse. Rather than teach traditional or even contemporary African literature, drama, and orature, European poetry, drama, and literature remained the subjects of study and the models for writing. The very system which introduced Greek cultural material to Africa was using that material as part of a larger system of imposition of European high culture on the indigenous peoples of Africa while simultaneously denigrating African culture and the people who produced and developed it. African culture was seen by the Europeans who organized the educational systems as comparatively primitive and inferior, easily understood and dismissed as one might understand and dismiss the stories a child makes up to entertain themselves.

In response to this Eurocentric discourse developed a counterdiscursive form of postcolonial, Afrocentric writing. These writings, by African authors, mark the beginning of a cultural struggle against European thought and its reductivist tendencies, especially where colonized peoples were concerned. As Ashcroft, Griffiths, and Tiffin contend, postcolonial discourse is rooted in a struggle for power, power over representation and evaluation. Postcolonial writers and artists seek to empower African thought, literature, and art, by demonstrating awareness of the power and meaning behind the choice of language, subject matter, approach, and style.

In many of the adaptations studied in this survey it is possible to interpret the act of adaptation as an instance of this Afrocentric discourse. As Elleke Boehmer observes, adaptation of classical texts "meant staking a claim to European tradition from beyond its conventional boundaries. Take-over or appropriation was in its way a bold refusal of cultural dependency" (205). In other words, adaptation of European drama to African milieus can also be read as an act of cultural resistance. In adaptation, European culture was appropriated and framed in an African context to serve the purposes of African artists. Mark Fortier argues that cross-cultural adaptation deals with "the complexities of post-colonial subjectivity," in which an African artist, by reworking a European text into an African context decenters the European text and instead privileges the African context (135). The African is now both subject and object of discourse, not the object of European creation or representation, but rather the subject and object of African creation and representation. By rewriting a Greek tragedy, an African playwright robs the text of its power by decentering the original text and not privileging the European original. The adaptation itself becomes an Afrocentric center.

Yet another discourse is also present in recent drama and theatre from Africa. In *Scars of Conquest/Masks of Resistance*, Tejumola Olaniyan notes that there exists currently in Africa three competing discursive formations: Eurocentric, Afrocentric, "and an emerging post–Afrocentric which subverts both the Eurocentric and the Afrocentric while refining and advancing the aims of the latter" (11). The post–Afrocentric approach to the study of the "cultural self" is unique because it "not only quests for different representation, but also, simultaneously, queries the *representation of difference*" [italics in original] (27). What Olaniyan calls "post–Afrocentric," Biodun Jeyifo calls "African interculturalism" ("Reinvention," 153). Regardless of nomenclature, this third discourse takes as its subject the issues which legitimize or problematize intercultural fusion of European and African cultures, or what Jeyifo calls the "complex relations of unequal exchange" (158). Much of the drama being written in Africa today is not only postcolonial but post–Afrocentric as well. While such plays as *Odale's Choice* reflect an Afrocentric mode, others, such as *Black Wedding Candles for Blessed Antigone* reflect this post–Afrocentric mode, questioning not only the manner in which Europeans have represented and constructed the African self, but also the manner in which Africans have represented and constructed the African self. The post–Afrocentric discourse does not automatically challenge and refute all things Western, but rather explores the complex relationship between Afroculture and Euroculture. The seeds of such a discourse are seen in the play *The Gods Are Not to Blame*, in which Nigerian Ola Rotimi posits that reacting to an African crisis by blaming Europe is a pointless, disempowering exercise, and that Africans must take into account European influence and oppression, but be responsible for their own actions.

In the colonial era, relations between Africa and Europe are classified by Jeyifo's "unequal exchange." The "modes of cross-cultural encounter," to use Fred Dallmayr's term, were conquest, forced conversion and forced assimilation of Africans by Europeans. In the post–Afrocentric era, however, African artists and writers attempt to guide African-Western relations into a new mode: an exchange of culture between cultural equals. This process is what Carl Weber calls "transculturation," i.e., "a transfer of culture" (27). Acculturation, "the appropriation of a foreign performance code without change or with merely superficial adjustments," is the first step of this exchange (Weber, 34). Yet, acculturation develops into transculturation in which the appropriated culture is rendered no longer foreign, but part of the target culture. Transculturation transforms its model while still respecting the original culture. The steps that Weber outlines for transcultural adaptation are the initial deconstruction of a "foreign" text, the "findings" of that deconstruction are rearranged according to the codes inscribed in the indigenous culture, the reconstruction of the performance text within those codes, and the disappearance of the model into the next text or technique within its own culture (34). This paradigm of transculturation is the format that the study of the plays considered herein will follow. As part of the post–Afrocentric discourse, African playwrights, drawing upon the similarities between African and Athenian cultures, deconstruct Greek tragedies and reconstruct them within an African context in which knowledge of the original tragedy and its context is no longer needed and the adaptation becomes its own entity with its own identity serving its own purpose within the African society for which it has been written.

This analysis does not suppose a Western notion of "universality." The tragedies of ancient Greece, despite the comments above, should not be read as a theatrical lingua franca, but rather a procrustean bed. Universality, as numerous critics have demonstrated, is a Western conceit, which ascribes to some texts a value which will mean the same thing to all who encounter the text, regardless of the individual's culture, gender, age, context, so on. The notion of universality excludes some texts from consideration while ascribing merit to others as ostensibly having no boundaries — a way for the European to believe his text somehow superior and boundless.

The inverse meaning of universality, that a non–Western text or form is universal, is equally problematic. Julie Stone Peters argues that the ascribing of "universality" to a non–Western work by a Western critic is merely a form of Orientalism, assimilating the Other on the virtue of being "like" the Self (205). Thus, universality either privileges Western texts and performances as being above cultural differences, or acknowledges non–Western texts and performances not as equal and valid on their own merits but only in their integration into a Western framework or their similarities to Western forms.

Greek tragedy is not universal in either of these senses. It was the product of a specific (albeit hybrid) culture, formed at a specific moment in that culture's history, which has transculturated both through time and space and across cultural borders into a variety of cultures which, in turn, transformed the plays into artifacts of their own cultures.

In the post–Afrocentric world, culture is not a possession that can be owned by anybody. Edward Said, in *Culture and Imperialism*, argues that, "Culture is never just a matter of ownership, of borrowing and lending with absolute debtors and creditors, but rather of appropriations, common experiences, and interdependences of all kinds among different cultures" (217). In other words, all culture is at least in part transcultural – the product of transference during cultural encounters. Julie Stone Peters similarly points out that cultural identities "are fluid composites with multiple genealogies" (210). When one acknowledges that all cultures are hybrid and all identity is fluid, then the procrustean nature of Greek tragedy becomes apparent. Rather than being universal, tragedy is a fluid bed that can be shaped to fit the context in which it is placed, becoming part of that culture in its new form.

Let us also recall that adaptation is the act of an individual, not an entire culture. A playwright does not impose his culture on all versions of a play, nor does he impose the play on the wholeness of his culture. Rather, the playwright takes a Greek text and transforms it into a new entity, different from the original, yet related to it. Furthermore, cultural forms are not appropriated from outside the culture, as in an American director using the original text of the play but imposing a *mise en scène* from another culture, such as the many *kabuki* productions of *Macbeth* and *Medea* demonstrate. Such a practice privileges text over culture, whereas adaptation privileges culture over text. In adaptation, the text is changed to meet the requirements of the culture, perhaps not always successfully as will be discussed below, but, in the end, it is the text that is transformed in an adaptation, not the culture into which it is adapted.

In adapting narratives from one medium to another, or from one culture to another, three things are of primary consideration: what is kept from the original, what is removed from the original — and what is changed or reworked from the original, in other words, retention, deletion, and alteration.[2] Michael Etherton, in his seminal study *The Development of African Drama*, observes that there are five forms of reworking a play from one culture to another: changing character and place names (i.e., small cosmetic changes), changing period or setting, adapting contexts, altering the story, and changing the theme or focus (102–3). Some adaptations do only one of these; many involve all these forms of reworking. The greater the number of changes, the further the play is from the original. All of the adaptations considered here change character and place names, settings, and contexts. Some use the original Greek play as a sounding board, metatheatrically referring to them in order to establish theme and focus. When considering the individual plays, we will look to these different ideas of adaptations: what is kept, what is cut, what is changed and, following Etherton, how it has been changed.

What enables many of these adaptations to "work," however, is their exploitation of similarities of cultures, or, more accurately, if the perceived gaps between the cultures are seen as small. The affinity that the target culture or the individual artist feels for the original culture enables the transcultural process to be smoother and more accommodating. This idea returns us to the notion of universality, or rather, an inverse of the Western notion of non–Western universality: what does the African playwright

---

[2] *I am in debt to Professor Keiko McDonald of the Department of East Asian Languages and Literature at the University of Pittsburgh for this theory of adaptation, shared during a roundtable discussion of Endo Shusaku's* Silence, *12 October 1998.*

see as similarity between his culture and Greek culture? What are the perceived likenesses between ancient Athens and contemporary (or historic) Africa?

Many African cultures, like that of ancient Greece, have anthropomorphic cosmologies. Greek gods and the polytheistic deity groups in African cultures have feelings and weaknesses, intervene regularly and in person in human affairs, and have offspring with human beings. The gods exist "somewhere else," and yet remain always present. In describing African religion to non–Africans, African scholars frequently use Greece as a model. For example, in writing about traditional African festival drama, Oyin Ogunba claims that traditional African religions have a pantheon of deities "much like the Greek gods" (8). As noted in the previous section, Mark Mathabane saw similarities between Greek mythology and the Tsonga stories that he was told as a boy (197). The similarities which allowed him to do so also allow African playwrights to seize upon Greek tragedy as a model for Modern African drama much more culturally suitable than Shakespeare, Molière, Racine, Wilde, Williams, or Miller.

The identity of the African self and the Athenian self both differ significantly from the modern European notion of identity, while being remarkably similar to each other. The modern European notion of self is constructed around the individual, and the European heritage from the Renaissance forward privileges the individual above the group. The Athenian identity was constructed beginning with the individual but not ending there. It was also defined by *oikos* (household), clan, and polis (city-state). The contemporary African identity also begins with the individual and is further defined by one's family, village or clan, tribe or ethnic group, and, finally, one's nation. The family and ethnic group are privileged over both nation (a European construction of which one may be a citizen, but loyalty and identity remain with one's ethnic group, a problem dramatized in Rotimi's *The Gods Are Not to Blame*) and individual (who is seen as part of the larger community). In other words, the European intellectual tradition privileges the individual, whereas African and Athenian tradition place the individual within the larger family community and privilege the community as a whole over the individual.

Another cultural similarity is the centrality of the marketplace in both African and Athenian culture. The marketplace reigns supreme as social center, economic center, and place of communal mixing. The *agora* of Athens played a major role in the economic, social, and political life of the polis. Will Durant writes in *The Life of Greece* that "Trade, not industry or finance is the soul of the Athenian economy" (275), which means that the marketplace is the site of "the soul of the economy." The trade which was the primary function of the *agora* (not just between citizens of the polis, but between Athenians and foreign merchants, as well as other visitors to the city) allowed the Athenian economy to grow and develop. The agora, however, was more than just a place of trade or exchange; it was, as Rush Rehm observes, "in both a real and metaphoric sense ... the center of the *polis*" (31). The *agora* was the place from which distances to and from Athens were measured. It was a place of public oratory. Philosophers would teach in the *agora* and informal philosophical and political debates were often held within its confines. The assembly, the law courts, the Acropolis, and the theatre of Dionysus were all located in the immediate area of the *agora*. According to one theory, the first tragedies, performed before the theatre of Dionysus was built, were presented in the *agora* (Rehm, 31). In short, the marketplace of Athens was in many ways the cultural, social, economic, political, and geographical center of the city.

Similarly, the marketplace in any African village is the center of everyday life. Martin J. Gannon believes that the "cultural metaphor" for "understanding the culture of the people of modern Nigeria is the marketplace" (234). The marketplace is the center of economic exchange and political and cultural discourse. The marketplace is where all groups come together to meet. In some areas of Nigeria the local chief or head clansman is called *Loja*, literally "owner of the market" (Gannon, 243). This title refers not only to the power of the ruler, but also the importance ascribed to the market; this is so much so in Nigerian thought that the marketplace *is* the village. Many festival performances are held in the markets of Africa. The market is the heart of information exchange and public announcements were and are traditionally made in the market to ensure wide dissemination to the population.

The market is of such cultural importance in Africa that many plays are either set in the marketplace, such as Soyinka's *The Beatification of Area Boy,* or else have important scenes which occur in or near the marketplace, such as in Rotimi's *Our Husband Has Gone Mad Again* or Soyinka's *Death and the King's Horseman.* As in ancient Athens, the marketplace is the heart and soul of the village, the city, and the traditional African social, cultural, and economic worlds.

Further similarities exist on many levels, from the existence of a wide variety of religious festivals, rituals, and societies to similar societal organizations. Many African ethnic groups have secret societies and traditional groups that serve political and cultural functions. The Greeks had mystery cults that functioned similarly. The Greeks allowed property-owning male citizens a voice in ruling the polis, as many historical African societies allow all adult males a voice in government, although the central authority may be hereditary. In both Africa and Athens, membership in the community entails responsibilities and duties as well as rights and privileges for the ruling group.

It can be reasonably concluded that, in many ways, ancient Athens and certain societies in Africa have some cultural similarities. Many African playwrights, seizing upon these similarities, use Greek tragedy as an outside matrix of interpretation which allows them to comment upon and analyze not only African society, but also the relationship between Africa and the West.

Such surface similarities, however, obscure much deeper differences. Three levels of cultural difference affect the adaptation of Greek tragedy into African settings by African playwrights. The first level of difference is conceptual. The European interpretation of Greek ideas of fate, the gods, the ancestors, death, the afterlife, and any and all aspects of religion and philosophy as taught as part of the Western intellectual tradition, differs significantly from an African understanding of these concepts. For example, the Greek concept of an unalterable fate is significantly different from the Yoruba idea of fate being a choice which one may change through action, as I will discuss in the analysis of Ola Rotimi's *The Gods Are Not to Blame*, a Yoruba adaptation of *Oedipus Rex*. Also included in this level of difference are the social roles. A Greek priest of Apollo is significantly different, plays a different role in the community, and is viewed differently by the citizens of the area he serves than a priest of Ogun in Nigeria. The role of a priestess of *Wonyinghi* among the Ijaw of Nigeria, itself an oracular office, is significantly different from the role of the oracular priestess of Apollo at Delphi. Even gender roles are conceptually different between African societies, some of which are matriarchal and vest supreme authority in a female leader, and ancient Athens, where women were not citizens and had no rights under the law in and of themselves, but only as members of the household of a father or husband.

The second level of difference lies in the interpretation of action. Many of the same actions occur in Greece and Africa, but the interpretation of that action is different, and the cultural meanings and implications of those actions may differ significantly. Such varied actions as suicide, homicide, sexual intercourse, homosexual relations, war-making, farming, hunting, offering animals for sacrifice, and other actions will be undertaken for different reasons and will be interpreted differently depending on cultural context. For example, the Japanese consider suicide an honorable alternative to living shamefully, whereas in the Christian West, suicide is an unforgivable sin that heaps additional shame on the doer. In ancient Greece, homosexual sex was acceptable within certain social situations, and even considered a positive and necessary action within that context, whereas in some African societies it is unheard of for two men to be intimate, and in some cultures punishable by death.

The third level of difference in adaptation lies in the theatrical traditions of both cultures. One could say that drama as the West understands it did not exist in Africa before colonial times, but the cultures of Africa have a rich performance history and culture. Greek tragedy was initially written to be enacted within a set of performance conventions. The transculturation process begins as soon as one removes these conventions. Yet the plays were written specifically to be performed in the theatre of Dionysus with an *orchestra*, a *machina*, an *ekkyklema*, with masked actors declaiming while wearing special robes and shoes. While African performance culture certainly has masks, special costumes, and stage devices and effects, it does not have these specific conventions. Therefore, the task of the playwright is to transculturate these, and other, conventions into a form recognizable and acceptable to the target audience.

For example, the most difficult aspect of adapting Greek tragedy is arguably the chorus. African playwrights have approached the chorus in a number of ways, from eliminating it entirely (*Orestes, The Island*) to using it as *the* driving force behind the play, even adding second and third choruses (Soyinka's *Bacchae of Euripides*). In *The Song of Jacob Zulu* the chorus not only fulfills the role of the traditional Greek chorus, serving as narrator, commentator, and occasional character, but also achieves significance and meaning because of who plays the chorus: internationally famous South African a capella singers Ladysmith Black Mambazo. The chorus in the Greek originals are social collectives who have a vested interest in the drama, such as the Furies in *The Eumenides*, the elders of Thebes in *Oedipus Rex*, Dionysus's followers in *The Bacchae*, or the women of Troy in *The Trojan Women*. Likewise, many of the adaptations present choruses who have a vested interest in the drama and who relate to the overall theme and structure of the play: the chorus of slaves in *The Bacchae of Euripides*, the chorus of Yoruba women in *The Gods Are Not to Blame*, the groups of neighbors in *Song of a Goat* and *Edufa*. Quite often the chorus not only stands in for the audience, or serves as a bridge between drama and audience, but also represents the larger community. In each of the following chapters the role of the chorus (or the lack thereof) will be of primary concern because the manner in which the playwright employs the chorus, or the particular group, individual, or African cultural form which takes over the role the chorus plays in the original, generates meanings not found in the original.

The African playwright inscribes the narrative of the Greek text within the performance codes of his or her culture. Many of the adaptations involve the blending of European performance techniques with indigenous African styles, many of which are appropriate only to a particular culture, or even a particular dramatist, whose reasons for adapting the Greek tragedy may prohibit or proscribe the use of certain techniques while simultaneously demanding the use of others. *The Island*, by Fugard, Kani, and Ntshona, with its two actors, invokes the township theatre performance styles of apartheid South Africa which would be completely inappropriate in *The Bacchae of Euripides*, Soyinka's communal celebration requiring three dozen performers, musicians, and dancers. Neither of these plays uses anything resembling ancient Greek costume, scenography, acting technique or music, as such elements would be irrelevant to an indigenous African audience.

In conclusion, then, the African children of Athenian tragedy no longer look like their parent. But, the original Greek tragedy is only one parent. Through the process of transculturation the other parent is the target culture and its performance codes. The narrative and other elements are ancient Greek, the context and performance codes are contemporary African — the drama is thus a hybrid, descended from two cultures but living with and within its living parent. The target culture, in the post–Afrocentric world, adopts and accepts this child as its own, despite its hybrid nature.

Tragic Theory and African Tragic Theory

Ketu Katrak holds that tragedy did not exist in Africa before the colonial period, quoting Anthony Graham White's statement that many African cultures feared that "to express sorrow was 'somehow to invite it'" (55). Only after colonization and exposure to European culture did Africans begin writing tragic drama and literature and theorizing about tragedy. Katrak maintains that this development occurred not only because of African exposure to tragedy as a form, but also because, of all the genres of drama and literature, tragedy best narrates the colonial experience. With the introduction of Greek tragedy to the African cultural milieu, African artists, scholars, and theorists began to examine the tragic theory of the West and then began to develop ideas about African tragedy that differed in their cultural specificity from Western tragedy.

Nigerian critic Biodun Jeyifo, writing in *The Truthful Lie*, argues that all African tragedies contain "an irreducible 'Africanness,'" and that this quality and the tragedies themselves are rooted in African history (26). Jeyifo is not alone in claiming an indefinable quality that is essential to all the writings of the continent from a particular genre; many critics, play-wrights, theorists, and scholars from both within and without Africa have made similar claims. Similar to Ketrak, Jeyifo argues that the colonial experience is responsible for much of the history which African tragedy is rooted in, thus further distinguishing it from the tragedy of the West.

Tragic theory in the West begins with Aristotle's *Poetics*, which not only set the definition for tragedy but has become the standard by which the drama of the West has often defined itself. Misreadings of Aristotle have resulted in the rigid dictates of neoclassicism as well as the Christianized idea of a "tragic flaw," a reading of the Greek word *hamartia* to indicate a quality in the character that accounts for a "tragic fall." Kenneth Telford, however, in his translation of *The Poetics*, observes that *hamartia* is an archery term, translated as a "missing of the mark" (23). In this interpretation of Aristotle's theory, tragic characters do not have a flaw that brings them to tragic ruin but rather suffer a change of fortune due to a mistake or tragic action. In other words, the hero is not punished for an innate flaw, the traditional Western interpretation; but instead the character commits to a course of action that results in tragedy. Telford notes that the *hamartia* "is an action, not a suffering or a flaw of character" (23). The characters of tragedy choose their fate; tragedy is the result of bad choice. The tragic hero has a choice in how to respond to a situation. Tragedy occurs when the character chooses wrongly.

Many African playwrights accept the commonly held misconception of a "tragic flaw" as introduced to them through the European colonial education system which unquestioningly accepted several centuries of interpreting Aristotle in this manner. Interestingly, however, the African playwrights adapt the Greek plays in a way that demonstrates the *hamartia* of the African character. In other words, African tragedy results from character choice, not character flaws. In many of the plays explored in this study I will examine the manner in which the African playwrights have shown a character's *hamartia*, tragic mistake, leads to tragedy.

Yet since Aristotle, tragedy has been remarkably difficult to define. Nietzsche, the French Academy, Schopenhauer, Hegel, Abel, Fergusson, Steiner, Williams and hundreds of others have attempted to define tragedy. In his examination of the tragic hero George Boas claims that it is hard to "play the genre game," as one is either defining the indefinable or using circular definition; i.e., a tragedy is a play in which a tragic hero, because of a tragic flaw, comes to a tragic end (143). More recently, Richard H. Palmer, in his survey of the history of tragic theory, observes that every definition of tragedy "possesses a degree of validity" in relation to a specific canon or methodology, but every definition conversely becomes a limitation (201). By defining tragedy we limit it, and every definition is then challenged by the next theorist or artist, hence articles such as Arthur Miller's "Tragedy and the Common Man," which argues that modern tragedy is possible, although such possibility had been declared impossible by previous definitions of tragedy. Definitions of tragedy are also culturally bound, and the tragedy of one culture may not intersect with that of another.

For the purposes of this study we may define (Western) tragedy in the following way, after Atillio Favorini, as this definition is a slight alteration of his own: tragedy is a form of drama in which the hero must transcend self and society while participating in an action, usually a struggle, in which the hero is paradoxically both victorious and defeated. The play must take place within the human sphere, and tragedy occurs when awareness exceeds power and the "loser" must then transcend failure. While still somewhat limiting, this definition attempts to be as little culturally bound as possible and attempts to encompass all the necessary formal requirements of tragedy while not being so open as to include everything or so closed as to exclude plays which do not conform to the rigors of neo-classical definition or even Miller's modern definition.

Such a definition also runs counter to George Steiner's dictate that "tragedy is dead" (10). In *The Death of Tragedy*, Steiner argues that tragedy is not only culturally bound by definition but that tragedy is only possible in the West. He writes, "All men are aware of tragedy in life. But tragedy as a form of drama is not universal" (3). In fact, he continues, tragedy is "distinctive of the Western tradition," as "this idea and the vision of man which it implies are Greek. And till nearly the moment of their decline, the tragic forms are Hellenic" (3). Steiner concludes this series of thoughts with the pronouncement that after the classical age and outside of the West, "we may have serious drama, but not tragedy" (3). Steiner essentially argues that tragedy is a Western, specifically ancient Greek form that died with Greek culture and is impossible in the contemporary theatre. Tragedy came about in Greece and slowly died out in the West. It never occurred anywhere else. It is with this theory of Steiner that many African tragic theorists begin.

David Kerr, writing of African theatre theory, responds to Steiner by arguing that the social conditions which Steiner asserts resulted in the death of tragedy in Europe, do not exist in Africa. European tragedy may be dead, but African tragedy is alive and well. Raymond Williams argues that Greek tragedy is "the only fully religious tragedy" (30). While this sentiment may be fact in Europe, the contemporary theatre of Africa is much more infused with religion and its attendant signs, symbols, tools, and roles than the contemporary theatres of the West.

Robert Plant Armstrong compares Greek and Yoruba tragedies from an anthropological point of view and concludes that Steiner is wrong — tragedy as a form of drama is universal because of the formal relationships between tragedy and audience, first and foremost through Aristotle's theory of catharsis, which Armstrong believes is universal (42). Armstrong compares *Oedipus Rex* with Yoruba dramatist Duro Lapido's *Oba Waja* (*The King Is Dead*) and identifies what he terms "an anthropologically probable definition of tragedy": tragedy is "a work of affecting presence which enacts at the substantive level a perversion or a denial of the cultural myth, doing so in such a way that with the defeat of the tragic protagonist a paradoxical terminal situation prevails, taking the protagonist down but the audience up" (43). Armstrong further refutes Steiner on the basis of similarities of dramaturgy, subject matter, use of myth, and audience response to both Greek and African tragedy. Similarity in function and source material (myth) demonstrate some of the possible universal qualities which tragedy may, by definition, have.

Armstrong's comparative tragic theory utilizes formalism, reception theory, and anthropology, which excludes him from the two groups of critics identified by P.J. Conradie as attempting to give some kind of definition of African tragedy (26). The first group looks to a metaphysical definition of tragedy, and includes such playwright-critics as Wole Soyinka and Zulu Sofola. While Soyinka's theories will be explored in the next chapter, we might summarize Sofola's definition of African tragedy as one in which unknown and unknowable forces bring about the suffering of the tragic hero and that suffering is of value to the community.

The second group, according to Conradie's typology, look to a Marxist definition of tragedy. The first task of Marxist theorists is to determine whether or not a tragic view is compatible with Marxism. Whereas Biodun Jeyifo believes tragedy possible because of colonialism, Andrew Gurr, noting that the "static world-view" of tragedy is in opposition to progress and therefore irreconcilable with Marxism, claims tragedy is impossible (140). Yet, as Kerr notes, theatre is inherently dialectical, which leads it "to mediate political and social controversies more passionately than other cultural forms" (3). This observation seems to confirm part of Sofola's definition: African theatre is community-oriented and tends to serve as a focal point for the debate of issues important to the community. African tragedy, regardless of whether possible under Marxism or not, must take into account this communal orientation.

The hero on stage may transcend society, but he or she is always a part of the community. Furthermore, African tragedy not only engages the community of the hero but also the community of the audience. The key word to understanding the audience dynamic of African tragedy is communal, as we shall see in the next chapter. African tragedy is "communal" in that it is focused on the community and is made by and for the community. In this sense, African tragedy represents a dramatization of Victor Turner's idea of communitas: a "model for human interrelatedness" in juxtaposition to everyday society (*Process*, 96). African tragedy can be and frequently is religious in nature, "communal" also meaning the need to communicate with the gods, ancestors, and supernatural world. The "communal" tragedy of Africa is thus both centered on the very real, physical community and its need, individually and collectively, to communicate with the metaphysical reality. The first "communing" creates the second — a concept which I will explore in depth in the next chapter.

African tragedy is therefore a form of drama in which the hero must transcend self and society while participating in an action in which the hero is paradoxically victorious and defeated, a condition which is of benefit to both the hero's community and to the audience who are brought together and not only purged of fear and pity, but raised up through the drama. African tragedy can never be far from the shadow of colonialism, which, while not always the theme or subject matter nevertheless always informs the drama. African tragedy is an evolving form, fairly recently developed, having emerged only in the 20th century. We must remember when defining it that further developments in African literature may eventually change the depth, scope, and definition of African tragedy.

Summary: Greek Tragedy in Africa

To understand African adaptations of Greek tragedy within their cultural contexts as hybrids and transcultural artifacts, we must understand the development of tragedy and its appropriation by African playwrights. Tragedy developed in fifth-century B.C.E. Athens out of particular cultural circumstances as the product of a religious festival, civic event, and artistic competition. Tragedy as a dramatic form marks the tensions inherent in a culture moving from orality to literacy and uses as its source material the myths of that culture as embodied in its oral epics. Tragedy is not a retelling of myth but an interpretation of it, for the purposes of commenting on both myth and society.

With the introduction of Greek cultural material through the colonial education system and cultural exchanges, African artists discovered an affinity for that material, noting cultural similarities between ancient Athens and colonial Africa. The result of these similarities was to make Greek tragedy compatible with African tastes in a manner in which other

European drama was not. Greek tragedy, though essentially European in origin, was not perceived as being part of colonial culture.

During the initial struggles against colonization, African writers, as part of a postcolonial Afrocentric agenda, resisted European-dominated discourse and rejected imperial culture. The post–Afrocentric view, however, neither rejects all things European nor bows down to them as cultural models. Instead, artists consciously choose to blend traditional culture with European culture in a transcultural process which creates a new artifact, a hybrid of both cultures which wholly belongs to the target culture. The perceived cultural similarities between ancient Athens and contemporary Africa facilitate the transcultural process, although that process is then problematized by the cultural differences that exceed the surface similarities. Differences of thought, belief, and conceptual understanding about the meaning of human action, combined with fundamental differences in dramatic and theatrical modes complicate transculturation.

In placing African tragedy within the larger genre of tragedy, some fundamental differences in tragic theory emerge. While "playing the genre game" is a complicated act, the cultural differences between Africa and the West necessitate different definitions of and developments in tragedy. While tragedy may or may not be dead in the West, it is alive and well in Africa. Two schools of African tragic thought have emerged: metaphysical and Marxist. Both agree, however, that African tragedy contains an essential "Africanness" and has the community as its focus.

When Kenneth Telford's interpretation of Aristotle's *hamartia* as a "missing of the mark," a tragic mistake, is applied to African tragedy we see that African tragedy is more compatible with Aristotle's definition than most Western neoclassical tragedies are. Rather than a "tragic flaw," *hamartia* is a rooting of tragic action in the choice of the protagonist, which, as will be seen below, is more congruent with the African belief system.

In conclusion, then, Greek tragedy proves to be a strong contender for an "acceptable" model of African drama in general and African tragedy in particular. Greek tragedy is adapted into African cultures by African playwrights through a process of transculturation and in order to illuminate or critique both the African culture and society for which it is produced and the culture of Europe that maintained the superiority of European culture during the colonial era. Nonetheless, African adaptations represent in some ways a return to the original impulse behind tragedy (combining art, religion, politics, performance, and socialization in an attempt both to critique society and yet simultaneously to reinforce the sense of community in that society) in a manner which the West has not achieved nor could.

With these conclusions in mind I will, in the subsequent chapters, discuss specific adaptations of Greek tragedy, examining the manner in which individual playwrights have transformed the originals. Each play's transcultural process will be examined, the *hamartia* of the protagonist will be considered, and, lastly, each adaptation will be framed in the larger social and political contexts of the cultures that have produced them. When relevant, I shall explore how such plays further illuminate African tragic theories.

Aristophanes in Africa

Finally, a word must be said about Greek comedy in Africa. Far more Greek tragedies are adapted or produced than the plays of Aristophanes. Most of the scholarly material available indicates that South Africa has had several Aristophanes adaptations, primarily in the 1970s. In 1971, Andre Brink, known for his adaptations into Afrikaans of classical plays, created *Hand vol Vere*, an Afrikaans adaptation of *The Birds*, for the Performing Arts Council of the Transvaal (PACT) Youth Company (Fuchs, *Playing*, 9). In 1974, Barney Simon adapted *Lysistrata* for The Company (Fuchs, *Playing*, 29). Not until 1996 was another adaptation of Aristophanes of national significance produced, although there were some university productions of *The Birds*, *The Clouds*, and *Lysistrata*.

In 1996, Chris Vorster, using students from the University of Stellenbosch Department of Drama, developed *Paradox*, an adaptation of *The Frogs* that utilized "rave" culture and explored issues of gender and culture. The Underworld of Aristophanes becomes a rave club "ruled by a bitch goddess Master of Ceremonies," where "W" (a woman playing the Dionysus role) and her slave debate the rave club denizens on "the issues at hand": South African cultures, feminism, and the role of classical culture in contemporary life ("Maties," 4).

Other than these three productions, Aristophanes remains relatively unadapted in South Africa. Furthermore, very few productions of straightforward translations of the Greek originals appear to have been performed in South Africa in the last half century, as reviews of only a handful of university and community productions indicate. Even less information is available about productions of Aristophanes throughout the rest of the continent. While, as noted above, absence of evidence is not necessarily evidence of absence, it seems fairly safe to conclude that Greek comedy is not nearly as popular in Africa as Greek tragedy, in any African nation. The reasons for this are many and varied.

First and foremost, the overall trend in world theatre is for the Greek tragedies to take precedence over the comedies. There does seem to exist a universal cultural prejudice that sees tragic drama as a higher form of art than comic drama. Tragedy is seen as "high art," whereas comedy remains the province of the "low" or "popular."

Furthermore, specific subject matter aside, tragedy tends to the universal whereas comedy tends to the topical. Douglas Parker argues that *Lysistrata* is Aristophanes's most popular play in production because "it is his most comprehensible, capable of assimilation with the least violence to preconceptions…" (342). It is this problem of contemporary comprehension of the plays of Aristophanes that makes their adaptation less popular than those of the tragedies. Aristophanes's plays rely not just on comedy of situation or character but on numerous puns and topical references. His plays are very referential — witness, for example, the sheer number of times Euripides appears as a character in Aristophanes's plays. In short, one needs a background in the era to truly understand the plays of Aristophanes.

In his 1988 book *Art, Dialogue, and Outrage*, Wole Soyinka wrote a brief chapter on the *Lysistrata*; but other than observing that "*Lysistrata* is a pagan hymn to life," and that "the idiom of *Lysistrata* is the idiom of fertility rituals," Soyinka makes no attempt to link this play or Greek comedy to indigenous African cultural concepts as he does with Greek tragedy and Yoruba drama in *Myth, Literature, and the African World* (36). Soyinka's article could have been written by any scholar with an interest in ritual, as he does not even apply an Afrocentric or Yoruba-based approach to the play. Not even Soyinka sees a connection between Greek comedy and Africa.

Perhaps most importantly, most African cultures have a rich indigenous tradition of satire, humorous storytelling, and bathetic parodying narrative. In short, Aristophanes's function is already fulfilled, and much more easily, by a native tradition. Whereas the tragedies can be used to critique colonialism from a distance or through the medium of Western culture, the comedies of Aristophanes could obscure issues and ideas that are already presented in a more accessible way within the culture. In short, why go Greek when one already has a system of public satire through performance?

In conclusion, apart from a handful of professional and university productions in the admittedly Eurocentric culture of South Africa (there are, after all, no Zulu, Xhosa, or Sotho adaptations, for example, only English and Afrikaans), there is very little, if any, adaptation of Aristophanes's works into African contexts. Even performances of translations of the Greek originals seem fairly nonexistent. For reasons of culture, topicality, and the presence of strong indigenous comedic traditions, Aristophanes does not occupy the same place culturally as Aeschylus, Sophocles, and Euripides. While this certainly does reveal some aspects of African culture, we should note that there is a tendency to privilege tragedy over comedy, especially for adaptation, around the world.

In short, the lack of Aristophanes in Africa can also be seen as a much larger trend in the theatres of the world — to mine the tragic vein of Greece much more than the comic.

Ritual, Roots, and Tragic Form

Action imprisons the world
Unless it is done as sacrifice;
Freed from attachment, Arjuna,
Perform action as sacrifice!
Foster the gods with this,
And may they foster you;
By enriching one another,
You will achieve a higher good.
Enriched by sacrifice, the gods
Will give you the delights you desire;
He is a thief who enjoys the gifts
Without giving to them in return.
                    —*Bhagavad Gita*
                     III: 9, 11–12

In 1859 Charles Darwin published *The Origin of Species*, introducing the concept of evolution into the larger discourse of European intellectual history. In 1871 Schliemann announced the discovery of the site of Troy, transforming both classical studies and the way in which Greek cultural material was interpreted. A huge amount of new information about the classical era was discovered as a result of archeological excavations. While the West was making these advances in the sciences, humanities, social sciences and the study and interpretation of "human" history, the political and economic imperialist aims of the West were also being advanced by rampant colonialism that had already been under way for several centuries. By this period in history, Europe began to organize collectively its colonialist exploitation of Africa. In 1885, only 14 years after the "discovery" of Troy in Asia Minor, the major colonial powers of Europe met at the Berlin West Africa Conference which partitioned Africa and established the colonial domination of the continent by a handful of European countries, notably Britain, France, Germany, and Belgium.

Explorers and anthropologists from the imperial countries went to Africa to study "primitive man." By the last decade of the century, Sir James George Frazer extended the ethnological approach to the classical past by "studying ancient cultures using the same techniques by which his contemporaries approached African societies," to quote Robert Ackermann (46). Frazer became one of the leading exponents of evolutionary anthropology, believing that cultures, like species, evolve from lower forms to higher. He and those who followed him compared the cultures, myths, and rituals of contemporary Africa with those of classical Europe. Such a comparison resulted in a racist conclusion: African societies had "evolved" to the point at which Europe had been during the classical era, and Europe had "evolved" far ahead of Africa. In other words, this theory states that early societies such as the Egyptians, Babylonians, and the Greeks, and contemporary African societies eventually evolve into more complex and technologically advanced societies such as those of Europe. This racist notion was used to justify colonization, in the name of facilitating the evolution of the "primitive cultures of Africa to a "higher" European standard.

We should note that the first conceptualization of the similarities between ancient Greece and contemporary Africa are made in this admittedly pejorative analysis of culture. Thus, the idea that ancient Greece and modern Africa are similar was introduced into the intellectual discourse of Europe and Africa as early as the late 19th century.

Frazer and those who followed him began to explore the relationship between myth and ritual, leading to an enquiry into the origins of tragedy and its relationship to myth and ritual. After *The Golden Bough* (1890), the Cambridge Ritualists, consisting primarily of Jane Ellen Harrison, Gilbert Murray, Francis M. Cornford, and Arthur Bernard Cook, studied the ritual origins of Greek comedy and Greek tragedy and possible examples of protodrama in the ancient Near East. They hypothesized that the origins of Greek tragedy, indeed of all drama, could be found in the rituals designed to illustrate and overcome the change of seasons in the agricultural cycles of the ancient world: the god died with the coming of winter and was reborn with the coming of spring. The type of ritual being celebrated was a sacrificial ritual: the god was sacrificed so that the land might be renewed. As the ritual that marked the death of the god and mimicked his sacrifice became more performative, the art of drama was born.

Subsequently, James B. Pritchard and Theodor Gaster explored the role of ritual in the origins of drama in many ancient cultures. Writing in the Foreword of Gaster's *Thespis: Ritual, Myth and Drama in the Ancient Near East*, Gilbert Murray summarized the Cambridge theory as the supposition that, "drama derived from a religious ritual designed to ensure the birth of the dead world" (vii). Gaster surveyed Canaanite, Hittite, Egyptian, and Hebrew literature for examples of the seasonal drama developing out of myths and rituals contrived to bring the dead god, and hence the dead world, back to life. He concludes that there is ample evidence to support the belief that protodrama developed in the ancient Near East out of these seasonal rituals.

While the specific conclusions of Frazer, Gaster, and the others are not universally accepted, there does appear to be a fairly pervasive consensus among scholars that tragedy is linked to ritual. There is much of ritual in theatre and there is much of theatre in ritual, though the two are neither identical nor homogenous or uniform in structure, approach, purpose, form, action, or efficacy.

More recently Victor Turner has analyzed the complex relationship between theatre and ritual. His theories of liminality, "Social Drama," and communitas facilitate the distinguishing of theatre from ritual while identifying and explicating their respective roles in society. According to Turner, while theatre may have its origins in ritual, it has grown into a different entity, liminoid rather than liminal as ritual is. Theatrical drama reflects the social and political crises of a society, while the crises themselves also reflect the theatrical conventions of the culture. As Turner wryly observes, "There was a lot of *Perry Mason* in Watergate" (*From*, 90). Finally, communitas is the term Turner uses to define the altered social structure that occurs in ritual and theatre, in which all participants are reduced to the same social status. In *The Ritual Process*, Turner contends that during ritual a "model for human interrelatedness" in juxtaposition to the everyday, commonplace model of society is generated, which results in an "unstructured or rudimentarily structured and relatively undifferentiated *communitas*" (96). Customary, normal society is a hierarchy that consists of the individuals of that society arranged in a vertical structure, from the leaders and the powerful at the top to the disenfranchised and powerless at the bottom. During ritual, communitas occurs, and the hierarchy is completely equalized, all participants of the ritual become of the same equivalent status before the gods, the ancestors, and each other. Ritual does not invert the social structure, it simply levels it, so that all members of the community are equals. Likewise, we can observe that regardless of social place, every member of the audience sees the same play. Theatre-going can become a form of communitas.

Turner was a symbolic anthropologist, employing semiotics and structuralism to interpret and understand ritual and its place in society. It was his observation of the parallels and similarities between the social relations and the rituals of the Ndembu of Zambia and the performance practices of Western theatre artists of the 1960s and 1970s which led him to formulate many of his performance theories as they relate to rituals and drama. Nevertheless, distinctions between various African ethnic groups and anthropologists' disagreements over the validity and usefulness of Turner's theories can limit their applicability.

Margaret Thompson Drewel, along with her husband, Henry Drewel, have copiously researched ritual and performance among the Yoruba of Nigeria, the ethnic group from which Wole Soyinka and Ola Rotimi come. Margaret Drewel critiques Turner's relevance to the study of Yoruba ritual, noting that, "The only point of correspondence between Yoruba rituals and Turner's liminal category was that they had a sacred dimension..." (198). She sees Turner's work as essentially limited and limiting in the study of the Yoruba, as the Yoruba are "structurally pluralistic," and Turner's theories work best within a more homogenous society (198). Communitas, in particular, argues Drewel, does not apply to Yoruba ritual: "If there was any common intellectual and emotional meaning, it was certainly not shared by all members of the community, not even all the participants in any of the rituals" (198). In short, the everyday social structure is not suspended within the actuality of being a ritual participant. While all might have the same experience, all participants experience it differently. According to Drewel, this is caused by the nature of Yoruba rituals which "accommodate optionality and individual choice," steering the experience away from possible communitas and towards a more individual experience of the ritual (199). In short, Yoruba ritual does not equalize all participants as Turner claims, but rather focuses the individual on the individual's experience. This is not to say that Yoruba ritual does not generate a sense of community, simply that it does not generate communitas.

However, as noted in the previous chapter, the community is a central part of African tragic theory. Whether or not communitas is possible in African culture is less important an issue than the prioritizing of the community over the individual, or, at the very least, the idea that the individual is part of a much larger community. Ebun Clark, writing in the introduction to the study edition of *Song of a Goat*, asserts that J.P. Clark's play is "a communal tragedy" (1). The twin meaning of "communal" as defined in the previous chapter is, first, being a community-gathering tragedy, a tragedy which affects the whole community and gathers the community together, and, second, suggesting "communion" or "communication," a tragedy which puts us in touch with the gods. The two meanings become inseparable. By "disconnecting" from the gods or by not giving the gods and the ancestors the respect they are due, we not only lose communion with the gods and the ancestors, we also damage the community.

In Africa, many playwrights utilize traditional religions and rituals as material for structure, form, and plot. These playwrights seek not only to connect to traditional culture, but also look to resacralize performance. These elements of traditional masks, clothing, music, language, dances, and rituals are also political. Ritual elements are used to resist colonial culture, Eurocentric representation, and imperial education, which sought to eliminate such practices and replace them with Western ones. Brian Crow affirms this idea, noting that in colonized nations, indigenous culture "has served as a potent weapon in the struggle for independence and liberation" (6). Ritual can be a powerful tool to resist oppression, connect to the sacred, and create community. The two plays considered in this chapter engage both African ritual and the ritual origins of Greek tragedy and combine these two disparate forms into a single ritualized drama (or dramatized ritual) for the sake of the community.

Greek tragedy is a particularly useful model for ritualized drama. James N. Amankulor links African and Greek theatre as examples of "Festival Theatre," described as "theatrical performances which occur under the auspices of a festival or that style of theatrical production which comes to assume the environment and functions of the feast," and which ultimately result in "communal affirmation" (44). Both Athens and traditional Africa framed theatre within a festival context containing both political and religious aspects. Both cultures used the festival performances to generate a stronger sense of community.

In order to better understand the efforts of African playwrights who turn to the ritual origins of Greek tragedy in order to craft modern African drama we must first examine Greek rituals and their relationship to Greek tragedy and similar uses of ritual sacrifice in ancient Greece and traditional Africa.

Ritual and Sacrifice in Greece and Africa

Walter Burkert, in *Greek Religion*, begins by observing the Cambridge ritualists' advancement of the ritual origins of tragedy as a unifying cultural link between religion and drama (3). He continues by approaching ritual "as a kind of language" by which humans can open up communication with the gods (55). He notes that ritual can take many forms in Greek religion: animal sacrifice, blood rituals, fire rituals, the pouring of libations, and the making of material offerings (54–84). All of these forms are actions performed by mortals in the world of the living in the name of the gods or the ancestors. Ultimately, ritual, and specifically ritual sacrifice, is devised to communicate with the gods or with the ancestors.

Writing in *The Encyclopedia of Religion*, Evan Zeuss defines ritual as "those conscious and voluntary, repetitive and stylized symbolic bodily actions that are centered on cosmic structures and/or sacred presences" (12: 405). For the purposes of this study, we might extract from this definition the idea that rituals are repeated actions that the performer chooses to do for the purpose of interacting with the divine or supernatural. Included in this definition would be a Roman Catholic Mass, a libation poured out for the ancestors, a morning prayer, or a week-long *Egungun* festival.

Sacrifice must be distinguished from ritual, as all religious sacrifices are rituals, but not all rituals are sacrifices. Sacrifice comes from the Latin words meaning "to make holy." Joseph Henninger, also writing in *The Encyclopedia of Religion*, defines sacrifice as a ritual offering in which the recipient of the gift is "a supernatural being ... with whom the giver seeks to enter into or remain in communication" (12: 544). It is the use of ritual which distinguishes sacrifice from merely "an offering" (12: 545). Henninger notes that sacrifice can have many intentions: praise, homage, thanksgiving, supplication, and expiation, all of which involve mortals giving a gift to either divine or supernatural beings (gods or ancestral spirits) (12: 549). He traces a variety of possible origins of sacrifice in various cultures: sacrifice can be gifts to the gods (as bribes or homage), communal meals, linking the sacred and profane worlds, reenactments of primordial events, designed to work magic or preserve the *status quo*, an anxiety reaction to misunderstood or unknown phenomena, and a mechanism for diverting violence (12: 550-553). In short, sacrifice is a ritual carried out by giving something to the gods/ancestors, in the hope of something in exchange.

Greek religion is polytheistic and pre–Christian, containing a pantheon of deities who require different observations, rituals, and sacrifices. The result of such a system is a pluralistic religious society in which ritual plays a very different role from that in a more heterogeneous or monotheistic society such as those of Christian Europe. Robert Garland propounds the idea that polytheism is, "by definition" pluralistic, as "god is not one but many" (1). One may choose from a variety of ways to engage and serve the gods. One may change allegiance or perform different rituals every time one wishes to communicate with the divine. Unlike monotheism, in which all engagement with the divine is with a single deity, in a polytheistic system different gods have different spheres of influence, and one may pray to one god for something and offer sacrifice to another god for something else. A polytheistic system, with more than one god to answer to, and those gods often at cross-purposes, is inherently in "a state of permanent flux," as Garland claims.

Similarly, in an African context several religious traditions may coexist in one context. Africans may be bireligious or trireligious, practicing or participating in several different forms of religion simultaneously or in conjunction. An African might attend a Christian church on Sunday, visit a diviner during the week to learn the will of his or her ancestors, perform a number of small daily rituals to appease the gods or his or her ancestors, make a small sacrifice in order to achieve success in work, love, or life, and attend a traditional ethnic festival the following weekend. Culturally, the polytheism of traditional Africa permits Greek tragedy, with its similar polytheistic background, to be more easily adapted than the plays of the Christian West, with monotheistic (and specifically Christian) ideas of ritual and sacrifice.

Greek religious belief and Greek ritual manifest their presence in Greek tragedy in two ways. First, as noted above, tragedy itself is rooted in ritual, at the very least having its origins in the ritual worship of Dionysus, in which groups of citizens would chant dithyrambs in praise of the god on his festival days. By 502 B.C.E. the City Dionysia received public sponsorship, transforming the ritual worship into a state-sponsored civic event, and the following year the choregic system of supporting tragedy at public expense was instituted (Garland, 175). The festival developed into a week-long event, in which tragedies were presented along with civic and religious rituals.

Second, the tragedians used ritual and religion as source material and models for form in their plays. As Jon Mikalson advances, the tragedians placed the contemporary religious culture of Athens on stage — the audience saw their gods, beliefs, and rituals presented and represented (203–5). The end result of this use of popular religion on stage during a festival is the reinforcement of those beliefs and practices, especially as the tragedians show such beliefs as true. The gods can predict and punish, and those who obey them are rewarded and those who disobey are punished. *Alcestis*, *Medea*, the Theban plays of Sophocles, and *The Oresteia*, among others, all demonstrate to the audience the power of the gods, the oracles, and fate. Greek tragedy, by its use of religion as a plot device and the gods as characters, reinforces the very rituals, beliefs, and oracles that it demonstrates.

Tragedy concerns itself with interaction between the human and the divine. Even in plays which do not feature gods as characters, such as *Antigone*, their presence is felt and their influence and will are made pervasive by the actions of the characters. The voice of Apollo speaks through Creon and Tiresias in *Oedipus Rex*, the priest of Zeus begs Oedipus for help in the name of the people, the oracle of Delphi is consulted several times and proven to be right every time. Antigone buries her brother because Creon's law forbidding his burial is not higher than the laws of the gods that demand she do it. Tragedy reinforces traditional models of interaction with the gods, even if they are not physically present.

Tragedy, rooted in ritual, demonstrates the efficacy of ritual and the reality of the gods. Furthermore, René Girard argues that tragedy both represents and replaces a real sacrificial ritual. In *Violence and the Sacred* Girard proposes that the Festival of Dionysus "commemorates a sacrificial crisis" (119). For Girard, tragedy "takes over the role of ritual," and the performance results in the offering of a surrogate victim, such as Oedipus, Antigone, or Dionysus, whose sacrifice protects and renews the community (168). Tragedy is thus derived from ritual, steeped in ritual and religious culture, and developed as a surrogate sacrifice.

Athens is the model for understanding sacrifice in Luc de Heusch's anthropological treatise *Sacrifice in Africa*. He observes that in the mythic prehistory of Athens, men and gods ate together and lived in the same "space" (18). However, ritual and sacrifice become necessary when a schism develops between mortals and immortals: "First we see Prometheus establish animal sacrifice, which confirms the definitive, tragic split between the gods and man" (20). Because gods and mortals share the meat of sacrificed animals, a togetherness is established. De Heusch reasons that sacrifice thus "abolishes the distance between the human realm and that of the gods … without destroying it" (216). Sacrifice is an action that unites the mortal world with that of the immortal.

In reaching this conclusion de Heusch is in agreement with Hubert and Mauss, self-proclaimed followers of Frazer. In *Sacrifice: Its Nature and Function*, they conclude that sacrifice is ultimately a physical, performed action that establishes communication between the mortal and the sacred "through the mediation of a victim, that is, of a thing that in the course of the ceremony is destroyed" (97). Many theorists agree that the process of sacrifice must destroy the object or person who is to be sacrificed, whether through consumption (by flames or by it being eaten) or disposal (in a volcano, in the ocean, in a river), or simply killing in the case of a living being.

Garland argues that Greek religion is "votive in essence" (1). Greek sacrifice involves giving in hopes of receiving — gift is given for gift, mortals sacrifice in order to receive the blessings of the gods. De Heusch argues that sacrifice has at its core the idea of debt — the gods (or ancestors) have already given first, and living mortals owe them, individually and collectively, gifts and offerings which are theirs by right. Both viewpoints have at their root the notion of an exchange. Whether the gods are owed sacrifice for their favor or are sacrificed to in order to gain their favor, sacrifice is a form of reciprocation that unites the realm of the mortals with the realm of the immortals.

Burkert further claims that in a group context sacrifice forms a communal bond that joins the participants into a community (*koinonia*) (58). He maintains the effect of the ritual on the gods did not matter to the Greeks; many festivals and rituals are actually designed not for the gods' benefit, but the community' benefit. Sacrifice also plays an important role in the life of Africans, both individually and communally. An individual may carry out personal sacrifices, the family must carry out other sacrifices, and the entire village may join in a ritual sacrifice during festivals. Even today the budget of many towns and villages in Africa includes money to buy animals for sacrifice as part of civic festivals. Margaret Drewel, reporting of a public rally to raise money for electrification of the area, was told by her informant that "The Development Council bought all the sacrificial animals" (165). Much like in ancient Athens, the public observation of ritual and sacrifice is (at least in part) a political act, supported and sometimes sponsored by the state.

In summary, noting that the origins of theatre are most likely located in ritual, and are linked to ritual sacrifice, some African playwrights attempt to resacralize the contemporary theatre through the use of dramatized ritual and sacrifice. The purpose of resacralizing the theatre through the use of ritual is to create communal drama, drama that creates a community and communicates with the divine simultaneously. Both J.P. Clark and Wole Soyinka, whose plays are considered in this chapter, attempt to create a genuinely African tragedy by returning to the ritual origins of tragedy: the seasonal rituals of ancient Greece. Both plays use ritual sacrifice both to advance the plot and to transform audience into community. Soyinka adapts a specific tragedy whereas Clark simply appropriates the form from its historic origins and places the form in an African context. Thus, the transculturation process, building on a similar climate of polytheistic religion and votive sacrifice in Athens and Africa, takes the

Greek tragic form and places it within an African ritual context. Rather than preserving the original Greek rituals, African ones are substituted, drawing the (contemporary African) audience into a community. The irony, of course, is that both playwrights return to the ritual origins of Greek tragedy and utilize traditional African rituals in order to develop a modern African tragedy.

A Return to Origins: Song of a Goat

The word "tragedy" has at its root the Greek words for "goat song." Walter Burkert, writing in *Homo Necans*, claims that goats were important sacrificial animals in many ancient Greek rites. Initially, goats were sacrificed to Artemis. The skin of a goat added to a *tropaion* (an oak stake adorned with an upturned helmet, spear, and shield) became a symbol of Athena (65–6). Goats and goat sacrifice were also connected to the Pythia of Delphi, oracular priestess of Apollo. Burkert relates the story that the oracular fumes from the cracks in the earth at Delphi had initially been discovered by goats that were subsequently driven insane by the visions (125–6). Lastly, John J. Winkler, after Burkert, argues that tragedy is so named because a goat was sacrificed to Dionysus at the festival (58). Goats, it would seem, are significant to Greek religion, Greek ritual, and possibly Greek tragedy.

Winkler translates *tragodoi*, Greek for "actors," as "billy goat singers" instead of simply "goat singers" (58). He argues, again, after Burkert, that other possible etymologies for tragedy include the Greek words for puberty and testicles, connecting these terms to goats through similar meanings of "rank smell" and "indiscriminate lust" (60, 61). In other words, tragedy, Winkler argues, is not simply rooted in the sacrifice of a goat, it is also rooted in lust, bodily change, and male sexuality. In the first plays, Winkler observes, satyrs comprised the chorus (60). Men whose lower quarters were that of goats and who were known for their lust and sexual prowess were the initial singers of Dionysus's praise. Thus, at its root, both in etymology and visual origins, tragedy is the song of a lusty goat.

Interestingly, many of the extant tragedies involve complex, difficult, forbidden, or problematic sexual relationships. Oedipus has an incestuous relationship with his mother Jocasta. Phaedra lusts after her stepson Hippolytus, the enemy of Aphrodite and eternal virgin. Clytemnestra takes a lover after Agamemnon leaves for Troy: his cousin Aegisthus. When Orestes, her son, comes to kill her, she bares her breast to him, in order to remind him of her breast-feeding him as a child. All of these are examples of the lust, desire, and tragic sexuality that sometimes cause and some-times are the effect of tragic circumstances.

Johnson Pepper Clark Bekederemo, better known in the West as J.P. Clark, poet, playwright, critic, theatre theorist, and former professor of English at the University of Lagos, utilizes both indigenous African nar-ratives and performative techniques as well as the model and language of European drama in order to develop a modern literary theatre in Nigeria. His book, *The Example of Shakespeare*, in addition to offering a morphol-ogy of Nigerian drama, argues in favor of relying on traditional theatre as a "unified combination of the arts lost to Europe," blended with modern realistic European-based theatre techniques to make "true Nigerian drama" (85). He observes that "the ascendant elements are those of music, dance, ritual, and mime" (85). It is the third of these elements that Clark invokes in his drama *Song of a Goat*, a drama which Martin Banham, writing in *African Theatre Today*, notes is firmly grounded in the "Ijaw world" (37). Clark himself is Ijaw, and, in many ways, *Song of a Goat* is not an African tragedy or even a Nigerian tragedy, but an Ijaw tragedy.

The Ijaw people occupy the southeast area of Nigeria, living in the mangrove swamps of the Niger River delta. Traditionally, they have been fishers and farmers (Olson, 236). The Ijaw language, which Clark speaks and occasionally uses in his dramas, does not resemble any other language in the area, which has led ethnologists to believe the Ijaw arrived in the area "long before the other groups" who live in the same geographic area (Olson, 236). The Ijaw live in villages along the river and have historically never been organized socially beyond the village level. Philip E. Leis asserts that the Ijaw have "never constituted a single political entity" (11). Much like the ancient Greeks, organized into city-states instead of nation-states, the Ijaw organize on the local level. This world is the unique environment that Clark seeks to capture in his writing. The Niger delta and the villages of the Ijaw are the setting of his plays.

Whether or not *Song of a Goat* is truly a Greek-derived or -inspired play is actually a point of contention among critics. In *African Theatre Today* Martin Banham reports that many of the similarities between Clark's play and Greek tragedy are "coincidence and not of intention on Clark's part" (38). Ketu Katrak, however, argues that the play "sounds so derivative in verse patterns, idioms, and characterization that it ... can hardly be given the status of an original African tragic drama" (37). Eldred Jones, writing of Clark's play *The Raft*, declares, "Good works of art are notorious for yield-ing more than their authors conspicuously put into them (5). In *The Exam-ple of Shakespeare* Clark himself argues that similarities in structure, form, theme, or development do not necessarily indicate influence or origin:

> The implication is not that one group of people borrowed this and that property from another but that there can and in fact do occur areas of coincidence and correspondence in the way of living among several peoples separated by vast distances and time, and who apparently are of distinct cultures, practices, and persuasions. For example, the orchestra and leader-chorus arrangement of characters occupies as much a principle part in Nigerian theatre as it did in Greek theatre. But this is not to say one is debtor to the other. It is a matter of correspondence and coincidence [83].

Clark argues vociferously for coincidence, and certainly similarities between Greek and Nigerian theatre are not the result of conscious borrowing, as traditional Nigerian theatre performance forms developed entirely independently of any contact with Europe and especially with classical Greece. Indeed, the first two chapters of this study have been spent arguing for similar cultural developments between ancient Athens and many African societies. However, Clark's work as a playwright is certainly influenced by his knowledge of European and specifically Greek dramaturgy. This influence is especially evident in *Song of a Goat*. While Ijaw culture does include ritual goat-sacrifice, and the play itself includes a live ritual goat sacrifice on stage, the title refers to the Greek origins of tragedy, the "goat song."

Clark acknowledges in the introduction to the study edition of the play that "It is quite possible that Sophocles and Euripides are in that play" (30). However, he also argues that García Lorca is "in there, too," yet Clark had never read Lorca before writing his play (30). Clark had read the Greek writers, though, before writing the play and the lack of familiarity with Lorca is in no way evidence that there is no Greek influence. While the play's Lorcaesque qualities can thus be ascribed to "correspondence and coincidence," the Greek antecedents were certainly part of the tragic milieu that Clark attempts to invoke by returning to tragedy's roots, as suggested by the very title of the play.

Clark knew the history and literature of Greek tragedy. His title evokes tragedy's origins. The three plays in the volume in which *Song of a Goat* was published (*The Masquerade* and *A Raft* are the other two) form a trilogy the events of which span several generations, much as in *The Oresteia*. Martin Owusu cautions, however, that unlike the Dionysian competitors, Clark did not write the three plays as a trilogy; rather, each play evolved separately (85). The Theban plays of Sophocles, however, were initially part of three separate trilogies and yet are linked by narrative and thematically. A comparison between these two nontrilogy trilogies can be drawn, as the playwright returns to the same story again and again for different reasons and to focus on different aspects of the theme. Which is not to suggest that Clark was modeling his writing process after Sophocles, merely that much "coincidence and correspondence" exists between Clark and the Greeks.

The similarities do not end there. Owusu further notes Clark's use of unity of place and action (85). Owusu fails to comment on the lack of unity of time, however. But we might note the similarity of staging, as the action of Clark's play takes place in front of Zifa's house, not within it. *Medea* unfolds in front of Medea's house, the action of *Oedipus Rex* takes place in front of the palace of Thebes, *The Bacchae* is set in front of the palace of Pentheus. Because of Greek scenic practice, Greek tragedy is set in front of a structure. Clark's play likewise occurs in front of a structure.

In terms of formal structure, as Owusu notes, *Song* has four major characters, a choral group, and an episodic structure (88). No violent deaths occur on stage; they are, reported instead, by the choral figures, much like in *Hippolytus* and *Agamemmnon*. The formal, structural, and many performative elements of Greek tragedy are present in *Song of a Goat*, intentional or not.

The areas in which Clark differs from the Greeks are the cultural conceptual differences between the Greek and Ijaw worlds, the African performative elements that Clark includes, and the live sacrifice of a goat during the performance. The Ijaw concept of fate differs significantly from the Greek concept. While Rotimi's *The Gods Are Not to Blame* (discussed in the next chapter) finds reconciling irreconcilable philosophies difficult and problematic, Clark's play does not entail as large a cultural shift. According to ethnographic anthropologist Philip E. Leis, who spent 20 months among the Ijaw, "free choice" is the guiding theme in Ijaw ideology and in "economic, social, political, and religious institutions" (3). First and foremost this belief is found in the Ijaw conception of fate and destiny.

The Ijaw believe every human being has a *teme* (soul) which appears before *Wonyinghi*, the mother goddess, before being born. The *teme* "informs the creator as to the nature of his future life" (Leis, 25). In other words, the soul freely chooses its own destiny, whether good or bad, up to and including the moment of death. In the case of individuals who suffer or die, Leis observes, "Ijaw explain why a *teme* chooses to request ill-fortune by referring to the naiveté to be expected of an unborn *teme*" (25). This freely chosen fate is referred to as "the Agreement" and it can be amended through sacrifice. One may offer ritual sacrifice to the ancestors and to *Wonyinghi* and, by doing so, change the Agreement to a better fate.

In a certain sense, this philosophy is not reconcilable with the Greek idea of fate, in which an individual's thread is determined at birth and nothing can change it. However, the Ijaw concept is not inconsistent with Aristotelian tragic theory as outlined in the second chapter. If a tragic character's tragedy is the result of a *hamartia*, a poor choice or a "missing of the mark," then we can compare tragedy with a naïve *teme* choosing a bad life. The major difference lies in the irreversibility of *hamartia*: Greek fate cannot be changed, but ritual sacrifice can reverse or alter an unwise choice by a *teme*. While irreconcilable within the realm of philosophy and religion, the Ijaw world-view finds correspondence with Greek tragic theory. Ijaw tragedy is the working out of poor *teme* choice.

Clark takes impotence and infertility as his subject matter — a topic that, as noted below, is both very serious and potentially tragic in the Ijaw world. Yet British audiences found such a topic "outside the range of tragic dimensions" when presented with Clark's play (Soyinka, *Myth*, 46). Here we see an example of how tragedy's subject matter is culturally bound. While the tragic impulse may arguably be a procrustean bed, the subjects of tragedy are culturally bound. Because of modern medicine and European cultural attitudes towards adoption, Western audiences do not find infertility or impotence a tragic subject. Yet, to the Ijaw, infertility is among the most tragic of circumstances. By using Greek form to explore an African tragic theme Clark develops a uniquely African tragedy.

The 1960 Masks, Wole Soyinka's company, first performed the play at the Mbari Club in Ibadan, Nigeria. Soyinka, who also played Zifa, directed the play. After a two week run in Ibadan, during which the play became a critical and popular success, the play transferred to Lagos for another two weeks. Finally, in 1965, Nigeria sent the production to London as an entry in the Commonwealth Festival of the Arts. Oxford University Press subsequently published the play along with Clark's *The Raft* and *Masquerade* as *Three Plays*. The text cited here is the one found in this volume, although the play is also found both in Clark's *Collected Plays and Poems 1958–1988* and in a study edition for use in the classroom, marking the importance and significance attributed to the text since its first publication.

The first movement begins as the Masseur examines Ebiere. The Masseur serves as a doctor, a therapist, and an oracle within the community, healing both physically and spiritually. Ebiere has come to him at the request of Zifa, her husband. The Masseur asks Ebiere why she has not had more children. She inadvertently reveals that after the birth of her first child, Dode, Zifa became impotent. The Masseur suggests that Zifa's brother be allowed to impregnate her, in order that she might bear more children. He tells her, "...That'll be a retying / Of knots, not a breaking or loosening / Of them" (5).

What the Masseur suggests is not at all unusual in many African communities. John S. Mbiti notes that "the supreme purpose of marriage according to African peoples is to bear children, to build a family, to extend life, and to hand down the torch of human existence" (*Introduction*, 110). The reasons for this belief are many and varied, but in a land with a high infant mortality rate and where families with many children are more economically stable and where children are expected to care for the elderly parents, it is imperative that a wife and husband have several children. Mbiti observes, "It is a very tragic thing when no children come out of a marriage," his very words confirming both the tragic nature of the subject matter and the seriousness with which it is approached (*Introduction*, 110).

In order to overcome the negative repercussions of a childless marriage, many African cultures allow for other family members to help the couple bear offspring:

> If the wife is barren, then she and her husband may arrange for him to have another wife so that children can be born in that family. If the problem lies with the husband, then a close relative or friend is asked or allowed to sleep with the wife in order that she may bear children for the family [Mbiti, *Introduction*, 114].

Such sex for procreation purposes would not be considered "outside the marriage," as it is carried out for the sake of the family. Therefore, such relations are not adulterous but necessary and even commendable. The child is recognized as a member of the family of the husband and wife, regardless of actual biological parentage.

Thus, the Masseur suggests a solution to the problem that is not only culturally acceptable, but also actually mandated by tradition and the gods. Childbearing is "a sacred duty," claims Mbiti (*Introduction*, 104). A childless couple is not only allowed to turn to a third party for procreation, they are expected to do so. In fact, in Ijaw culture, a woman who fails to conceive after marriage may divorce her husband and return to her family (Leis, 29). In the Ijaw world, it is the man's responsibility to ensure that his wife conceives, either through his efforts or those of an agent acting on his behalf.

Ebiere, however, refuses the suggestion. She initially claims such an action would be improper, but the Masseur allows that such an arrangement would be acceptable with proper sacrifice. He explains to her:

> Blood of a goat
> So large a cowrie may pass thro' its nose
> A big gourd of palm wine and three heads of

> Kola-nut split before the dead of
> The land, and the deed is done [5].

In other words, if Zifa makes the proper ritual sacrifice to the ancestors ("the dead of the land"), they will allow Ebiere to bear her husband's brother's children as his own without repercussion. The ancestors not only allow this solution, they demand it, and demand it be accompanied by the proper ritual sacrifice. The Masseur has thus introduced the theme of proper ritual sacrifice.

Ebiere still refuses to listen to the Masseur. She states that Zifa sent her for a cure because the problem is hers. She claims the Masseur has not cured her. She exits in a fury, as Zifa enters looking for her. The Masseur then takes Zifa to task for not impregnating his wife. He indicates Zifa's "sacred duty" to turn to a family member if there is a problem:

> All this is folly, Zifa. No
> Man ever built a house or clear
> A piece of ground all by himself. You ought to have
> Asked for help in your plight [6].

Zifa refuses to ask for help, arguing the problem is his alone. This refusal is Zifa's *hamartia*, taking a problem which tradition dictates is the family's and claiming it is his own to solve alone. Zifa denies his sacred duty and refuses to accept the socially required solution.

Zifa then confesses to the Masseur that he thinks he is under a curse that is causing his impotence, and thus it is not his fault that he cannot procreate with his wife. Zifa's father died of leprosy, given him by the gods because he killed members of his own clan. Zifa, as his oldest son, was required to oversee the funerary rites. Zifa "brought him back home among his people" too early for one who had died of leprosy (10). In other words, Zifa performed the rites too soon after his father's death, which was an offense to the ancestors.

In Ijaw culture, as Leis reports, the ancestors protect the village, "causing illness and death only if they are offended for some reason" (25). Leis further notes that when their descendants act immorally, the *opuduwoiyou*, or "great dead people," will "cause the offenders to be ill or barren until they are propitiated" (25). In other words, within an Ijaw cultural context, Zifa's curse of impotence is appropriate punishment from the ancestors for his actions. An Ijaw audience would immediately recognize in Clark's play both the cause of the problem (offending the ancestors) as well as its cure (sacrifice and following their wishes).

Clark demonstrates that Zifa has a history of ignoring the proper ritual actions. He carried out his father's rites too soon. He does not sacrifice to his ancestors so that they will lift their curse. Now, he does not allow his wife to be impregnated by this brother. Zifa's father also offended the gods and was cursed. Similar to Greek tragedy, Clark's play contains the idea of a curse that is passed down through generations. The house of Atreus was cursed; Atreus, Agammemnon and Orestes all suffered for it. The house of Laius was cursed; Laius, Jocasta, Oedipus, and all of their children met tragic ends. Zifa has a history of not performing rituals and sacrifices properly and of ignoring the will of the ancestors. Clark thus literally sets the stage for tragic action.

The Masseur serves as an oracle, suggesting Zifa allow his younger brother to "take over the tilling of the fertile soil" (11). Zifa, again demonstrating pride, stubbornness, and ignorance in the face of the will of the ancestors flings curses at the Masseur and thunders that he will never allow such a solution. Zifa's *hamartia* is reinforced. The first time he did not carry out the proper sacrifices required of him he was cursed with impotence. This curse brings about with it a second crisis, and Zifa is offered an opportunity to perform the proper sacrifices to overcome the curse. He again refuses to do so.

The second movement begins with the cries of Orukorere, Zifa's "half-possessed" aunt who lives with the family. She cries out that she hears "the cry of a goat" (14). The neighbors enter, serving as a chorus. They comment on Orukorere's situation and pronouncements, calling her mad. Zifa returns home, finding the crowd surrounding his home and aunt and he asks who gave her wine. She, however, announces that she is not drunk but that she sees the future. She warns of a leopard "that will devour my goat" (16). Tonye, Zifa's brother and fellow fisherman, helps Orukorere inside.

The neighbors observe that "a curse lies heavy" on Zifa's family. In her youth Orukorere was chosen to be a handmaiden for the people of the sea, but, "She was so proud she would / Not listen to what the oracle said" (18). She was cursed, Cassandralike, to become a prophetess who would never be believed by those around her. This fact demonstrates again that the family of Zifa ignores the will of the gods and ancestors and suffers as a result. Ebiere and Dode enter and Tonye and Zifa tell them about what has happened with Orukorere, who reenters herself and warns the four of them that terrible things will happen soon.

James Ndukaku Amankulor observes that Orukorere is "a spirit medium of the [Ijaw] possession cult known as *orukoro*" (425). Although she most resembles Cassandra, Amankulor sees her as a Tiresias figure: "She may be a dramatic counterpart of Tiresias but she is certainly *not* borrowed from Greek mythology" [emphasis in original] (425). While Amankulor is essentially correct in that Orukorere represents a class of person occurring in Ijaw culture and is used often as a character in Ijaw literature, she also represents a transculturated prophetess character who appears in Greek tragedy, as Cassandra is cursed not to be believed, but members of the *orukoro* cult are believed when they pronounce. Her character is a transcultural blend. She has been deconstructed and rewritten using the cultural codes and contexts of the Ijaw.

The third movement begins with a domestic scene: Ebiere bathes Dode while Tonye works to repair the nets he and Zifa use to fish. Dode angers Ebiere who strikes him. Tonye displays kindness towards Dode and chastens Ebiere for being an unkind mother who does not understand children. She insults him in return and the two provoke each other until they physically struggle with each other. Tonye tells Ebiere to take her hands off him but, instead, she begins to make love to him and he, hesitant at first, joins in enthusiastically. Dode calls for help, believing his uncle is hurting his mother. Orukorere, however, guides him away from them to elsewhere in the house, telling him that his mother and uncle are "two dogs at play" (28). She recognizes Ebiere as the leopard who devours the goat in her vision, and further demonstrates her prophetic understanding of the ramifications of what has happened by telling Dode, "Only the gods and the dead may separate / Them now, child" (28). While Tonye and Ebiere are mandated by the gods, the ancestors, and cultural tradition to have intercourse for the purpose of bearing children, the required sacrifices were not performed that would make such intercourse acceptable to the gods and ancestors. Furthermore, Clark makes it clear that Ebiere provokes Tonye intentionally, for the purpose of seducing him, and that their actions are not motivated entirely by the need for children, but also by lust. Without the proper sacrifice, their actions are considered incest in this particular cultural context. Similar to *Oedipus Rex* and *Hippolytus*, Clark's play invokes the themes of incest and forbidden love within the tragic frame.

In the final movement, Zifa returns to find Tonye completely unconscious and still in bed. Zifa then delivers a monologue about his suspicions that his wife and brother are having an affair, threatening to kill both of them should his fears prove to be true. His anger against family members for their sexual sins, real and imagined, is similar to Theseus asking Poseidon to kill his son in *Hippolytus* (885–890).

Orukorere enters and hints at what has happened. She continues to recite dark prophecies, but is ignored by Zifa. Tonye awakens and is rude to Zifa, who regards this behavior as confirmation that something has happened in his house. Orukorere suggests that he clean himself and make sacrifice to the ancestors to resolve the situation. Zifa responds, "I do not need cleansing, perhaps others do" (33). Zifa sends Tonye for a sacrificial goat so that sacrifice might be made to the gods. Orukorere suspects that the sacrifice may not be the true motivation for Zifa's actions, warning him, "Be careful, son, and do nothing that is / Rash. When the gods ask for blood it is / Foolish to offer them oil" (36).

Tonye returns with the goat and the family gathers for the sacrifice. Tonye holds the goat's head while Zifa decapitates it with a single stroke. This particular stage direction caused many problems in the initial production when the actors attempted to actually sacrifice a goat on stage. Abiola Irele, writing in the introduction to Clark's *Collected Plays and Poems 1958–1988*, observes, "The play, which consists in the ritual slaying of a goat as part of the dramatic action, was calculated to impress, even if its motivation was not a crude sensationalism, but to awaken the sense of drama as communal rite" (xl). Clark was attempting to resacralize drama, to add a real sacrificial ritual to the onstage action so that the play transcended mere drama and became a genuine communal tragedy. However, the sacrifice of a live goat on stage at the Mbari Club proved to be problematic in the initial production, as Martin Banham observed in his review in *The Journal of Commonwealth Literature*, "Nigerian Dramatists," as the ritual decapitation of a real goat on stage "without, for obvious reasons, adequate rehearsal" was a "chastening experience" for actors and audience (132–3). More than "a single stroke" was required to decapitate the goat. After the first show, a symbolic gesture was substituted for the actual sacrifice, allowing for a smoother performance, but obviously changing both the onstage action and the meaning thereby generated. The play no longer contained a "real sacrifice," which proved to be too difficult and too messy, and ultimately did not draw the audience into a communal ritual, but rather disturbingly broke through the liminoid state of the theatre, shocking and alienating the audience. The actors were not the characters, the stage was not the Niger delta; thus, the real death of a real goat in front of the audience conflicted with the obvious artificial enactment onstage. The substitution of a symbolic gesture was more in keeping with the symbolic nature of the theatre.

The use of real rituals and sacrifices as part of a staged performance complicates the attempt to resacralize performance or to reintroduce a genuine religious element to the theatre. As Kacke Götrick questions, when modern university-trained professional actors perform "real" rituals onstage, are these acts "meant to be perceived as fictional or efficacious" (162)? In other words, how real are the "real" rituals and what effect are they intended to have? The framework of a professional theatre performance is in direct contradiction to the purpose, function, and working or religious ritual. While the ritual contains performative and theatrical elements, and theatre contains ritual elements, the two are not the same.

In *From Ritual to Theatre*, Victor Turner notes that theatre "resembles without being identical to" ritual (32). One of the major differences between the two is the distinction made between participant and observer and whether or not attendance is mandatory. Theatre distinguishes between performer and audience; ritual does not. Theatre involves audience choice; one chooses whether or not to go. In Nigeria, those who attend the theatre for plays such as *Song of a Goat* tend to be highly educated Western-minded, urban citizens. They choose to attend the theatre as a cultural event. Ritual does not involve choice: one either attends or faces consequences including, but not limited to, excommunication and rejection by the community or divine punishment. Ritual has efficacy: the performance of ritual achieves a real effect. Theatre does not necessarily have efficacy; it need not do anything.

The initial mistake that Soyinka as director and Clark as writer made in actually sacrificing a live goat is that such an act attempts to cross the boundary between ritual and theatre. Regardless of the intention behind such an act, audiences would not accept such a shift in action. Götrick explains that modern urban audiences in Africa will be skeptical of traditional world-views: "Few spectators can be expected to perceive a religious ritual, performed on stage, as an authentic non-mimetic act of worship. The majority of the audience is likely to interpret the theatre according to the present Western theatre concept..." (169). As noted above, the audience at the Mbari Club was a typical, modern urban African theatre audience: highly educated and not comprising a single homogenous "community." Unlike the audience for a traditional ritual, modern theatre audiences come from different ethnic and religious groups and from a variety of professional and economic backgrounds. Soyinka is not Ijaw. As the character is fictional, no actual ancestors are being sacrificed to. The lack of community other than as a theatre audience meant that the ritual could not be a real ritual. African audiences will no more accept a "traditional" ritual as being real when performed onstage by actors than would a Western audience accept as real the performance of a Catholic mass by actors. Even the Greeks, while perhaps using real animal parts on stage, would not have sacrificed a real goat during a tragedy. To do so violates the sacredness of ritual and the mimetic nature of theatre, and offends the audience. *Song of a Goat* could not cross the line between theatre and ritual because the theatrical frame could not be broken.

As a piece of theatre, however, and as a tragedy, the play was very effective. Femi Osofisan, assessing Soyinka's work in the context of theatre on the Nigerian stage, observes that Soyinka's portrayal of Zifa was particularly powerful during the sacrifice scene. Osofisan claims that Soyinka "led participants into collective panic – Aristotle's 'terror' – at the climax of sacrifice" (154). Aristotle writes that tragedy must purge the audience of terror and pity precisely by subjecting them to terror and pity. By watching tragedy we, the audience, have a cathartic experience. Osofisan does not explicate the source of this "collective panic," that is, whether it is caused by the action of the sacrifice, the use of a live goat the first night, the psychological situation played onstage, or the realization that the sacrifice comes too late. Yet it is interesting to note that Osofisan interprets the audience's visceral reaction to the sacrifice as an embodiment of the Aristotelian "terror and pity." Osofisan's analysis is another example of how the Greek model of tragedy and tragic theory becomes a litmus test for African tragedy: does the tragedy have a cathartic effect for the audience?

As the play continues, the blood from the goat accidentally soils Ebiere's clothes, symbolically representing her own ritual impurity, having slept with her husband's brother without making the proper sacrifices first. Zifa, seeing the stain, asks her to place the goat's head into a pot that is too small for it. Ebiere, recognizing that Zifa knows what has happened, faints as the pot shatters, symbolically representing the family shattered by a sacrifice that has come too late. Tonye flees the house, and the neighbors enter as Zifa gets his cutlass to kill his brother.

Zifa enters the house and the neighbors follow him inside. They return to report the offstage action, as a messenger or chorus in Greek tragedy would. They tell the audience that Tonye has killed himself by hanging from the loft. Interestingly, in Greek tragedy, hanging is reserved for women. Nicole Loraux reports, "Hanging is a woman's way of death" (9). In addition to Jocasta, Antigone, Phaedra, and Leda hang themselves. Loraux theorizes that hanging is "the death of a grieving wife," although the grief is not necessarily for a lost husband, but for a marriage that has been defiled or compromised (31). Jocasta learns she is married to her son. Phaedra makes an unsuccessful pass at her stepson, then falsely accuses him to her husband. Antigone first has her marriage to Haemon canceled; she then claims death has her husband. In Clark's play, Tonye has defiled his brother's marriage and committed incest.

According to Paul Bohannon, within African society suicide occurs in three forms: "jural," or suicide because the person has committed a crime which he or she must atone for; "domestic," or suicide because the person's domestic role or domestic situation is threatened; and "status-linked," where a person commits suicide because of a lowering of status within the community (262). Tonye's suicide bears elements of all three reasons.

Furthermore, whereas in Greek thought hanging may be a woman's way of death, in African thought both genders hang themselves. Bohannon notes, "As in many other areas of the world, the overwhelming method of suicide in Africa is hanging" for men, who usually carry out the act inside the house (263). In other words, regardless of the Greek influence in Clark's play, Tonye's suicide by hanging within the house is not only plausible within an African context, but also his reasons for killing himself are common and acceptable to an African audience.

Interestingly, Bohannon notes that it is "characteristically African" that suicide is not seen as "a volitional act" (263). When a person commits suicide, even if the reasons for doing so are apparent, people still believe that the person acts under the influence of the ancestors, the gods, or witches. No one would consciously choose to end one's life. Therefore, if someone does commit suicide an outside influence must be working on that individual. In the context of Clark's play, Tonye's suicide, and Zifa's that follows it, would be seen as a working out of the ancestors' curse on the family.

Zifa then leaves the house, reentering the stage space. He delivers a monologue in which, according to the best Aristotelian guidelines, the recognition and reversal have occurred at the same time. Zifa recognizes that Tonye was attempting "to keep / What his brother was powerless to keep / In the house" (41). Zifa recognizes that the tragedy came about as a result of his refusal to carry out the proper sacrifices and allow his wife and brother to procreate for the sake of the family. By putting his own selfish pride before his wife, the family, the house, the ancestors, and the gods, he has brought about the ruin of his house. His brother is dead and his marriage has been destroyed because of his shortsightedness. His house, that he believed he was preserving, has collapsed because of his actions. His suicide must be the final sacrifice to the ancestors to atone for his errors.

The neighbors follow Zifa as he goes to "find a place to rest" (41). They return a moment later to again relay the offstage action. They tell Orukorere that Zifa went to the river which was the source of his livelihood and drowned himself. Orukorere gives the closing monologue of the play. Thrown into a hysterical fit because of the tragedy which she foresaw, she tells the neighbors to take away the lights and to allow darkness to literally fall on the house that already has a metaphoric tragic darkness about it. Both brothers are dead and with them, the family. The neighbors agree to leave, taking all the lights with them. The closing lines of the play, spoken by one of the neighbors, "Come away, tomorrow is a heavier day" (45), suggest the choral ending of such tragedies as *Oedipus Rex*.

Clark also wrote an alternative ending at the suggestion of one of his former university professors who proposed a return of the Masseur. Ebun Clark, writing in the introduction to the study edition of the play, argues that the alternative ending "weakens" the play, as the Masseur's presence is not needed after the tragedy has occurred (29). In the alternative ending, the Masseur enters after Orukorere's monologue and learns from her what has happened. As the neighbors flee the site of tragedy, the Masseur gives the moral of the tragedy:

> Do not, my people, venture overmuch
> Else in unraveling the knot, you
> Entangle yourselves. It is enough
> You know now that each day we live
> Hints at why we cried out at birth [87].

Certainly this closing reflects a tragic view of life found in such Greek plays as *Oedipus Rex*, which ends with the choral lines, "Count no man happy till he has passed the final limit of his life secure from pain" (1529–30). The tragic view sees the human condition as one in which we are born to suffering, and death is a form of release, and reminds reader and spectator alike of the transcultural nature of life and death. Regardless of the meaning given to living and dying, all human beings do both.

In conclusion, in *Song of a Goat*, J.P. Clark developed a hybrid tragedy. He used Greek form and structure, including the illustration of the *hamartia* in the case of Zifa, followed by a recognition and reversal. The *hamartia* concept finds a correlation in the Ijaw belief of the Agreement between a *teme* and the creator. By his use of a series of rituals (and absence of ritual) in the play, including an initial (if misguided) attempt to sacrifice a live goat, Clark also connected his tragedy to the origins of tragedy in ritual sacrifice. He placed the story in an African setting, used African subject matter, and ensured that his characters' actions were appropriate and believable within an African context, regardless of Greek conceptualization of those actions. Clark has transculturated Greek form and structure through the Ijaw world-view into an African context, creating a truly African tragedy and a true transcultural artifact.

Dionysus and Ogun: The Yoruba Tragedy of Wole Soyinka

The Yoruba are one of the largest single ethnic groups in the Federal Republic of Nigeria. However, as Ato Quayson explains, "'Yoruba' is a generic term [that] conceals a wide variety of peoples often holding allegiance primarily to specific tribal groupings," such as the Oyo, Ekiti, Ijebu, Egba, Ilesha, Ondo, and Ketu (10). Together, these groups compose the entire Yoruba nation.

Ile Yoruba, Yorubaland in English, is the Yoruba homeland, reaching from "the swamps and lagoons of the coast" to the "woodland savannah and the distant bend of the Niger," covering an area roughly the size of Great Britain (Smith, *Kingdoms*, 7). Ife, a city in the northeast of *ile Yoruba*, maintains primacy within the religious and cultural life of the Yoruba: *ile-Ife* is the cultural heart of the Yoruba. Historically, the Yoruba have existed in the western area of modern Nigeria for many centuries.

The Yoruba past is orally preserved, as the Yoruba had no written language until the advent of the Europeans. According to Robert Smith in *Kingdoms of the Yoruba*, a number of factors contributed to the development of Yorubaland as a nation within pre-colonial Africa. The presence and agricultural base of the yam, kola tree, and palm tree (for palm oil and palm wine) signified "food production capable of supporting an organized society" (4). The geographic proximity to both the coast and many rivers allowed for trade with Europeans on the coast and Islamic merchants near the Sudan (5). With trade from Islamic merchants came exchange of ideas and philosophies, and although Islam did not take root among the Yoruba as it did among the Hausa, the Islamic concepts of political organization combined with indigenous ideas about government enabled the Yoruba to organize themselves politically on a national level, as opposed to the groups which never organized beyond the village level, such as the Ijaw. Wole Soyinka, Nobel laureate, teacher, essayist, poet, dramatist, novelist, and Nigerian national hero has theorized a "Yoruba tragedy," based on the transculturation of Greek tragic theory into Yoruba culture. Soyinka primarily presents his theories in "The Fourth Stage," subtitled "Through the Mysteries of Ogun to the Origin of Yoruba Tragedy," found in *Art, Dialogue, and Outrage*, although elements are also found in *Myth, Literature, and the African World*. Soyinka analyzes tragedy using the Nietzschean Apollo/Dionysus dichotomy. He identifies both of these tragedy-forming impulses within one Yoruba deity: Ogun, Yoruba god of iron, war, creativity, and hunting. Although Obatala represents some aspects of Apollo, Soyinka concludes that "Ogun, for his part, is best understood in Hellenic values as a totality of the Dionysian, Apollonian, and Promethian virtues" (*Myth*, 140). He calls Ogun "the first actor" and notes that "Yoruba tragedy plunges straight into the chthonic realm," which is "the transitional yet inchoate matrix of death and becoming" (*Art*, 22). Ogun, as the first being to enter that gulf and cross it into the world of the living, became the first actor.

Ogun is a changing, transforming, mutating deity, altering himself to meet whatever needs modern Yorubas have. He began as a god of iron, war, and hunting, but today his realm includes everything from "modern technology to highway safety – anything involving metal, danger, or transportation," according to Sandra T. Barnes in "The Many Faces of Ogun" (2). Barnes claims that Ogun operates under the "inclusive principle," in which "no one feature gives definition to a domain" (12). In other words, the boundaries of Ogun's sphere of influence are not limited; he incorporates anything which he is required to by his followers, including, in this case, Yoruba tragedy.

Ogun is a paradoxical deity, and this fact is perhaps paramount to Soyinka's theories. As Barnes writes, "Ogun kills and he creates," and an unending "tension is maintained between the two sides of the equation" (16–17). Ogun manifests contradictory principles in the same deity, thus also making him the god of balance. Like Dionysus, who presides over both wanton madness in the form of bacchanalia and highly organized creativity in the form of the tragic theatre, Ogun is a paradoxical figure who inspires artists and dramatists, yet is also the patron of warmakers and destroyers.

Soyinka draws upon the parallels between the forms of worship given to the two gods to further make his case. He notes Dionysus has the *thrysus* and Ogun has the *opa*, an iron-tipped pole used in his worship (*Art*, 33). Ogun is also the god of wine in Yoruba cosmology. Soyinka argues that the parallels between the two deities allow Yoruba theatre artists to develop a tragic form similar to the Greek, one that is a manifestation of Ogun instead of Dionysus.

Yoruba tragedy, maintains Soyinka, begins in Yoruba metaphysics. According to the Yoruba, a gulf exists between the gods and the mortals, between mortals and ancestors, and between mortals and the unborn. This gulf separates mortals from all they have been and all they will be. The gulf between mortal and immortal can be diminished through sacrifice, but it can never truly be bridged (*Art*, 23–4). Soyinka writes, "Tragedy, in Yoruba traditional drama, is the anguish of this severance, the fragmentation of essence from self" (*Myth*, 145). Tragedy originates in a person's "severance" from his or her true "essence," which is what he or she was in the world of the unborn and will return to in the world of the ancestors. Tragedy also originates in the anguish of humanity's severance from the gods (*Myth*, 145). The moment of Yoruban tragedy occurs when the tragic hero, voluntarily or involuntarily, undergoes a third separation, away from society. The tragic hero thus exists in "the fourth stage," a liminal area in which the hero is disconnected from the community, the gods, and himself and has plunged into the above-mentioned gulf.

Soyinka postulates that this character undergoes some kind of suffering for the sake of the community while in this transitional phase. The final result of the suffering is not what happens to the hero but what happens to the community as a result of the hero's suffering: "Whether the protagonist is alive or dead at the conclusion of the drama, his tragic experience itself is profitable both for his self-knowledge and for his people" (Katrak, 19). This idea is a variation on the Aristotelian idea that tragedy is not necessarily what happens to the hero, but rather what happens through the hero. The focus of the tragedy is the community and the effect of the tragedy on it, rather than a hero and his or her fall.

The result of this shift in focus is of paramount importance to Yoruba tragedy. Katrak asserts, "The goal of Yoruba tragedy is to energize the community at the conclusion; therefore the need for calamitous endings is eliminated" (19). It should also be recognized that this elimination of calamitous endings connects Yoruba tragedy to Aristotle's contention that tragedy is not defined by a tragic ending but instead is a function of structure, in which likelihood and necessity bring about catharsis for the audience (read: community).

Soyinka further focuses on the importance of ritual in Yoruba tragedy, connecting myth to ritual and tragedy. Katrak asserts that in "Soyinka's universe" the gods are "a felt presence"; audiences are not only aware of the deities but believe in them as real beings (40). The death of tragedy, asserted by Steiner for the West, does not hold true in the African context. Katrak argues, correctly so, that "tragedy functions as a productive genre in modern Africa because of a definite living tradition of myth and ritual" (40). The Yoruba gods are present and active in Nigeria in a manner which the Greek gods are not anywhere in the world in the modern period.

Ritual, as Katrak observes, is "the bridge between myth and tragedy," and the enacting of ritual connects myth (belief system) with tragedy (imitation of an action for communal cathartic purposes). Ritual is an active manifestation of myth. When narrative and Ogun's rituals are blended, Yoruba tragedy is born. For Soyinka, the heart of these rituals is language and music, corresponding to Aristotle's notions of diction and music. Language and music become the tools through which ritual is enacted and Yoruba tragedy is created, implying an interesting inversion of Aristotle's hierarchy.

To summarize the paradigm, Yoruba tragedy is based on the myths and rituals of the Yoruba, utilizing their language and music. The action is "the disintegration of the Self," as Soyinka terms it (*Myth* 145). The tragic hero, already separated from his "true essence" and the gods (as are all people), is then separated from his people and undergoes a kind of suffering which has a direct result on the community of the play, with the overall goal of energizing the community watching the tragedy unfold (the audience). The hero enters a "fourth stage" in which he is no longer himself and completes the tragic action which will bring life, change, or energy to the community.

Yoruba tragedy is informed by both Greek tragic theory and Yoruba ritual and belief. Katrak explicates: "The final 'restitution' in the formal structure of Yoruba tragedy is always beneficial for the community, though it may or may not include the protagonist's coming to self-knowledge" (31). By "restitution," I take Katrak to mean "reversal" in the Aristotelian sense: a change in the hero's fortune that may be either good or bad. In other words, the final component of the formal structure of Yoruba tragedy will always be a reversal of the community's fortune to a positive one from a negative one. The hero's fortune may change from positive to negative, but the change of the hero's fortune must always result in a positive fortune for the community. "Recognition," on the other hand, defined by Aristotle as a change in the hero from ignorance to knowledge, is possible in Yoruba tragedy, but not necessary.

Soyinka has come under criticism and acclaim for his attempts to locate a tragic base within Yoruba culture. Biodun Jeyifo, in his introduction to Soyinka's *Art, Dialogue, and Outrage* calls Soyinka a "mythoclast," claiming Soyinka uses tragedy to "debunk" the myths of his own people, demonstrating how these myths are used to support an oppressive class structure. Jeyifo argues that in order to formulate his tragic theories, Soyinka "drew both from the historical realities of the period and more particularly from mythological sources" (xvi). Jeyifo further argues that the positive strength of Soyinka's pieces is drawn from the myths, as Soyinka displays "pessimism concerning the realities of Africa" (xvi). Soyinka is a mythoclast. Like the Greek dramatists before him, he is a conscious interpreter of myth, using the myths of his people to critique both the myths and the institutions that those myths support. Yet, like the Greeks, Soyinka does not merely "debunk," he interprets and uses the myths to guide the Yoruba, Nigerians, and all Africans towards a potentially better future rooted in traditional, indigenous metaphysics.

Soyinka is criticized, however, for his problematic use of the word "ritual" in his writings and his seemingly limited yet transforming definition of the word. Derek Wright refers to the essay "The Fourth Stage" as "tangled metaphysics," noting that Soyinka's theoretical writings shift the meaning of the word "ritual" from context to context (31, 35). Wright further observes that "Soyinka's reading of ritual as the drama of transition is in itself a narrowly selective one" (37–8). Soyinka is a playwright, not a ritualist, priest of Ogun, or a theologian. He is a Yoruba writer of literature who consciously interprets myth and ritual for ideological reasons.

The Yoruba notion of ritual is much more open than Soyinka's writings imply it to be. Margaret Thompson Drewel, writing of Yoruba ritual, maintains that even the language used to describe ritual and related phenomena is ambiguous: "Yoruba often use ritual, festival, spectacle, and play interchangeably ... so that any generic distinctions have to acknowledge that, as categories of performance, they are open and inclusive rather than closed and exclusive" (12). Drewal argues that the Yoruba "play" ritual, "constructing identities, transforming consciousness— their own and others— through spontaneous interruptions and interventions in ritual..." (171). Yoruba rituals are inclusive performances, experienced individually (as noted above), which remain in a state of flux and fluidity, changing as the participants change. This definition differs from the more serious and fixed image of ritual that Soyinka implies in his writing.

We should note, however, that by applying ritual to theatre, Soyinka *is* creating a sense of ritual play in which identities are literally constructed. The audiences are included in the rituals, so to speak — they are distanced observers who are nevertheless drawn in through narrative. While Soyinka's theories might be rendered problematic by shifting and limiting definitions, his actual plays are arguably excellent examples of Yoruba ritual and "play."

Yet Soyinka has constructed his own ritual world. Ogun, his patron, Yoruban Dionysus, and originator of Yoruba tragedy, is, as defined by Soyinka, more a construction of the playwright than the actual Yoruba deity. Donald J. Cosentino wryly observes (quite rightly, though) that "Soyinka has made Ogun world famous. He is the deity's press agent and apostle to the non–Yoruba literate world" (305). Yet, the portrait which Soyinka paints of his patron is one filled with "Afro-Wagnerian pomposity" (306). Cosentino contends that Soyinka takes "enormous liberties" with oral tradition, changing Ogun to meet his needs. While the god is inclusive and fluid by nature, as noted above, Soyinka has transculturated his deity, making him a tragic god for the whole literate world, and not necessarily the Ogun worshipped in shrines and households in Nigeria.

Soyinka's interpretations of Greek culture and religion also suffer from occasional inaccuracy. Joseph Henninger reports that there exists in Greek culture two kinds of blood sacrifice, one for ouranic gods and one for chthonic. Ouranic gods require a sacrificial meal; thus pigs and cattle are sacrificed to the gods and then consumed by the participants. Chthonic gods require a blood sacrifice of destruction, in which the entire carcass is burned, and thus only inedible animals are used in chthonic sacrifice (12: 555). Soyinka does not distinguish between the two types of sacrifice, but claims that his ritual drama originates in the chthonic realms. The difference between the types of gods, types of sacrifices, and manners of sacrifice is important, and Soyinka's failure to distinguish in his theories implies that Soyinka uses Greek culture as he does Ogun – taking what he needs and ignoring that which differs.

Gods are what we make them. Soyinka uses a fluid and inclusive deity to preside over the creation of a transculturated art form. He is not writing for a Greek audience, but for a contemporary African, specifically Yoruba, audience. He has developed a transcultural African theory of tragedy that seemingly reflects a number of Aristotle's observations of tragedy. He confirms, as postulated in the previous chapter, that African tragedy involves the actions of a tragic hero that influence the community of the play and the audience. Soyinka is not without his critics, many of whom offer legitimate criticism of his theories and use of terminology and concepts. Yet, Soyinka's entire body of work, both dramatic and theoretical, may be viewed as part of a larger project of developing an African tragic form that is rooted in African metaphysics. Unlike in mathematics, not all parts of the formula must be entirely accurate in order for the form to begin to take shape and develop.

As a playwright, Soyinka has written a number of Yoruba tragedies. As a theorist he has analyzed *Song of a Goat*, the plays of Ola Rotimi, Duro Lapido, and other African dramatists, and the work of non–African dramatists. Soyinka clearly speaks with authority when engaging tragedy. Interestingly, for a dramatist who has based his own theories in part on the similarities between Ogun and Dionysus and on the Greek theories of tragedy, Soyinka has actively adapted only a single Greek tragedy to an African setting: Euripides's *Bacchae*. Furthermore, this adaptation, entitled *The Bacchae of Euripides* was first written and performed in the United Kingdom, not in Africa. The National Theatre of Britain commissioned the play. The play makes an interesting test case to examine how Soyinka's tragic theories manifest themselves in practice.

Ritual and Revolution: Soyinka and The Bacchae of Euripides

In August 1973, the British National Theatre Company premiered Wole Soyinka's commissioned adaptation of Euripides's tragedy of the god of theatre at the Old Vic. Soyinka's play is in many ways a paradox that also contains a number of paradoxes that ultimately contribute to its meaning as well as embody the paradoxical nature of both ritual and Yoruba tragedy.

To begin, the title itself is paradoxical. Though named by Soyinka *The Bacchae of Euripides*, the adaptation is not *The Bacchae* of Euripides. It is an adaptation, very different from the Euripidean original, yet it remains faithful to the Greek tragedy in spirit, in its embrace of Dionysus, and in its metatragic nature, all of which will be analyzed below. The title is misleading and ambiguous, but reveals many of Soyinka's intentions behind the adaptation.

Charles Segal argues that Euripides's original play was so named because, "In the absence of any single center of values or meaning, the vacuum is filled by the Maenad-chorus in their ambiguous, problematical way" (*Bacchae*, 165). The Bacchae themselves are the center of the play. They are the people affected by Dionysus, who follow him. Segal, in arguing that Euripides's play is a metatragedy, claims that the chorus does not stand in for the author, but rather represents the audience: those who are directly affected by the power of Dionysus.

Dionysus is an ambiguous and problematic god. He is the god of wine and tragedy and, as Burkert reports, "has many forms" (*Greek*, 166). Even within *The Bacchae*, which presents the god as a young man, Dionysus remains mysterious and difficult to interpret. The audience learns only of his birth and of his intention to bring his worship to Thebes. Interestingly, this play remains the only known tragedy which concerns itself with the patron god of drama, Apollo and Athena being the gods who make very regular appearances in the extant tragedies. Even in the worship of Dionysus through theatre, the god remains a shadowy figure.

Worship of Dionysus is connected with madness, drunkenness, transformation, and inversion. The mania which possessed his followers, however, was "not the ravings of delusion," claims Burkert, but rather "an experience of intensified mental power" (*Greek*, 162). Much like the peyote visions of Native American shamans of the southwest, the illusory effects of being possessed by Dionysus actually allow the "victim" to achieve a state of hyperawareness, to be in touch with a greater reality than the mere physical plane. It is this power which both Euripides and Soyinka choose to represent onstage, although for different reasons and to different ends, as will be outlined below.

Soyinka differentiates his adaptation from the original in a number of ways. He changes the plot, moves events around, adding and removing scenes and lines. Soyinka introduces a host of characters not present in the original: the Slave Leader, a slave chorus, priests, floggers, a chorus of vestals, and a "Christ-Figure." These characters fulfill a variety of functions within the play. In his production note to the text, Soyinka mandates that "The Slaves and the Bacchants should be as [racially] mixed a cast as possible, testifying to their varied origins" (xix). By doing so, he sets a play which is informed by Greek tragedy, Yoruba culture, and early seventies British theatre practice in a landscape and culture of the imagination which is, ostensibly, separate from any one particular culture.

The opening to Soyinka's play is similar to the Greek original's. Both plays begin with Dionysus addressing the audience before the palace of Thebes, near the tomb of Semele. The staging is somewhat similar, as well, although Soyinka's stage directions call for some slaves to be harvesting in the background of the scene, thus establishing visually at the outset the significance of the slaves and their labor (which, as evidenced by the harvest, is connected to the agricultural cycle). The fact that the slaves are harvesting also indicates to the audience that the play is set as the earth is dying at the end of the agricultural cycle. As tragedy's origins are in the ritual sacrifice that renews the earth and starts the cycle over again, the audience learns that a sacrifice will be needed after the harvest in order to bring about the rebirth.

In the Greek original, Dionysus delivers a 63-line speech retelling the mythic origins of his birth as well as his reasons for returning to Thebes. He begins:

> I am Dionysus, the son of Zeus,
> Come back to Thebes, this land where I was born [1–2].

He continues with the story of the insemination of Semele, daughter of Kadmus, by Zeus, and the birth of Dionysus from Zeus's thigh, following the death of his mother. From lines 20 to 30, Dionysus relates that he has heard rumors that his father was actually a mortal and the Zeus story a clever lie told by Semele to hide her son's illegitimacy. He further declares that Thebes "lacks initiation in my mysteries" (40), but that he will eventually "stand revealed to mortal eyes as the god / she bore to Zeus" (42–3).

Soyinka's adaptation differs significantly in this opening monologue. Dionysus's speech is much shorter, much more direct, and much angrier in tone. Rather than retell the legend, Soyinka's version begins around line 25 of the original, stating, "Thebes taints me with bastardy. I am turned into an alien, some foreign outgrowth of her habitual tyranny" (1). Dionysus is an outsider, an outcast from the city, and, worst of all, has had his divinity denied and is considered a bastard. Of particular note is the declaration that Thebes has "habitual tyranny." Dionysus claims that Thebes is, by tradition, an oppressive state, and his outcast status is an example of Thebes's oppression.

From the opening lines, Dionysus is a Soyinka type of figure. Soyinka is the native son transformed into an alien, an outsider, by the "habitual tyranny" of the state. Soyinka brings truth and freedom, but the Nigerian government has imprisoned him, exiled him, and tried to silence him during his career. *The Bacchae of Euripides*, while an adaptation of a Greek tragedy commissioned by a British theatre company, fits quite comfortably within the context of Soyinka's more direct critiques of the Nigerian state, including such recent works as *The Open Sore of a Continent*, whose very title is a direct criticism of the regime of Sani Abacha. The Dionysus of Soyinka's play may be read as a Soyinka-like figure: one who wants to liberate the people and bring truth, but is oppressed by a tyrannical government.

Soyinka's Dionysus does not intend to reveal himself as a god; he does not want to initiate Thebes into his mysteries, as his Greek forebear did. Soyinka's Dionysus wants only total and unconditional submission. He tells the audience, "I am the gentle, jealous joy. Vengeful and kind. An essence that will not exclude, nor be excluded. If you are Man or Woman, I am Dionysus. Accept" (1). He ends with the simple command, "Accept." One does not choose to believe in Dionysus. One does not contemplate and attempt to provide a theosophy for Dionysus. One simply accepts Dionysus. He "will not exclude, nor be excluded," and, therefore, is all encompassing. To reject him is to reject life. The Dionysus which Soyinka presents is the Ogunian Dionysus of his theories. J. Michael Walton, writing of the original, explains, "Dionysus exists, the play tells us. Good or bad is irrelevant. What is essential … is respect for that power" (*Living*, 170). This aspect of the original is summarized in the one word, "Accept." Both the original play and Soyinka's adaptation concern themselves with respect for the divine and natural orders, respect for the power which those orders bear, and willing submission to that power.

The power that one must accept, however, is not merely the power of a god. Two other kinds of power are suggested by Dionysus's dictate to accept him. Soyinka links Dionysus with the political power of the masses, represented by the slave chorus. Good or bad, the masses also have power, and one must respect and accept that power or be overthrown by revolution. Elizabeth Hale Winkler, in comparing three different transcultural adaptations of *The Bacchae*, observes that Soyinka's is unique in that it equates "Dionysiac possession with political rebellion" (226). Dionysus's mania is freeing, not only from the constraints of society and morality, but also from political oppression. Dionysus, therefore, becomes a symbol of subversive and revolutionary power that must be respected and accepted, lest it overwhelm habitual tyrants.

The other power that must be accepted is the power of theatre as represented by its patron, Dionysus. Charles Segal writes that the Euripidean play makes the god of theatre "a visual and tangible presence on the stage," the only Greek tragedy to do so ("Bacchae," 162). The paradoxical nature of Dionysus manifests itself in the paradoxical nature of the theatre: tragedy uses illusion to create truth (156). (This notion also applies to African theories of theatre. Biodun Jeyifo, after all, called his book *The Truthful Lie*.) We can only appreciate and learn from the theatre by "surrendering ourselves" to the drama performed in the name of Dionysus (157). The mania that possesses the followers of Dionysus is a metaphor for those who get caught up in watching a drama and "lose themselves" in the play. Segal argues that *The Bacchae* is a metatragedy, a tragedy about the power of tragedy. Soyinka's adaptation is a political metatragedy, as will be outlined below. It is a play that deconstructs tragedy and the political power of surrendering to Dionysus, both literally and metaphorically.

Following this introductory monologue, in Euripides's play the chorus of Asian Bacchae enter, singing the praises of Dionysus in a lengthy (103 lines!) ode that closes by calling the citizens of Thebes to the mountain to worship Dionysus. As they exit, Tiresias enters wearing the ceremonial clothes of Dionysus, carrying a thyrsus, and calling for Kadmus, who comes in response.

Soyinka's play diverges from the original after the introductory monologue. As Dionysus exits, a herdsman and the Slave Leader enter instead of the Bacchae. We learn from their conversation that a slave is to be sacrificed – flogged to death – in an annual ritual. When the Slave Leader asks why a slave must die each year, the herdsman replies, "Someone must cleanse the new year of the rot of the old or the world will die" (4). Soyinka thus firmly roots the play in the agricultural ritual sacrifice origins of drama. His adaptation further develops Segal's metatragedy theory by introducing the ritual origins of tragedy into a tragedy.

Soyinka, however, pairs the theatrical significance of the ritual with its political importance. The Slave Leader warns that the oppression of the slaves will lead to unrest, noting that the ritual itself is capitalism at its worst. He argues that slaves should not be the victim of a sacrifice: "Because the rites bring us nothing! Let those to whom the profits go bear the burden of the old year dying" (4). The herdsman warns him that such talk is treasonous. The audience is thus shown a further example of the "habitual tyranny" of Thebes, in which one is not even allowed to speak dissent against the established order. The ritual enactment has both theatrical and political significance.

A huge procession enters in which the Master of Revels leads priests

The Bacchae of Euripides, Workshop Theatre, University of Leeds. The Slave Leader and the Herdsman argue as Dionysus and the Slave Chorus look on. *Photograph courtesy of Dr. Amanda Pierce.*

and vestals while a bound Tiresias is flogged by men with lashes. Dionysus appears, proclaiming, "Sing Death of the Old Year, and welcome the new god" (6). The slaves are reluctant to welcome Dionysus for fear of punishment, though they wish to; but his presence unnerves the members of the procession who are members of the establishment. The priests, the servants of gods, ironically flee the presence of the god, and, at Dionysus's behest the slaves and vestals begin dancing. The Slave Leader announces that the presence of Dionysus is a sign to resist Thebes's oppression: "Nature has joined forces with us," he proclaims (7). The vestals and slaves abandon both procession and fields in order to go to the mountains, to dance and worship Dionysus.

Tiresias is left on stage with the floggers, whom he upbraids for doing their job too well: "Can't you bastards even tell the difference between ritual and reality.... Symbolic flogging, that's what I keep trying to drum into your thick heads" (9). With this statement, the play begins to deconstruct its own metatheatricality, acknowledging that the ritual of flogging is more "symbolic" than real, just as the play itself is more symbolic than real. Interestingly, Tiresias seems to view ritual as being the opposite of reality, which is inconsistent with the traditional African viewpoint, which maintains that ritual not only has efficacy and that its performance or absence can and will have a very real effect, but also that ritual and the worlds to which it connects the performer are more real than reality.

Tiresias already wears the ceremonial clothes of Dionysus under the sackcloth he wears to be whipped. Dionysus approaches Tiresias as the floggers exit and, through their conversation, we realize not only that Tiresias and Dionysus know each other, but also that Tiresias is a high priest in Thebes—this, too, marks a departure from Euripides. Dionysus asks why Tiresias must be flogged, to which Tiresias responds, "The city must be cleansed. Filth, pollution, cruelties, secret ambitions—a whole year's worth" (10). By volunteering to be flogged, Tiresias becomes the same ritual sacrifice as Dionysus, dying for the sins of the old year so that the new one may come. When Dionysus asks the mortal what might happen if this symbolic act of renewal should kill him, Tiresias responds that he will be transformed by his death and become new himself. He then turns the question on Dionysus in a self-conscious questioning of the myth pattern: "Is that not why, Dionysus? ... Why you all seem to get torn to pieces at some point or the other?" (11). Tiresias's cynicism reveals an awareness of the ritual paradigm; unlike his Greek predecessor, he has read *Themis, Thespis, The Golden Bough,* and *The Hero with a Thousand Faces.* Yet, in his cynicism, he wishes to partake in the ritual. When pressed further as to why he volunteered to be flogged, Tiresias claims that he wished to touch the life force.

Tiresias is emblematic of the educated elite whose very knowledge and cynicism isolate them from the truth of the traditional ways. While lip service is given, Tiresias is disconnected from the life force and attempts to connect to it in a symbolic ritual. But a symbolic ritual can only get one in touch with a symbolic life force. Tiresias must discover real ritual, not seek reality in an empty, theatrical, state-sponsored ritual. As opposed to the slaves and vestals, who simply accept Dionysus and go to the mountains and dance, Tiresias engages in an intellectual exercise of symbolically acting out the myth pattern. He must learn to let go of the intellect and simply accept. Dionysus commands Tiresias to dance, and he does, finally getting in touch with the life force from which an empty, symbolic ritual kept him.

Kadmus enters and watches Tiresias, who stops his dance in order to warn Kadmus that his divine grandson has returned to Thebes in order to challenge his other, power-mad, mortal grandson. Kadmus acknowledges the approaching conflict between his two grandchildren, and the two old men then hide as the Bacchants enter, dancing and singing. The slave chorus follows them and the Slave Leader approaches the first Bacchant,

The Bacchae of Euripides, Workshop Theatre, University of Leeds. Dionysus speaks to the Bacchants as the slaves and Slave Leader look on. *Photograph courtesy of Dr. Amanda Price.*

interrupting the frenzy. The first Bacchant and Slave Leader recite a prayer of blessing on those who follow Dionysus, as the orgiastic singing and dancing rages anew, with the slaves joining the Bacchants in the celebration. Eventually, the other slaves must drag the Slave Leader to safety, as the Bacchants grow even more frenzied. The Bacchants run off in their mania while the slaves fearfully exit, seeking safety.

At this point, Soyinka's play converges with Euripides's again. Tiresias and Kadmus emerge and, in light of what they have witnessed, excitedly discuss their own garb and the worship of Dionysus. Kadmus argues with himself about dethroning Pentheus, his grandson who rules the city of Thebes. Tiresias, however, refocuses him on the worship of Dionysus. Kadmus laments his age, but Tiresias invokes the inclusiveness of Dionysus: "...It is the will of Dionysus that no one be excluded from his worship," to which Kadmus responds, "Except those who exclude themselves"

(26). Dionysus, as has been repeatedly acknowledged, is an inclusive god whom some choose not to accept. The line also foreshadows the entrance of Pentheus.

Pentheus enters, as in the original, with a monologue explaining his absence from the city and his concern for the rumors he has heard about Dionysus. In Euripides's play he claims he was away (without giving reason for his absence), but returned to the city upon hearing that the women of Thebes, including members of his own family, have fallen under the spell of someone who claims to be Dionysus. Euripides's monarch claims he will stop the mountain revels, calm the women, and arrest and execute the "foreigner" who has come to Thebes claiming to be Dionysus.

Pentheus is distanced from the gods, far more than Tiresias. In terms of Yoruba tragedy, Pentheus is a man who believes that the gulf separating him from the gods is impenetrable by either side. The original play concerns itself with politics and religion as well as the points where both intersect in the personal lives of the leaders. In direct opposition to Pentheus's beliefs, as J. Michael Walton points out, exists Dionysus, who is a demigod, a living bridge between mortality and divinity (*Living*, 170). Like Ogun, by his very existence Dionysus bridges the "fourth stage," the gulf between mortal and immortal.

Page DuBois argues that the play and its divine character manifest the blurring of boundaries: "In *The Bacchae*, Euripides' greatest masterpiece, the tragedian collapses all boundaries, fuses male and female, human being and animal, Greek and barbarian" (119). Dionysus is the god who removes difference and limits, and therefore, privilege. Soyinka's adaptation takes this concept into the religiopolitical sphere: Dionysus is the original Marxist, abolishing all social and political barriers through ritual. The slave is the equal of the king, the equal of the high priest, the equal of the Bacchant. No one is to be excluded from the worship of Dionysus, and all worship equally, in the same manner. Gender, social, national, and even ontological boundaries collapse.

In Soyinka's play the force arrayed against the egalitarianism and inclusiveness of Dionysus is the militaristic, egotistic Pentheus and his thuggish soldiers. The stage direction for Pentheus's entrance indicates that he is "militaristic in bearing and speech" (26). Both his appearance and his language are suggestive of a militaristic dictator, perhaps even intended to evoke the military dictators of Nigeria, whom Soyinka has habitually parodied, attacked, satirized, mocked, criticized, and condemned in such plays as *A Play of Giants*, *Kongi's Harvest*, *Flowers from Zia*, and, most recently, *The Beatification of Area Boy*. Soyinka frequently presents leaders on stage as being power mad and obsessed with their own

The Bacchae of Euripides, Workshop Theatre, University of Leeds. Pentheus as arrogant young dictator. *Photograph courtesy of Dr. Amanda Price.*

self-importance. The dictator characters in *Kongi's Harvest* and *A Play of Giants* move to silence and destroy not only any threat to their power, but even any who dare to speak a critical word about their reigns. To these characters we must add Soyinka's Pentheus—Greek tyrant manifested as African military dictator.

Interestingly, when Pentheus enters, the language of the play, prose to that point, switches to verse. Pentheus speaks verse and only responds when spoken to in verse. His language pattern thus further distinguishes him as being artificial and distanced from what is natural, normal, and accepted by both slaves and gods. Pentheus's speech artificially heightens and distances him from the people he rules, the people whom he considers beneath him. It also distances him, however, from the prose-speaking god Dionysus.

Soyinka's Pentheus establishes himself with his first lines, even stronger and harsher than Euripides's: "I shall have order! Let the city know at once / Pentheus is here to give back order and sanity" (27). From his first words, the audience is reminded of the speeches of military heads of state after a coup, promising to reestablish "order and sanity." Unlike the original, this Pentheus explains why he was away: "I'm away only for a moment / Campaigning to secure our national frontiers..." (27). Soyinka's

Pentheus is a general, a man obsessed with security and order, both within and without the nation. He moves against perceived threats, whether from neighboring lands or his own people's religious mania. Pentheus is the embodiment of the oppressive military dictator so common to postindependence Africa, bearing similarities to his forerunners, Ghaddafi, Mobutu Sese Seko, Idi Amin, or even Nigeria's own General Yakubu Gowon, ruler of Nigeria since a 1966 military coup, whose politics led to a bitter, bloody civil war from 1967 to 1970. Soyinka has always been a voice of opposition to the military governments of Nigeria, and has returned to the problem of military rule in his writings again and again, from the autobiographical *The Man Died* to the recent *The Open Sore of a Continent*.

Pentheus, as in the original, sees Tiresias and Kadmus and grows greatly offended. He condemns them for wearing the ceremonial garb of Dionysus. Tiresias argues in favor of accepting Dionysus, stating that if one considers the power of wine over individuals, Dionysus must be a great god indeed. Kadmus and Tiresias encourage Pentheus to join in the worship and thereby become part of the community. Pentheus further scorns them and sends a detachment of soldiers to arrest Dionysus. As Kadmus and Tiresias exit, Tiresias again draws the play into metatragedy by asking, "Kadmus, in Greek the name Pentheus signifies sorrow. Does that mean anything? Let's hope not" (36). Soyinka's characters are self-aware and aware that they are in a Greek tragedy. By asking Kadmus this question, Tiresias tells the audience that Pentheus is destined to stand against Dionysus and lose. Soyinka's Tiresias's prophetic knowledge in this play is less that of the chosen sayer of Zeus and Apollo than that of a well-read literature instructor. Foreshadowing rather than foreknowledge is his forte.

As with the characters in *Song of a Goat*, Pentheus could avoid his fate through proper piety and communication with the gods, but he will not. He is concerned with only his own power and how that power is reflected through his control of the nation and the people. Pentheus does not even recognize the god in their midst. His power-hungry politics results in a blindness to reality which demands his ultimate downfall, in particular since his myopia has a negative impact on the community. As he disdains the community, both individually and collectively, such impact does not matter to him. In short, Pentheus, as a military dictator, causes a problem in the community. The freedom which Dionysus represents grows like the mania which Dionysus's touch brings, until all in the nation are engulfed and under its power, except for those who do not accept the idea of freedom for all. The oppression of Pentheus is matched and overwhelmed by the revolution brought about by Dionysus.

The slaves begin to question Pentheus about Dionysus, who rebukes them, draws his sword, and threatens to kill anyone who approaches him. The slaves begin a group prayer in praise of Dionysus. In the face of such faith, the Slave Leader recites a messianic poem about Dionysus, referring to him as "the autumn sacrament," but also "the fearful flames" which will "melt as wax the wilful barriers of the human mind," but not "to the tyrant mind" (38–9). Soyinka ties together in this poem the idea of the ritual sacrifice of the god to renew the world with the idea that Dionysus also represents a freedom that must be stopped according "to the tyrant mind." Ritual sacrifice and political revolution against a tyrant are synonymous actions as they both represent acceptance of a natural order of things.

The entrance of the soldiers with the captive Dionysus interrupts the liturgy of Dionysus. The attendant of Euripides becomes an officer who reports the capture to Pentheus. Pentheus, not believing in the divinity of Dionysus, interrogates him as to his identity and his agenda. Dionysus simply tells Pentheus that his worship is everywhere and all nations will eventually fall before him.

Pentheus responds, "We have more sense than barbarians. / Greece has a culture" (45). This line is the first real indication of a geographic location: not Thebes, not Africa, but "Greece." This Greece, however, is not historic Greece, modern Greece, or mythic Greece. Rather, Soyinka creates an amalgam of the mythic Thebes of Euripides, contemporary Africa, and his own transcultural, imaginative landscape. As noted above, the slave cast has varied ethnic origins, which gives the lie to a possible real-world locale. Likewise, Soyinka does not use any characteristic Africanism, African language, or site-specific reference to Africa. Like Euripides, Soyinka is a self-conscious interpreter of myth who uses the story of Pentheus to craft an object lesson about ritual, revolution, and tyranny. Soyinka's play occurs in an imaginary landscape, a metaphor for any land in which oppressed people come under the sway of a freedom movement, and the self-serving militaristic dictators intent on maintaining their own power attempt to stop that movement.

Interestingly, Pentheus attributes his land's ability to resist Dionysus to the fact that his Greece has "culture," as if culture is an antidote that provides resistance to religious mania, freedom, and mass movements. By culture, Pentheus makes the same mistake Tiresias did at the beginning of the play: believing ritual and religion to be the opposite of reality. By culture, Pentheus means "high culture"; his people are too intelligent and sophisticated to worship Dionysus. Such a belief only reinforces how out of touch Pentheus is, both with reality and with his own people.

Pentheus has Dionysus chained, shorn, and imprisoned. Dionysus clearly warns him, "Set me free" (45). Pentheus refuses and the slaves and Bacchants wail and protest. The slaves are initially crushed that a seeming messiah figure has been defeated, but the Bacchants continue to cry for Dionysus to come to them. Their prayer builds to a frenzy, calling out, "Now. Now is the time... Be manifest! Come, the new order!" (52). The language suggests both popular revolution and the promise of a better political and social future under the religious rule of Dionysus. The chorus calls out for "the new order," suggesting both the end of the oppressive social structure and the coming of a revolutionary rule.

As in the original, the palace is destroyed in an earthquake, and Dionysus emerges. After assuaging his followers he prepares to face Pentheus in his true form. Pentheus enters and demands an accounting for the destruction of the palace. The herdsman enters and warns Pentheus that the Bacchants and the women of Thebes are running amok in the mountains and in the area around the city. Pentheus instructs the officer in charge of the detachment of soldiers, "Set in motion / The standard drill for a state of emergency.../ I want the troops massed here directly. / We attack the Bacchae at once" (62). Different from his Euripidean counterpart, Soyinka's Pentheus is military in mind and bearing, planning a military operation to stop his own people. The play of Euripides has become the tale of the conflict between the god who, like a rebel leader, would bring the people to freedom, and the military dictator who would stop him, all framed in metatheatrics and ritual.

As Pentheus plans his campaign against the women, Dionysus offers to bring the women to Thebes without the use of force. Pentheus refuses, demanding his weapons and armor. Dionysus tells Pentheus that Pentheus fears him because Dionysus can free him. The tyrant then asks which of them is the prisoner, reminding Dionysus of his place. But Dionysus replies:

> You, Pentheus, because you are a man of chains. You love chains. Have you uttered one phrase today that was not hyphenated by chains? You breath chains, talk chains, eat chains, dream chains, think chains. Your world is bound in manacles [65].

Pentheus is just as confined by his rule as are the people under him, but he knows only that he must keep power. By reinforcing a rigid social hierarchy, Pentheus is just as confined by the system as those under him.

Dionysus offers to guide Pentheus to the mountain himself, so that the dictator might see for himself what is happening. Pentheus accepts this offer, deciding to go to the mountain alone with Dionysus, wearing what he believes is his armor, but is, in fact, a Maenad costume, just as in the Euripidean original.

As Dionysus dresses Pentheus in woman's robes, Pentheus asserts he shall have to punish Tiresias and Kadmus, and possibly kill his own mother for dishonoring the royal house. Anything Pentheus perceives as a betrayal is punishable by death. Pentheus is a ruler who will kill his own family members in order to maintain control and order — a Theban Saddam Hussein.

While Dionysus dresses Pentheus, the slaves recognize that the moment of reckoning is approaching. They remark:

> We will call them
> Spirits,
> Gods,
> Principles,
> Elements,
> Currents,
> Laws, Eternal causes.
> But they are born in the blood
> Unarguable, observable and preserved before time...
> As freedom. No teaching implants it
> No divine revelation at the altar.
> It is knotted in the blood, a covenant from birth [77].

As human beings, we are born to life and to freedom. This is the human condition. Those such as Pentheus resist it and oppress their nations and people. But no one can deny freedom for long, for, like Dionysus, it is an irresistible force that will overwhelm those who try to repress it. As Pentheus marches off in his dress to stop the Bacchants, a wail is heard off stage and the slaves begin celebrating freedom.

The chorus acts out a stylized mime of the hunt as the officer tells the story of the death of Pentheus at the hands of his mother and the Maenads. The freedom that the slaves were celebrating begins to seem less sweet to them. As one remarks, "Oh this is a heartless / Deity, bitter, unnatural in his revenge. / To make a mother rip her son like bread / Across a banqueting board! I pity her" (86–7). The slave expresses distaste for the violence that was necessary in order to bring about freedom. Soyinka's play fuses the theories of ritual and revolution, of Victor Turner and Franz Fanon. Both sacrifice and revolution are rooted in violence, both require that something be destroyed in order that power be unleashed. Both also absolve the destroyer, as the violence is necessary and justified. The death of Pentheus is both the sacrifice which will renew the earth and the violent act of overthrow which ends a repressive regime and allows for a more free society.

As if on cue, Agave enters with the head of Pentheus. She tells the assembled group that she has killed a lion and all must join in "a feast of celebration" (89). After a maypole dance, the head is nailed to the palace wall. As Kadmus and Tiresias enter with Pentheus's body, Agave realizes it is her son and not a lion that she has killed. She wants to remove the head from the wall, but it begins to act as a fountain, spraying blood in every direction.

Tiresias, however, not seeing that it is blood, tastes the flow, and tells the gathered crowd that it is wine. One by one they approach the head and drink from the fountain of blood wine, including Kadmus and Agave. It is this final image which transforms the metatragedy of Euripides into the sacrificial ritual drama of Soyinka. At the end of the revolution, the play enters the realm of the metaphysical. The death of Pentheus frees the nation from his political oppression, but also draws the people together into a community with communitas. The final image of the play is of Theban royalty, slaves, and foreign Bacchants all drinking together at the same fountain.

Unlike in earlier rituals, Dionysus is not the dying god — he is the freeing god. Pentheus, not Dionysus, is the one who dies so that the world might have life. The fountain which flows from his head becomes, literally, communion wine, the drink of the communal rite. The fountain flowing is both the completion of the ritual and the divine response to it: the gods have looked favorably on the sacrifice of Pentheus and allowed a miracle. The divine world approves of the revolution and the ritual.

Yet simultaneously the Greek original posits the ending of the play as a "disconnecting" from ritual reality. Segal argues that Agave's awakening in Euripides's play "symbolizes the process by which drama frees itself from the bondage of ritual" ("Bacchae," 170). The return to conscious reality separates drama from ritual, and yet the effects of ritual are real: the sacrificed object is still destroyed. The effect of drama is also real, yet illusory, as the actor who plays Pentheus lives to be sacrificed again, yet the audience has been moved by what they have experienced.

Soyinka's play, however, reverses this process. The ending of his play, differing as it does from the original, places Soyinka in opposition to Segals's conclusion. Ritual is real and inseparable from reality. While Euripides's play celebrates the Dionysiac freeing of tragedy from ritual and celebrates the metaphor of "surrendering to Dionysus" by attending and being affected by the theatre, Soyinka's play is a transcultural attempt to resacralize drama, as well as celebrate the freeing link between ritual and revolution: both free the oppressed from habitual tyranny. Whereas Euripides's play celebrates freedom, Soyinka's play celebrates the process of freeing.

As a theatrical performance, the initial run in London was successful, but critics have judged the play to be below Soyinka's usual standards.
Martin Banham, writing in *African Theatre Today*, argues that the play
"fails to show the quality that is evident elsewhere in Soyinka's work," and
disparages its "inconsistency of style" and "inaccessibility" (35–6). Admittedly, the initial production in London was an African transculturation of
a Greek tragedy using a British cast, performed before a British audience.
The play would most likely be better understood by an audience who had
lived under an oppressive military dictatorship, although its blend of style
and reliance on the original might make the play problematic for an African
audience as well.

Norma Bishop, on the other hand, praises the play as a brilliant amalgam of Greek and Nigerian cultures, considering both the participatory
nature of theatre in each culture, the postwar environments in which each
play was written (post–Peloponnesian for Euripides; post–Biafran for
Soyinka), the use of choral criticism of the ruling powers, and the use of
Dionysus as a mediating figure between non–Western and Western worlds,
having originally come from Asia Minor himself (115–7). The play certainly does draw upon similarities, both between Greek and Nigerian cultures and also between historical situations. When Soyinka wrote his
version, the four-year Biafran War had devastated Nigeria and left the
country in ruins, literally as well as economically. Similarly, the Peloponnesian war proved the downfall of Athens. Both playwrights blame the
leaders for the wars.

Interestingly, however, the play had subsequent productions in New
York and Jamaica, but never in Nigeria itself (Gibbs, "Masks," 57). Thus,
The Bacchae of Euripides is ultimately a great paradox: not only is it not
The Bacchae of Euripides, but it is arguably the best-known transcultural
adaptation of Greek tragedy which has never been performed in the cul-
tural context into which it was transposed. The play blends ritual and rev-
olution, African and Western, literary and political, and, accordingly is like
Dionysus: all-inclusive.

The final irony of the adaptation is that it does embody aspects of
Yoruba tragedy, as theorized by Soyinka, and yet the community which
was rejuvenated at the end of the initial production was not Yoruban, but
British. Onstage, the sacrifice of Pentheus both brings about communal
benefit and diminishes the gulf between gods and men. The onstage
sacrifice removes a tyrannical ruler from power, his death renews the world
and seasons, and wine flows from his head, creating communitas as all in
the community share this divine gift from the god of wine. The audience
that celebrated this sacrifice, the revolution that it encompasses, and the

freedom that it brings, however, were an upper and middle class British audience at the Old Vic who had come to see an adaptation of a Greek tragedy. Soyinka takes the Greek original and plunges through the transcultural depths of Yoruba tragedy and Yoruba performance codes in order to create a play that was presented in an entirely British context.

The play does embody paradox, metatragedy, and communal ritual. The play does fuse ritual and revolution. Although the conditions of its initial performance limited the possibility of it being well-received, Soyinka has firmly ensconced the play within both the concerns of the original and his own prescriptions of Yoruba tragedy. Therefore, ultimately, one might argue that the play is an interesting experiment in transculturation which, like Dionysus, one must simply accept.

THE VOICE OF THE *POLIS*

In matters that belong to the public, training for them must be the public's concern. And it is not right either that any of the citizens should think he just belongs to himself; he must regard all citizens as belonging to the state, for each is a part of the state; and the responsibility for each part naturally has regard to the responsibility for the whole.

— Aristotle, *Politics*, Book IV

Political Theatre in Athens and Africa: Myth as Civic Lesson

In his work *Writers in Politics*, Ngugi wa Thiongo observes that "The poet and politician have certainly many things in common. Both trade in words. Both are created by the same reality of the world around us. Their activity and concern have the same subject and object: human beings and human relationships" (71). From the writings of Aristotle, the Greek historians and tragedians, to the work today of such politically involved writers as Ken Saro-Wewa, recently executed by the government of Nigeria, Vaclav Havel, imprisoned playwright turned president of Czechoslovakia, and Salman Rushdie, still living in hiding because of the *fatwa* pronounced against him by the Ayatollah Khomeini, politics and literature are mutually influencing spheres of human activity. Writers attempt to influence politics as much as politicians attempt to control writing. The history of censorship by the state and its representatives is long and complex, beginning with the Greeks. Plato would ban drama from the ideal republic because of its power to influence. Phrynichus was censured and fined for writing the politically unpopular *The Fall of Miletus*, and, as a result, playwrights were discouraged from writing about contemporary events in the Greek theatre.

Ngugi further argues that the relationship between writing and politics in contemporary Africa is especially crucial as African culture is "developing under the strangling embrace" of colonialism, industrialization, and Western capitalism (72–3). Writers in Africa often become far more politically active than their Western counterparts, sometimes paying with their lives for their writings and their activism. As noted above, the Nigerian government executed Ken Saro-Wewa for his involvement in Ogoni politics. Likewise, Christopher Okigbo died for the cause of Biafran freedom. Other writers, including many in this survey, such as Wole Soyinka, Athol Fugard, and Femi Osofisan use their drama to speak out against the political order of their homelands and, as a result, have been incarcerated, had their passports seized, been placed under surveillance, and been the victims of police harassment. In South Africa alone, during the apartheid era, the very act of writing might place the author at odds with the government, and hundreds of South African authors saw their works banned, themselves "banned," and were driven to exile or suicide.

The very act of writing, therefore, can become an act of resistance to on oppressive political situation. South Africa alone has demonstrated the full range of the development of political and protest drama, which Loren Kruger refers to as "an instrument in the struggle" to overcome apartheid (150). The use of drama as a tool of resistance has been documented by many authors such as Orkin, Kerr, Larlham, Kavanagh, and Gunner. As noted above, Greek tragedy can be used to "disguise" protest and resistance drama.

The political uses of drama, however, do not end with protest and resistance. Many nations use drama for development. I. Peter Ukpokodu notes that some African nations "use theatre as a vehicle for promoting social awareness among the rural communities" (257). These nations have had success in using theatre to teach about farming techniques and health considerations or to educate voters in new democracies or warn of the dangers of disease (see Mda, Salhi, and Abah). This type of popular theatre, however, which is performed for the marginalized rural and urban poor in order to develop solutions to widespread problems such as AIDS, does not usually employ the model of Greek tragedy. While perhaps simulating the original Greek experience, as theatre for development is a forum for addressing the peoples and problems of the nation, the actual texts are completely unrelated. Most, if not all, of the political plays based on Greek models are rooted firmly in the urban cultures of modern African, written by those connected to the universities and performed for both elite and popular audiences.

Rather than protesting colonialism and neocolonialism, in the manner that much early African political drama did, these plays engage the problems of a postindependence Africa. While still acknowledging the problems created by colonialism, the new political drama explores postcolonial politics. These plays are less plays of resistance than plays that examine and question the newly independent nation from within. The sole exception to this rule, *Demea*, initially written as a play of resistance, was not performed until after the conditions it was resisting had begun to end. Thus, Guy Butler's play took on a new role: that of questioning the nation's future in terms of its past.

Greek tragedies, after all, were not initially plays of resistance written and performed by an oppressed people, but rather served to educate the people and question the polis and its actions from within. According to J. Peter Euben in the introduction to *Greek Tragedy and Political Theory*, "Greek tragedy directly shaped classical political theory" (6). The chief theoretician in both cases was, of course, Aristotle who wrote what many consider to be the defining classical definitions and arguments in his *Politics* and *Poetics*. Plato, as well, wrote extensively on the drama and politics. Drama questioned, affirmed, and sometimes refuted the actions, both individually and collectively, within the political sphere of the polis. As noted above, the festival surrounding the tragedies was nothing short of a full affirmation of the status quo in fifth-century Athens. The festival and plays reinforced the community's self-image and reflected the political traditions of the polis as held by the elite of the city who sponsored and attended the *City Dionysia*.

Not all plays or playwrights, however, unquestioningly accepted and supported the status quo. The plays of Euripides, in particular, stand out as an example of the questioning not only of the polis, but of the places and roles of the disenfranchised, such as women and foreigners, and of the morality and practicality of the political decisions of the polis. Euben notes that Greek drama, both tragedy and comedy, were "preoccupied with membership and community..." (36). These plays concern themselves with the rights and responsibilities of the people, with citizenship and belonging, and asking the question to whom does the polis belong? Greek tragedy represents one of the first self-explorations by a community of what it means to be a member of that community and what it means not to be.

Greek political life in the city was volatile and noisy. Rather than a homogenous view of the polis and the status of its various residents, those residents held a wide variety of perceptions, which often came into conflict with one another. The dominant discourse in Athenian politics (held and presented by the ruling elite of citizens) was always under attack by a variety of viewpoints and beliefs. Greek tragedy, rather than always supporting the dominant discourse, frequently became a site of opposition to the hegemony of the Athenian elite. The theatre gave voice to women and foreigners (*Antigone, Medea, The Trojan Women, Persians*), as well as called attention to the silence of those same groups (*Alcestis*). The dissenting voices of tragedy opposed the status quo even as the celebratory nature of the festival upheld it.

By questioning the dominant discourse, the playwright also assumes a voice of authority, as Justina Gregory points out in *Euripides and the Instruction of the Athenians*, which, by its very title, suggests the nature of drama as a political teaching tool. Gregory notes "three strands of political reflection in the plays of Euripides" (9). The first is the "evocation of democratic institutions and practices," a reflection of the power structure of the polis and the manner in which such power is in the hands of the citizens (9). Second is "access to the political process, guarantee of free speech, and the impartial protection of the law," the rights of all citizens in the polis, which also reflects on the fact that noncitizens (including the women of citizen families) did not have these rights (10). Lastly, "Athenian imperialism" is a large theme in Euripides's work, and as citizens of the polis, even Athenians not directly involved in imperial practices participated in, supported, and benefited from them (11). While one's own imperialism is and was not a large concern of African playwrights, the first two reflective strands play an important role in the adaptation of Greek tragedy, by African playwrights. These plays, while not all Euripidean, all concern themselves with the realities of national institutions and practices, the political process, and the rights of the members of the community.

Like the Greek tragedians, the African playwrights do not simply write political tracts, but rather examine the effects of political actions and policies on the lives of the individuals who live (and die) under them, from the leaders of the nation down to common citizens and even those who are outsiders within the community in which they live. In this chapter I will analyze three plays by three different playwrights from three different African countries, all of whom adapt a Greek original to an African setting in order to voice political concerns and, like Euripides, give instruction to the citizens. In Ola Rotimi's *The Gods Are Not to Blame*, the playwright uses Sophocles's *Oedipus Rex* to explore the causes of the Nigerian civil war. Guy Butler adapted Euripides's *Medea* into *Demea*, creating a tragic protagonist out of the South African political system, destined for tragic fall unless, unlike Medea, the dispossessed of that land can be assuaged so that they do not wreak vengeance. Efua Sutherland sets the *Alcestis* of Euripides in postcolonial Ghana in *Edufa*, examining the new pressures which modernization brings about on the lives of Africans. All three plays do not necessarily utilize the original political content or "message" of the tragedy adapted, but rather, through a process of transculturation, place the original narrative in an African political content where a new meaning, relevant to a contemporary African audience, is generated.

Fate and the State: Ola Rotimi's The Gods Are Not to Blame

Nigeria, a nation of over 90 million people and one of the largest and most prominent countries in Africa is "as a geopolitical entity ... essentially a creation of British imperialism," notes Martin J. Gannon (233). In 1914 the British combined three West African territories into a single unit of colonial administration which, after independence, remained unified together but were fraught with strife and conflict culminating in a civil war and continued unrest to this day.

The nation consists primarily of four large ethnic groups. According to the 1991 census, in which 65 percent of the population was counted, the Yoruba, the ethnic group from whose culture Soyinka's theories discussed in the previous chapter were derived, comprise 20 percent of Nigeria's population. The Hausa represent another 21 percent, the Ibo another seventeen percent, and the Fulani another 9 percent. The remainder of the population consists of a variety of other groups and subdivisions of these four main groups (Gannon, 236). Nigeria is a federation, consisting of 19 states that are largely organized along ethnic lines. The northern area of the country is mostly Hausa and Muslim, whereas the southern section is primarily Christian, Yoruba and Ibo (Gannon, 251). Gannon notes that "deep rooted ethnic allegiance often takes place over national allegiance," which indicates that the country is divided not just geographically, but ethnically; this fact creates a number of problems, the greatest of which is perhaps the continuing instability of the government (237). The military has ruled Nigeria for all but ten of the more than 40 years since independence, as of this writing. The primary cause, according to Gannon, of the inability of Nigeria to establish and maintain a Western-style democracy is "interethnic mistrust" (237). This mistrust was also a primary cause of the Nigerian civil war and the very danger that Ola Rotimi warns against in his play *The Gods Are Not to Blame*.

Nigeria attained independence in 1960. In the following six years, regional rivalries, largely ethnic in origin, developed and grew within the nation, with central political power growing in the north, but the economy bolstered by the discovery of oil in the south. In January 1966, a military coup overthrew the elected civilian government and further eroded civil rights and regional and ethnic equality in the nation. The Ibo, who lived in the oil-rich south, were persecuted and the region had inadequate representation on the federal level (Davidson, *Modern*, 201). In May 1967, ruler General Yakubu Gowon began restructuring Nigeria into federated states. The Ibo then declared southeastern Nigeria a separate republic under the name Biafra. The federal government fought the secessionists and a civil war raged from 1967 to 1970. Federal Nigeria won and the union of Nigeria was preserved, but the war itself was "very bitter" (Davidson, *Modern*, 201). Both sides fought hard and many Nigerians were killed or brutalized. The Nigerian Federation remained intact after the civil war, but was badly scarred and still struggling with deep ethnic divisions and much mistrust. To this day the ethnic problems of the Nigerian nation continue to plague its people and the current military government uses those problems to its advantage to keep the nation unorganized for democratic elections. In his book *The Open Sore of a Continent*, Wole Soyinka outlines many of the same problems of 30 years ago which remain unsolved in Nigeria today.

During the civil war, in 1968, Ola Rotimi, a Nigerian dramatist who was educated at Yale and who studied under John Gassner, adapted Sophocles's *Oedipus Rex* into a precolonial Nigerian setting in order to create a cautionary tale of leadership and fate. Rotimi himself hailed from a multicultural, multiethnic background. Born on April 13, 1938, in Sapele, Bendel State, Emmanuel Gladstone Olawale Rotimi was the youngest of three children born to Yoruba and Ijaw parents (Okafor, 24; Coker, 60). Rotimi grew up speaking Yoruba, Nembe (the Ijaw language), pidgin, and English and was raised Christian. Educated through secondary school in Nigeria, he attended school in Boston and earned a master's degree from the playwriting program at Yale Drama School. He then returned to work at the Institute of African Studies at the University of Ife (Coker, 60–1). During the time of the civil war, Rotimi was teaching and writing in Ife, the "spiritual and cultural center" of the Yoruba, and his adaptation of *Oedipus Rex*, called *The Gods Are Not to Blame*, was first presented at the Ife Festival of the Arts in 1968 (Coker, 61; Banham, "Tribesmen," 67). The play was subsequently mounted several times again during the war by the Ori Olokun Acting Company at the University of Ife (Coker, 69).

In this version of the Oedipus story, Laius, who appears on stage, unlike in Sophocles, is named King Adetusa. Oedipus is called Odewale,

Jocasta is Ojuola, and Tiresias is named Baba Fakunle. Rotimi has also added a narrator. The play begins with narration to a mined prologue, as metal objects are "clinked" to play "the rhythm of Ogun, the Yoruba God of Iron and War" (1). Interestingly, in the original production at Ife, Rotimi himself played the narrator, transforming the authorial voice into literally a voice onstage. He who crafted the story literally tells it to the audience: literary author as oraturist, the teller of the tale.

The narrator begins the tale:

> The struggles of man begin at birth.
> It is meet then that our play begin with
> the birth of a child.
> The place is the land of Kutuje.
> A baby has been born
> to King Adetusa and his wife Ojuola,
> the King and Queen of this land of Kutuje [1].

With this opening passage Rotimi not only sets time and place, the Kutuje people (a fictional tribe), he also introduces the very Greek idea of life being a struggle that begins at birth and does not end until death. The closing lines of *Oedipus Rex* reflect this sentiment, as do those of *Antigone*. Here, Rotimi demonstrates the paradoxical idea that, despite birth being the moment when the suffering of the individual begins, it is also a cause of great joy to the family and community. While Rotimi, the playwright and narrator, speaks the words which let us know that the child's suffering has only begun, he counters that sorrow by mounting on the stage a celebration and procession of King Adetusa and Queen Ojuola to "merry singing and drumming" (1). They joyfully carry the child to the priest of Ogun in order for him to divine the child's future. With the opening moments of the play, Rotimi has already concretely embraced the theme of the paradoxical nature of life as both joyful and painful.

The narrator then tells the audience that Baba Fakunle, the blind soothsayer who serves the function of Tiresias, and shares the oracular role of the Delphic original with the oracle at Ile-Ife, has arrived to pronounce the child's future:

> He tells them
> what it is that the boy has brought
> as mission from the gods
> to carry out on earth [3].

These lines demonstrate the Yoruba idea of destiny and fate, called *iwa*. *Iwa* is chosen by the person, rather than being given by the gods. It is this difference between the Greek concept of fate as unalterable and the Yoruba concept of fate as chosen by the individual and alterable which is both the message of the play and a cause of contention for the critics who see the events of the Greek original impossible in a Yoruba context.

Baba Fakunle pronounces that "This boy, he will kill his own father and then marry his own mother" (3). It is fairly safe to say that in almost every culture, African and Western, both patricide and maternal incest are among the greatest taboos. Paul Bohannon, in his study of homicide and suicide in Africa, found that only among the Gisu does any large percentage of parent-murder occur (242–5). For the most part, parricide remains a largely nonexistent crime in Africa, and is certainly regarded with great horror in those rare instances when it does occur. Similarly, maternal incest is forbidden in most, if not all cultures, and also regarded with great horror in those instances when it does occur. Thus, the killing of one's father and marrying of one's mother for which Oedipus is famed does not need a cultural contextual shift, because to the Yoruba, as to the Greeks, these actions are among the greatest crimes one can commit.

The prologue continues as the narrator explains that the priests of Ogun bind Odewale's feet and that Gbonka, special servant to the king, abandons the child in "the evil grove" to die of exposure (4). In order to comfort the cursed royal couple, Obatala, the Yoruba god of creation, sends them another son Aderopo. The narrator then relates that after the passage of 32 years, King Adetusa meets with "rough death," and the Ikolu attack the kingless Kutuje (4). The war goes badly for the people of King Adetusa until Odewale arrives, seemingly from nowhere, and gathers the people of Kutuje to him. He leads an attack on the Ikolu, destroying their ability to make war on Kutuje. The people crown him king as the narrator relates that Odewale has ruled the land for 11 years, having taken Ojuola for his wife. They have four children: Adewale (Polynices), Adebisi (Antigone), Oyeyemi (Eteocles), and Adeyinka (Isemene). The history of the characters and events which shape the drama, familiar to the Greek audience of the original, are thus presented to a Nigerian audience through mime, stage pageantry, and verbal narration.

The first act of the play proper begins with the people of Kutuje complaining to Odewale and his chiefs about a plague killing the people of the town. Odewale orders his children brought forth. He shows to the crowd that Adebisi, the Antigone figure, has been stricken, demonstrating to his people that the plague has affected him as well. When the suggestion is made that a ram be sacrificed, Odewale cries out, "To what gods have we not made sacrifice, my chiefs and I?" (11). In the Greek original, a priest makes the plea to Oedipus in the name of the people, and Oedipus's family is not touched by the plague. Rotimi puts the plea in the mouths of the citizens themselves; they need no representative to tell the king. Rotimi shows citizens giving voice to their suffering and petitioning the central authority themselves, rather than through an intermediary. Rotimi also shows that when the nation suffers, the leaders and those close to them will suffer as well.

The crowd is told that Baba Fakunle has been summoned and that Aderopo, now grown, has been sent to Ile-Ife to consult the oracle. Odewale then challenges the crowd: "…But what about you yourselves? What have you done to help yourselves? Answer. Or is the land at peace?" (12). When no one in the crowd responds, Odewale tells them, "Well, let me tell you brothers and sisters, the ruin of a land and its peoples begins in their homes" (13). With these lines, Rotimi places the main theme into the mouth of the play's central authority figure: ultimately, responsibility for what happens to a nation is in the hands of its people. Control of the nation occurs only with a mandate of the masses; if the people will not follow the leaders when bad decisions are made, then the nation will not suffer. Rather than simply complain about the problems of the community, the people should take action. These lines are the first of many calls to action in the play. The irony is that the call to fight corruption and plague is coming from the authority figure who is himself the cause of the plague.

Aderopo returns from Ile-Ife, and meets with Odewale and the chiefs. Much like in the Greek original's message from Delphi which Creon brings, the message from Ile-Ife is that a curse on the land brings suffering, and the suffering will continue until the source of the curse is purged. Much like Creon, Aderopo wishes to give this message to the king in private, not in public before the gathered chiefs. When Odewale insists that all information be shared publicly, Aderopo admits the curse has come about because the land shields the murderer of King Adetusa, king before Odewale. Aderopo brings a riddle from Ile-Ife that reveals the identity of the murderer. Unlike his Greek predecessor, who bested the Sphinx, Odewale is not known as a riddle-solver. He is a warrior, a general who has defeated his enemies in military battles, not battles of wits.

The chiefs and Ojuola then relate the story of the death of Adetusa, just as in the Greek original Oedipus is told of the death of Laius. Adetusa was killed on the Oshogbo road, with only one of the five bodyguards accompanying him returning alive to tell the tale. Odewale concludes that someone in the kingdom paid to have Adetusa killed in hopes of gain. He then grows suspicious and fearful, noting his own ethnic difference from the group he now rules and fearing that if they would kill a king of their own tribe, why would not the same people kill an outsider, for Odewale is "an Ijekun man, a stranger in the midst of your tribe" (23). He no longer trusts those he has lived among and ruled for 11 years. He swears an oath that he shall find the murderer of King Adetusa and "bring him to the agony of slow death" by having his eyeballs crushed and then "be expelled from this land of his birth" (24). In short, the murderer will be blinded and exiled, not only so that the curse will be lifted, but also so that none will dare challenge the rule of Odewale, who ostensibly was not born in this land, although, ironically, he was not only born in this land but also, like Oedipus, is himself the murderer whom he seeks.

In the second act, Baba Fakunle cries out to Odewale, "You are the murderer!" (27). Odewale chooses to misinterpret this outcry as Baba Fakunle's fear that Odewale will punish Baba for knowing of the conspiracy which robbed Adetusa of his life. Odewale responds, "Why, I have not killed you yet..." (27). Odewale deliberately misinterprets Baba Fakunle's outcry. After all, Odewale is looking for a murderer. Baba Fakunle makes further veiled accusations that Odewale is the man he himself is searching for, calling him "bedsharer," a reference to Odewale's incestuous relations with his own mother (29).

Odewale is shaken by these accusations, just as Oedipus is in the original, believing the blind prophet is part of a conspiracy to dethrone the king. In the original, in response to the statement that Oedipus is the murderer, Oedipus asks Tiresias, "Was this your own design or Creon's?" (378). He adds threats to his counteraccusations: "And now you would expel me, because you think that you will find a place by Creon's throne. I think you will be sorry, both you and your accomplice, for your plot to drive me out" (398–403). Upon the entrance of Creon, Oedipus attacks him as well, accusing him of "highway robbery of my crown," and asking why Creon would "lay a plot like this against me?" (536, 538). With no justifiable proof, Oedipus believes Creon and Tiresias plot against him because Tiresias tells Oedipus that he is the murderer whom he seeks. Oedipus has no grounds for believing in a conspiracy against his throne. Unlike Odewale, Oedipus is not an outsider, or at least never identifies himself as such. He calls Creon "my kinsman," and tells Tiresias that by withholding information Tiresias would "betray us and destroy the city" (553; 331). Oedipus is not an outsider, but an accepted member of the polis who regards himself as one with the city. When Creon suggests Oedipus should not rule if he rules badly, Oedipus cries out, "O, city, city!" (629). In his own mind, Oedipus is one with the polis. He loves the city and does not see himself as different from its citizens or from the members of the family into which he has married. Sophocles's character is threatened by the accusations, and wishes to retain power. Odewale, too, wishes to retain power, but he sees the root of the threat in his ethnicity. Like Oedipus, he moves to stop any perceived threat to his power, but Odewale sees himself as different, an outsider, set to rule over a city of schemers of ethnic origin different from his.

In the next scene, Odewale attributes the accusations against him to his different ethnic origins: "I am an Ijekun man. That is the trouble. I, an Ijekun man, came to your tribe, you made me king, and I was happy, ignorant that plots, subversion, and intrigues would forever keep me company" (30). He begins calling the first chief "son of Kutuje," further emphasizing his own ethnic otherness (31). Odewale emphasizes the differences between himself and the people he rules, ascribing to them all sorts of fiendish characteristics. By distinguishing between himself and his adopted people, he constructs them into the Other. The perceived sinister nature of these people, which Odewale never felt before this crisis, allows him to justify his seemingly irrational and repressive actions. This process is similar to what occurred in Nigeria at the time of the civil war, when military leaders (note: Odewale became king because of his skill on the battlefield) divided the country into separate regions based on ethnicity and geography. Ethnic strife and distrust undermined both the central authority of the government and the unity of the nation. The governed who initially accepted leaders of a different ethnic group found themselves as a nation distrusted and alienated by those leaders who did not trust the people precisely because of their ethnic differences.

Odewale, like Oedipus in regards to Creon, suspects Aderopo of jealousy. Aderopo, Ojuola's son from her earlier marriage to Adetusa, was not made king upon the death of his father. Aderopo, functioning in the Creon role, is of a different relation to Ojuola and Odewale than Creon is to his sister Jocasta and her husband, Oedipus. Aderopo has a much better claim to the throne than does Creon. Interestingly, Odewale condemns Aderopo for his possible desire to rule, citing the fact that Ojuola is queen: "So, let him come and marry his own mother. And not stopping there, let him bear children by her" (31). He accuses Aderopo of desiring to do what he, Odewale, has unknowingly done himself. Odewale accuses Aderopo of this desire, knowing how heinous the chiefs would find this possibility. Odewale accuses Aderopo of prejudice: "Just because I am an Ijekun man, and do not belong to your tribe, the sight of me as your king gnaws your liver and rips your heart asunder (34). Again, Odewale locates the site of Aderopo's jealousy in Odewale's supposedly different ethnicity.

Odewale takes an oath upon his sword, thus making it sacred to Ogun, the god of war and iron, swearing, "May my eyes not see Aderopo again till I die" (35). Not only does this line foreshadow what is to come, especially to those familiar with the original, but also reinforces Rotimi's theme of the dangers of bad leadership. The original audience would take a leader swearing a sacred oath very seriously. Yet the audience is aware that Odewale's suspicions are misplaced, and thus his oath is equally as wrong and potentially damaging, not only to himself personally, but also to his credibility as a leader and to the land which he rules.

Ojuola and Odewale speak in private as Odewale prays to Ogun, asking, "Who can I trust?" (40). A bodyguard informs Odewale that a madman has come to speak to him. When Ojuola asks how the guard knows the man is mad, the guard replies, "He is not a man of our tribe, your highness" (41). The tribal distrust which Odewale has begun to exhibit thus begins spread among those around him. A man of another tribe who has come to the land of Kutuje is automatically constructed as mad by the guard. The people of Kutuje, having a leader who fears them for being ethnically different from him now begin to see the threat in those from other tribes. The madman is revealed to be an Ijekun, a man of Odewale's own tribe, named Alaka.

Alaka reveals that 13 years before, Odewale left Ishokun village, instructing Alaka not to look for him "until his mother and father are both dead" (43). Odewale explains to Alaka how he came to be the king of the Kutuje, rather than a farmer in Ede, the village to which he had initially fled. In a flashback sequence the audience sees Odewale kill an old man after using a talisman to slow down the old man's bodyguards. The old man had been using a charm to kill Odewale, but Odewale overcame its power and uses his yam hoe to strike down the old man. Odewale then flees, begging Ogun's protection. When asked why he and the old man had fought in the first place, Odewale claims the man had insulted his ethnicity: "The old man should not have mocked my tribe. He called my tribe bush. That I cannot bear" (50). In the Greek original, Oedipus kills Laius over the right of way at a crossroads, demonstrating his quick temper and pride. Odewale here demonstrates his own tribal pride and prejudice. We sense a Greeklike curse of tribal pride through the bloodline: Adetusa, after all, insulted Odewale's tribe and asserted his own tribe's superiority; now Odewale accuses Aderopo and the Kutuje of also being prejudiced because of Odewale's ethnicity. "Ethnic unrest" was therefore the cause of Adetusa's death, and "ethnic nationalism" the "flaw," or, more accurately, the *hamartia*, over which unknowing father and unknowing son came into conflict, resulting in father's death and son's exile from his own adopted people.

As the search for the murderer continues, Odewale grows more "ethnically aware." Rotimi again demonstrates the ethnic-based identity and distrust of Odewale furthering the tragic action. When Ojuola tells him he is of the people of Kutuje, as he is their leader, Odewale responds, "Wife, I am an Ijekun man" (51). "You have now become one of our tribe, my lord," she tells him (51). He responds, "Mmm… Mmm… The monkey and gorilla may claim oneness but the monkey is a Monkey and the gorilla Gorilla" (51). Despite having fought with and for the people of Kutuje, despite having lived among them and ruled them for 11 years, despite having a Kutuje wife and children raised in the land, customs, and beliefs of Kutuje, Odewale considers himself different. He ascribes essentialism to ethnicity; therefore differences can never be removed or overcome regardless of context or circumstance. While it is Odewale whose view constructs this reality, he blames it upon the Kutuje, who he claims will never accept him because he is of a different ethnicity.

Ojuola reveals Baba Fakunle made her kill her first son. The chiefs then tell Odewale how, when, and where Adetusa was killed. Odewale begins to suspect that he may not be what he has believed himself to be. His entire identity, constructed on the belief that he was Ijekun and not Kutuje, is called into question, and he orders that Gbonka, the servant who abandoned Ojuola and Adetusa's first child, be brought in from Ilorin, the city where he now resides. The shift that occurs in the Sophoclean original is also repeated in Rotimi's adaptation. In the original play, the action moves from Oedipus's quest for the murderer to Oedipus's quest to find out his own true identity. Likewise, Odewale, who has sworn a sacred oath to find the murderer, relinquishes that search in order to discover his own identity.

Alaka reveals to Odewale that Odewale's father died peacefully in bed in Ishokun. Odewale, visibly relieved at the news, announces to the gathered crowd that "the gods have lied" (59). He relates through a flashback that a priest of Ifa told him he would kill his father and marry his mother. The death of his father proves the oracle wrong. As noted in the previous chapter, the oracles of gods and ancestors are never wrong, and tragedy occurs when a stubborn individual ignores an oracle of bad fate. To take action, other than to commit sacrifice, or to flee is to give into the bad fate. Odewale, by fleeing rather than sacrificing, dooms himself to the fate he is fleeing.

Before him, Adetusa and Ojuola, having failed as parents by killing their child rather than sacrificing to the gods and ancestors, have also allowed the curse to continue. Unlike the Greek original, in which fate is unavoidable, in this adaptation, the tragedy occurs because the correct steps to avert it (ritual sacrifice after consulting an oracle) were not taken, and because the leaders allow themselves to make bad decisions based on ethnic nationalism and prejudice. By ignoring the greater good of the greater community, they endanger the community.

Alaka reveals, as in the Sophoclean original, that the people Odewale believed to be his parents, Ogundele and Mobike, were, in fact, his adoptive parents. He further reveals that he himself "picked [Odewale] up in the bush" when he was just a baby, and that he observed a limping man with Oyo marks who delivered that baby to the bush (62). The priest of Ogun confirms that this description matches Gbonka, both in appearance and action.

Gbonka enters and serves the function of two characters from Sophocles's play. He was not only the one who abandoned Ojuola's baby, he was also with Adetusa when he died. Gbonka tells Odewale that an Ijekun boy killed Adetusa when Adetusa insulted the boy's tribe. He further reveals that the priest of Ogun ordered him, Gbonka, to kill Ojuola's baby at birth, but that, instead, he gave the baby to Alaka. In response, the priest of Ogun tells Odewale that Ojuola is therefore his mother. The rest of the play unfolds very much like the Greek original.

In true Greek fashion, Ojuola flees the stage to kill herself out of view of the audience. She stabs herself with a dagger, unlike Jocasta who hangs herself. Although suicide by hanging is more accurate in an African context, stabbing oneself is not unheard of in many African ethnic groups (Bohannon, 263). One possible reason for the change could be the prevalence of Ogun in the drama. As Odewale swears on a dagger to find the murderer and then swears again on a sword not to see Aderopo until he dies, an iron dagger is an instrument of Ogun. The priest of Ogun has been involved in the unfolding of the tragedy. It seems only appropriate in a Yoruba context that a symbol of Ogun would serve as the instrument of death for Ojuola.

Her body is then revealed to the audience. Upon viewing her body Odewale, instead of using the brooches of his mother-wife as Oedipus does, puts out his own eyes with the dagger she used to kill herself. Thus, the same instrument is used to bring both of them to their fates. Odewale, true to his oath, prepares for exile.

Aderopo, upon seeing the body of his mother and the eyeless king, cries out that the gods must have meant for all this misfortune to happen. Odewale responds with the final message of the play:

> No, No! Do not blame the gods. Let no one name the powers. My people, learn from my fall. The powers would have failed if I did not let them use me. They knew my weakness: the weakness of a man easily moved to the defense of his tribe against others [71].

In the Sophoclean original, when the blinded Oedipus is asked who brought him to his tragic ruin, he responds:

It was Apollo, friends, Apollo.
that brought this bitter bitterness, my sorrows to completion.
But the hand that struck me
was none but my own [1329–1333].

Oedipus acknowledges the role he played in bringing himself low, but he also blames Apollo for allowing him to be born to this terrible fate. Oedipus may have to bear the burden, but he knows he is not to blame for his fate. In comparison, Odewale claims that the gods had nothing to do with his fall; he allowed himself to become the instrument of his own fate and his fall could not have happened without his consent.

Odewale and his children then leave to begin their exile. As he exits, the townspeople kneel, "in final deference to the man whose tragedy is also their tragedy" (72). This final stage direction on the part of Rotimi acknowledges the communal nature of African tragedy discussed in the previous chapters. Rotimi's play in this sense is a complete inversion of Sophocles's. In the closing lines of the original, the citizens of Thebes are called upon to "behold this Oedipus," though none view his tragedy as theirs (1524). In the original, the man who saw himself as part of the city and one with the city is established as being different from the city. His fall brings about the restoration of the community, his exile will end the plague. The citizens of Thebes are called upon to note the difference between themselves and Oedipus and take moral warning from it. In Odewale's tragedy, the ruler who always perceived himself as being different from the people he ruled is demonstrated to be one of them, a member of the royal family, in fact. Oedipus is made an outsider by his tragedy; Odewale is made a part of the community he fears by his.

Rotimi's play was not only a popular success as a theatrical piece, enjoying critical and popular acclaim in its original run, as well as in numerous revivals, but it also rapidly became a Nigerian classic and a required text in many African classrooms. As a result of its popularity and the critical debates as to the play's meaning which the text has sparked, Rotimi published *Understanding The Gods Are Not to Blame*, an interview with Rotimi by his nephew who was required to write about the play for a class.

Asked to explain the title and its relation to the theme, Rotimi observes that during the Nigerian civil war, the federal government accused foreign nations, especially the former colonial powers, of helping Biafra. Conversely, Biafra blamed foreign nations for encouraging the federal government to attack Biafra (qtd. in *Understanding*, 1). The title thus refers to "political nation gods": the United States, the Soviet Union, the United Kingdom, and France, all of whom became politically and economically involved in the civil war (*Understanding*, 1). Odewale's closing speech about who is to blame for his tragic fate is a direct reference to the interference of these "political nation gods." Rotimi claims, "These *foreign* nations will continue to do just what they like with our lives *so long as we let them*" [italics in original] (*Understanding*, 1–2). Just as Odewale observes about his own fate: the gods cannot make us victims without our consent.

Rotimi constructs the relationship between the foreign powers and Nigeria as being similar to the relationship between gods and mortals in both Greek mythology and Yoruba cosmology. Both religions are votive: sacrifice is offered and rituals are performed in order to gain a boon from the gods. In *Understanding The Gods Are Not to Blame* Rotimi notes that Nigeria "sacrifices" oil, natural resources, and raw materials to the "gods" of the West in order to win the blessing and support of those entities (2). Rotimi uses a Greek tragic narrative, adapted from a specific Sophoclean play, in a fictive African context, based on Yoruba history and culture, in order to provide a model of analysis for the political situation of the civil war era of Nigeria. Rotimi gives an object lesson for the "polis" of Nigeria: tragic fate can only be overcome if we do not blame the powers that would help us destroy ourselves and rather look within the community for the solution. The nation should not blame "the gods" for problems that could have been avoided by correct action. Odewale's *hamartia* lies in his basing his actions upon his ethnic pride and identity, not in anything the gods have done.

Rotimi's own analysis of the play is useful for providing the author's insights into the play he created, but Rotimi does not extend his analysis to the significant differences between the Greek original and his adaptation. Oedipus's tragedy, written at the time of the Peloponnesian war, is of the ruler of the polis, who moves from inside the polis to outside, warning the viewer about the danger of ignoring oracles or of misguided action in the name of the polis. Odewale's tragedy, written during the Nigerian civil war, is of the ruler of the nation who moves from outside the community to inside, warning the viewer of the dangers of ethnic distrust and of considering the community to be only those of one's own ethnic group.

If the gods are not to blame for the social and political tragedy of the Nigerian civil war, one may ask, then who is? Rotimi's play makes two suggestions. The first suggestion is that poor leadership is responsible for the nation's problems. Odewale, a military man, quick to anger and quick to fight, is made king. Chris Dunton refers to the plays as "a study in leadership," observing that Odewale is "certainly unfit to rule" (16–17). I. Peter Ukpokodu writes that the cry for good self-government is a major theme in Nigerian political drama, and one can view Rotimi's play within this wider context (69). *The Gods Are Not to Blame* adapts a Greek tragedy into an analytical framework which shows a ruler relying on ethnic distrust to preserve his power while solving a crisis situation which he and his predecessor (literally his father) have created themselves. Bad leadership perpetuates bad leadership, and the frequent result is a political situation in which the rulers work to preserve their own power rather than working for the common good of the citizens. Rotimi demonstrates the tragedy of several generations of poor leadership.

The second suggested group to blame is the people themselves. Odewale tells the crowd, as noted in the quotation above, that "the ruin of a land and its people begins in their homes." The citizens, individually and collectively, are to blame for allowing the situation to move out of control. Rotimi, rooting out the causes of the civil war for which the gods are not to blame, criticizes a society that allows unfit leaders to continue to lead and perpetuates the problems of the nation. Citizens must resist tyranny and bad leadership. The power to rule comes from a mandate from the masses, and thus the masses are partially to blame for allowing poor leaders to implement bad decisions.

The need for individuals to take responsibility for the community, the nation, and the greater good of all is a theme that runs through much of Rotimi's work. When one considers *The Gods Are Not to Blame* in the context of Rotimi's other plays, the Greek adaptation is part of a much larger body of dramatic work that considers the role of the individual citizen in shaping history. From the historical tragedies *Kurunmi* and *Ovonromwen Nogbaisi* to the more contemporary critiques of Nigerian society *If...* and *Hopes of the Living Dead*, Rotimi returns to the themes of the dangers of bad leadership, the need to overcome ethnic distrust, and the responsibility of the individual citizen to participate in the community. *The Gods Are Not to Blame* is Rotimi's attempt to frame these themes within a Greek narrative.

In *Make Man Talk True: Nigerian Drama in English Since 1970*, Chris Dunton outlines four points of criticism which reviewers and scholars have often made against *The Gods Are Not to Blame*. First is the language, which is neither contemporary, nor historical, but rather a forced amalgam of English and African dialects, occasionally in verse which many read as "false" (14). The other three areas of criticism are interrelated: the viability of transferring this story from the original Greek to a Yoruba context, the emphasis in the play on "individual responsibility in a hierarchical system," and the relevance of the theme of ethnic distrust as it relates to the play as a whole, structurally and thematically (14). The final two criticisms stem from the issue of the viability of transference, as it seems

Rotimi attempts to insert Nigerian issues into a Greek narrative unconcerned with them.

The largest cultural roadblock to a Yoruba adaptation of *Oedipus Rex* is the concept of fate in each culture. Although different concepts of fate was an issue in the development of *Song of a Goat*, Clark does not have as many difficulties to overcome as he was not adapting a specific tragedy, and especially not *Oedipus Rex*, which is rooted in the Greek concept of fate. For the Greeks, fate is both a mysterious concept of destiny that is even stronger than Zeus, as nothing can escape fate, and the inevitable result of the work of the fates (*moirae*), the three sisters who, according to Hesiod, "give to men at birth evil and good to have" (Hamilton, 27, 42). Clotho spins the thread of each individual life; Lachesis disposes lots, assigning each person their unchangeable fate at birth; Atropes cuts the thread at death. The Fates are implacable; fate cannot be changed. As Oedipus himself observes, the fates will not allow an individual to die when the individual thinks he should, but only when he is fated to (1457–60). Fate cannot be changed. What is left to mortals, then, is how one responds to this fate, as noted in Oedipus's lines at the end of the play: "But the hand that struck me / was none but my own" (1331–2). The three sisters may decree Oedipus's fate, Apollo may prophesy it, but Oedipus alone chooses the manner in which he responds to that fate, first by fleeing it, then by seeking it out, and finally by embracing it and accepting the consequences.

This reading stands in direct conflict with the Yoruba world-view. Meyer Fortes, in his seminal work *Oedipus and Job in West African Religion*, examines the "Oedipal Principle," or Fate, and the "Jobian Principle," or supernatural justice, in several West African cultures, including the Yoruba (viii). In Yoruba, fate is *iwa*, or one's destiny. *Iwa* is not chosen by the gods or assigned randomly by the *Moirae* as in Greek cosmology. Rather, before birth, when one is in the world of the yet to be born, the individual spirit performs what is called *akunleyan*, "to kneel and choose," in which the spirit kneels before the creator god and chooses its *iwa* (7). The *iwa* is not inherently good or bad, negative or positive; it is simply the destiny that the spirit has chosen. The way in which that destiny is then pursued determines whether or not one is acting in accord with the gods and the world. The *iwa* cannot be avoided, but the person chooses the *iwa* freely. Furthermore, as in Ijaw culture, sacrifice (called *ebo* in Yoruba) can influence events, allow the gods or ancestors to interfere, and even change not *iwa*, but the manner in which destiny is achieved (7).

Robin Horton, in the afterword in Meyer's book notes three ways in which the African concept of fate differs from the Western (primarily

Greek-derived) one: "personality versus impersonality," "flexibility versus rigidity," and "a matter of choice" (73–4). The Western view of fate shows fate to be impersonal, rigid, unyielding, and random. In Africa, specifically in Yoruba culture, fate is personal, is chosen by the individual before birth, and "can be modified or sometimes even revoked by proper negation with the agency that sustains it" (75). These last two factors play an important role in the transcultural adaptation of *Oedipus Rex* to an African context. In Yoruba culture one chooses one's fate, and thus is personally responsible for it. The tragedy of Oedipus, in which he learns that the fate of which he has been warned (that he will kill his father and marry his mother) has not only come true but that there was never any way to avoid it, is somewhat ludicrous in a Yoruba context where Oedipus, as soon as he learned of this fate (one he hardly would have chosen) could and would have made sacrifices to change it. In the Sophoclean tragedy the only choice which Oedipus has is how to respond to fate. In a Yoruba context, where fate implies a personal responsibility, Oedipus doesn't have to respond to fate; he can change it.

In support of Rotimi's adaptation, however, we should note that the Yoruba concept of fate does embrace a certain sense of inescapability or fatalism. Looking at Yoruba proverbs such as "Ay'anm'o 'o gb'o'ogun" ("Destiny has no cure") and "Aw'aye I ku o si" ("He who lives shall die") one sees an acknowledgment not only of the certainty of death, but of the certainty of "destiny" as well (Ibitoku, 3–4). This reference to destiny may indicate that there is no escaping the choices one makes at *akunleyan*; although one is free to choose one's destiny at this moment, the results of the choice are inescapable. On the other hand, Benedict M. Ibitoku suggests that one does have the opportunity to experiment with destiny in the world of the unborn before *akunleyan*, noting, "man before birth has to rehearse and get himself well prepared before he dares come into the world" (22). Such a belief system indicates freedom to experiment with choice before choosing, although the results of that choice are fairly binding once actually chosen.

Perhaps a better example of the highly complex Yoruba concept of fate is seen in the proverb "Enti ti a ba ni aje ma pa je ki n fi epo para," quoted in Oluremi Omodele's essay on the presentation of African leaders on stage. This proverb, roughly translated, means "The individual who has been labeled as food for witches must not use palm oil as a body lotion" (261). It means that one should avoid any situation which might allow a negative *iwa* to come to pass. Omodele cites this proverb as evidence that Odewale was not a prudent leader, nor even a good Yoruba, as he had been forewarned about a potential fate and not acted appropriately. In Yoruba belief, once Odewale had been warned of his fate he should never have killed any older man or married any woman older than himself. In not doing either of these things he would have avoided the negative version of his *iwa*. In simpler words, Odewale should not have tempted fate, literally. Omodele argues that *The Gods Are Not to Blame* is not a bad adaptation because it attempts to reconcile two irreconcilable cultures. Rather, the play very accurately depicts "the impairment of judgment" of leaders who ignore all of the evidence that their actions will lead to the ruin of both themselves and the land, as in *Oedipus Rex* (260).

Michael Etherton, on the other hand, is particularly critical of Rotimi, claiming that not only can the two cultural belief systems not be reconciled, but that Rotimi is misreading Aristotle and Sophocles, thus compounding his interpretational errors. Etherton claims that "the Yoruba gods are not capricious, least of all Ogun," whereas the Greek gods are highly so: flawed, vengeful, and all too human (125). In other words, Greek and Yoruba cosmologies, theologies, and philosophies are irreconcilable, and therefore the Greek narrative cannot be transferred to a Yoruba setting. Etherton accuses Rotimi of "misreading" Aristotle, particularly in the concept of *hamartia*, which Rotimi reads as the traditional interpretation of "tragic flaw or fault" (125). Etherton comments: "It is a particularly Christian interpretation of the Greek play to see Oedipus as *deserving* his punishment from the gods because of his pride" (125). While Rotimi has given such an interpretation of the play's action in the past (see *Dem Say*, Lindfors, ed., and *Understanding The Gods Are Not to Blame*), we might note that Rotimi is himself Christian, and writing in the context of a Western interpretation of the Oedipus story. However, in postmodern literary theory, the author's opinion is but one of many, and by no means authoritative. We can examine the text of *The Gods Are Not to Blame* and see not Odewale's "tragic flaw," but a true *hamartia*: an action and not a character condition. Rotimi claims neither to be representing Greek culture nor a historically accurate Yoruba culture; the play is set among a fictional tribe, the Kutuje. Rotimi is not writing an academic exercise designed to display the similarities between ancient Greek and early modern Nigerian cultures. Transcultural adaptation does not necessarily claim to be an accurate portrayal of either source material or target culture; it is a bridge between two cultures in which the narrative of the first is rewritten in the codes of the second producing a new unique artifact which is part of the target culture. In short, one can argue the merits of Rotimi's play based on whether or not it is a good play qua play. But as a creative work, the play need not conform to anyone's notion of what is Yoruba drama or whether or not two cultures have similar enough cultural concepts to allow adaptation. As noted above, the original audience of Rotimi's plays would not necessarily have known or cared about the Greek original; they would only watch and evaluate the experience of the play on its own merits. To argue that the adaptation fails because Greek fate is different than Yoruba fate is similar to arguing that the play fails because a Greek drum is very different than a Yoruba drum, and therefore the drumming is "irreconcilable." The Nigerian audience does not care about the Greek concept of fate, only their own. Rotimi's adaptation succeeds for precisely the reason some critics think it fails: he transculturates the narrative so that everything is in the codes of an African context.

Rotimi is also criticized, however, for misrepresenting the Yoruba context. As Bernth Lindfors observes, in the historical context of the Yoruba culture in the period in which Rotimi has set his play, King Odewale would have more than one wife (63). Even more importantly, objects Lindfors, it is highly unlikely that a stranger, especially someone of a supposed different ethnic group who came of age in a different community, would be appointed sole leader of the people (64). The story of Oedipus as handed down from the Greeks does not mesh well into the Yoruba cultural landscape without much more radical changes, which would even further remove the story from the Greek original. Lindfors' objections represent a very real and legitimate argument against "successful" transculturation: that Rotimi has not fully recorded the original narrative into the codes of Yoruba history and performance. Under these criteria, Rotimi does not succeed at fully bringing the Oedipus narrative into an African context.

Yet, Rotimi does succeed in a larger, metatheatrical sense. In his examination of Ola Rotimi's work, Martin Banham notes that "Rotimi employs indigenous theatrical means … to create a trans–Nigerian idiom, whilst at the same time relying predominantly upon English as a language of expression" (68). Like the colonial language he writes in, Ola Rotimi's work becomes a national unifier. His play is meant not just to appeal to the Yoruba, but to all Nigerian cultures. As the point of the play has been to discourage tribalism and encourage national unity in order to bring about better leadership, Rotimi is practicing what he preaches by ensuring that the drama is not solely Yoruban, but rather open to all citizens of the Nigerian federation. In this sense, Rotimi's play is a success because the target culture into which he is transculturating the story of Oedipus is not actually the Yoruba culture, but Nigerian culture, an artificial invention which Rotimi must almost create from whole cloth himself. As "Nigerian culture" includes many different indigenous cultures, Rotimi must pick and choose (and sometimes even fabricate) which cultural and performance codes he uses to create a successful adaptation. The play, while problematic in many ways, is a transcultural bridge, not between merely Greek and Yoruban cultures, but between all of the cultures of Nigeria.

Rotimi's "trans–Nigerian idiom," to use Banham's phrase, has successfully passed through the ethnic barriers to make Rotimi one of the most popular playwrights in Nigeria. Okafor reports Rotimi's popularity, noting that he occupies "a special place in the Nigerian theatre," as he does not simply represent his own ethnic group, but tries in all of his plays to present the multiethnic face of Nigeria (29). Like his other plays, noted above, *The Gods Are Not to Blame* transculturates across Nigerian cultures, in addition to transculturating from the Greek. Rotimi's cautionary play does what the governments of Nigeria past and present could not: overcome ethnic differences and embrace the idea of a nation instead of an ethnic identity. He also, through the use of a play whose very name is synonymous with the concept of fate, reminds the nation that the fates of its peoples are inextricably linked together and to its leaders. *The Gods Are Not to Blame* is not Sophocles's play, but it is Nigeria's.

The Household Suffers as Society Suffers: Edufa

Efua Sutherland is the mother of modern Ghanan theatre. Born in 1924 in the Cape Coast, educated in Ghana and England, she began to organize the theatre world in Ghana immediately after independence and under the eye and support of President Kwame Nkrumah. In 1957, the year of Ghana's independence, Sutherland founded the Ghana Drama Studio, a "small open air theatre on the outskirts of the city" in Accra, the capital (Banham and Wake, 52). Unique among contemporary African nations, the theatre community supported the government rather than serving as the voice of resistance and opposition, and, in turn, was supported by the government. Such a healthy relationship and cultural environment enabled Ghanan theatre to develop differently than the theatres of resistance in South Africa and Nigeria.

Sutherland went on to develop the School of Music and Drama at the University of Ghana at Legon, and founded and led the Studio Players (see Banham, Hill, and Woodyard, 38). In her role of running both the top professional theatre of Ghana and the training program at its major university, Sutherland effectively guided the development of the contemporary theatre for the nation. She began writing plays to be performed by both the university students and the professional company, many of which were based on Akan or Ashanti myths and stories, such as her best known play *The Marriage of Anasewa*.

One of Sutherland's early experimental pieces was an adaptation of Euripides's *Alcestis* entitled *Edufa*. *Edufa* was first performed at the Ghana drama studio in 1962, eventually seeing publication in 1967. Banham, Hill, and Woodyard link the play to a larger theme in Ghanan theatre: "the extraordinary domestic crises that result from secret and dubious short-cuts to material prosperity," seen in such plays as *Kivuli* by Asiedu Yirenkyi, Jacob Hevi's *Amari*, and Martin Owusu's *The Sudden Return* (40). Certainly *Edufa* does engage this theme, as the character of Edufa believes himself to be fully "modern" and therefore able to ignore traditional ways with impunity, a theme certainly relevant in a newly independent Ghana.

Sutherland has adapted an ancient Greek tragedy in order to explore the crises which modernization brings about within the household in a "new" African country. As Rotimi explores the macrocosm of the nation and the individual's responsibility to it, Sutherland, not writing in opposition to the government, is more concerned with the microcosm of the household and how national attitudes can damage it.

In Greek mythology, Alcestis was the daughter of Pelias and Anaxibia, and stepcousin to Jason. Her husband Admetus was the son of Pheres, an Argonaut. Alcestis did not help her sisters, the Peliades, kill their father at Medea's behest, having already been won by Admetus with the help of Apollo before the return of the Argo (Bell, 18–19). Admetus is granted a boon by Apollo as well: when he is to die, someone else may take his place. When no other family member or friend agrees to die for Admetus, his wife volunteers to take his place. Two versions of the myth exist in the writings of Apollodorus. In the first version, after Alcestis dies, Heracles, another friend of Admetus, journeys to Hades and brings Alcestis back. In the second, it is Persephone who grants Alcestis a boon for dying for her husband, allowing her to return to life (41).

J. Michael Walton observes that Euripides's play based on the myth is the fourth play in a tetralogy, but it is not a satyr play. He believes it is "an experimental piece" in which Euripides creates a "realistic evaluation of the myth" (*Living*, 102–3). The problem with the play, Walton offers, lies in Apollo's boon: what is the gift in allowing another person, especially a loved one or kinsman, to die in one's place (103)? Walton concludes that Euripides uses the play to explore "the public and private faces of death" (103).

Nancy Rabinowitz, however, views the play as presenting a model for women to follow: silent and sacrificing for husband and household, a political rallying cry written during a time of war in Athens: "The play is, then, political in that it participates in the process of recruiting women as wives and prescribes a model of female virtue useful to Athens on the brink of war" (68). Unlike Walton, Rabinowitz doesn't see the play as a philosophical exploration of responses to death, but rather as a political play which affirms the societal standard of the oppression of women as being for the greater good of both *oikos*, household, and polis, city.

As an experimental piece, however, Euripides's play provides a strong framework for Sutherland, who is less interested in the "public and private faces of death" and the oppression of women than in the individual characters' choices. Ampoma, Edufa's wife, has an even smaller role than Alcestis does in the original, because her actions are not the focus of the play. Both plays present the events of the day in which a wife dies for her husband, and the consequences of this sacrifice. Yet while many Ghanan playwrights, Sutherland included, explore the problematic status of women in modern Ghanan society, especially as that society undergoes the flux and difficulties of modernization, Sutherland does not focus on this issue in *Edufa*. Most critics agree that, regardless of the title, the play is Admetus's, focusing on his actions and reactions. Edufa, the Admetus character, is Sutherland's focus, as her title suggests. Much like Rotimi, she uses the structure, story, and characters of the Greek original, not to update it, but only as a vehicle for the larger themes which are her concern, and which are not present in the original.

The play takes place in "the courtyard and inner court of Edufa's expensive house," much as the Greek original unfolds in front of the house of Admetus (vi). Edufa is a wealthy merchant, prosperous because of his willingness to embrace modern ways of commerce and trade. The Greek original begins with Apollo relating the history of his friendship with Admetus and the boon that he has given him. Death enters and debates with Apollo, announcing that he has come for Alcestis who has agreed to die for Admetus. After this supernatural prologue, a chorus of male citizens gathers and frets over death in general and Alcestis's death in particular. A maid enters to announce that Alcestis is dying: "the life is breaking from her now" (143). Only then do Alcestis and Admetus enter.

Unlike the Greek original, death is not personified and no god introduces Sutherland's play. Instead, it begins as a chorus of women from town enter before the house of Edufa. They wail and chant as death approaches, but they do not know who is dying. Sutherland, in removing the supernatural from the beginning of the play, sites the play firmly in the contemporary real world, and in the realm of dramatic realism. The chorus of female citizens remind us of the people who will be affected by the tragedy about to unfold. Furthermore, by changing the gender of the chorus from male to female (an act of appropriate transculturation, as it would be the women who would mourn the death in Akan culture), Sutherland also presents a feminine voice in the play other than Ampoma, thereby removing many of the gender issues which the silence of the resurrected Alcestis generates in the original. Sutherland's play does not engage gods and boons; it engages the repercussions and consequences of the actions of an individual on the household and on the community of which that household is a part.

The chorus moves past the house, chanting. They exit, hoping to protect the community against death. The audience learns what the chorus does not: Ampoma is dying and Edufa has given orders to the household that no one be told of his wife's death. We might contrast this with the original, in which Alcestis's maid publicly announces her death, and the action takes place outside the house, in public.

Ampoma and Edufa enter and Edufa swears he will not marry again, just as Admetus does. Edufa expresses his grief: "Oh, wife of my soul. You should never have made that fatal promise" (10). Unlike the Greek original, in which the original audience presumably was familiar with the story and in which Apollo narrates the situation in the prologue, this line is the first indication in Sutherland's play that the wife's death is anything but natural. Whereas in Euripides's play the story is known and therefore the focus is on the reaction of Admetus to the actual unfolding of events, in the adaptation Sutherland must allow the audience to discover the truth behind Ampoma's dying.

Seguwa, the servant of Edufa, also serves as a choral figure. Observing Ampoma fainting into Edufa's arms after telling him, "My love has killed me" (10), and Edufa carrying his wife to her sick bed, Seguwa responds:

> Let those who would gamble with lives
> Stake their own.
> None I know of flesh and blood
> Has the right to stake another's life
> For his own.
> Edufa! You have done Ampoma wrong.
> And wronged her mother's womb (11).

This speech both introduces the idea that Edufa has "gambled" with his wife's life and that Ampoma is wrongly dying because of Edufa. The reference to "her mother's womb" also serves to remind that the death of one person has repercussions on family, household, and community.

With the arrival of Kankam, Edufa's father, who three years before declared Edufa "not fit to be his son," the audience learns more about

Edufa's character (12). Kankam has returned to the son he has forsworn because of rumors about the occurrences in Edufa's household. African audiences would immediately recognize that the rift between father and son indicates that Edufa, in offending his father, has disconnected and alienated himself from his family, his clan, his own household, and, by extension, the ancestors. Like Odewale and Zifa, Edufa is a man prepared to disregard traditional values. He is disconnected from his kin and community.

The audience is made further aware of this fact by the disrespectful ways in which Edufa treats his father. In addition to the verbal taunts and insults which he hurls at him, Edufa fails to show the courtesy and hospitality due any guest in his house, but especially to a father. Kankam tells him, "Don't let us fail, however, on the sacredness of courtesy. Had I entered the house of a total stranger, he would have given me water to drink, seeing I'm a traveler" (12). Even when chastened by his father for ignoring the traditional mores regarding the treatment of guests, Edufa fails to show respect. Seguwa finally is the one to give Kankam water and Kankam "pours a little on the floor stylistically for libation" (12). With this simple action we see Kankam as a man who respects tradition and who gives honor to the household even if the head of the household does not give honor to him.

Kankam then confronts Edufa about the tragedy building in his home. Edufa initially denies any knowledge of the situation, but Kankam reveals that he knows Edufa has been to a diviner for questionable purposes and, by using a diviner himself, he has learned about his son's actions. Edufa admits to visiting a diviner four years before, but claims that he does not believe that any actions a diviner performs have efficacy in the real world. Kankam tells him, "...Most of us consult diviners for our protection. All men need to feel secure in their inmost hearts." To which Edufa responds, "I am not all men. I am emancipated" (14). It is in this exchange that we come to the heart of the play and Edufa's *hamartia*: in the interest of being "modern" and "emancipated," Edufa has rejected all things traditional, including things he himself once did believe in. By rejecting traditional culture Edufa considers himself emancipated and superior to those who hold to the old ways, yet he has consulted a diviner. He has placed his modern personal beliefs in direct conflict with traditional culture which he cannot bring himself to dismiss entirely.

The audience finally learns that, in visiting the diviner four years ago, Edufa was told he would die soon. Kankam asks why he did not offer a sacrifice of some kind to change this fate, for, as has been shown above, sacrifice is the way to change a bad fate. Instead, Edufa bought a charm from the diviner which would allow someone else to die in his place. At that time, wearing the charm in secret, Edufa returned home and asked who was willing to die for him. Kankam remembers the event, and recalls that the whole thing was treated as a joke, a game: "'Not me, my son,' I said joking. 'Die your own death. I have mine to die'" (16). But Ampoma said, "I will die for you, Edufa" (16). What was intended as an expression of love became the catalyst for the charm Edufa was wearing; Ampoma was given the death Edufa was to have.

Edufa argues, however, that even if the charm is to blame for his wife's illness, modern medicine will cure her: "Indeed, in this age there are doctors with skill enough to sell for what's ailing her, and I can pay their fees" (17). The irony, of course, is that Edufa did not trust these doctors to cure him when it was to be his death. Instead, he went to a traditional diviner and bought a charm. Edufa did not believe in modern medicine enough to save himself, but now his faith in money seemingly outweighs his belief in the traditional ways. As a result, his wife is dying.

When the chorus of women arrive in order to "drive away evil," by performing funeral rites, Seguwa asks whose funeral they will perform. The chorus responds, "While we mourn another's death, it's our own death we also mourn" (22). The chorus's response indicates an empathy for dying things which was lacking in Edufa. We mourn the death of even a stranger, for some day, too, we must die. The response can also be read as to indicate the communal nature of death: when one member of the community dies, the entire community is lessened.

Edufa, however, will not allow funeral rites to be performed. He tells the women that his wife is getting better, and so they perform "the ceremony for the benevolent one" (24). Edufa lies to the women about his wife and they wrongly give thanks to the goddess of healing. Edufa is thus even further removed from tradition and the community as he allows the wrong rituals to be performed for her, rather than letting the community know the truth. With each choice Edufa makes, the audience sees him choosing the wrong action based on his fear of death and his need to be "modern."

The themes of empathy for the dying and the communal impact of death is continued in the face of Edufa's errors. The chorus exits, chanting:

> Crying the death day of another
> Is crying your own death day.
> While we mourn another,
> We mourn for ourselves.
> One's death is the death of all mankind [25].

Their words haunt Edufa, as his wife's death day literally should have been his. He knows that the chorus feels an empathy for his wife, while he only feels fear for his own death. Furthermore, the chorus invokes the complex Akan attitude towards death. John S. Mbiti in *African Religions and Philosophy*, records a traditional Akan dirge sung in Ghana:

> Man's hopelessness in the sight of death
> Alas, mother! Alas, father!
> We are being carried away,
> Death is carrying us all away... [158] .

Death is the great unifier. Just as all are born of a mother and father, so, too, all must die some day. All people who are born must die, and thus it is a common experience and the fear of it is common. All humans are "hopeless in the sight of death," and the death of others reminds us of our own demise. The death of someone close is a human and communal event.

On the other hand, death is also a solo experience. A human being can experience firsthand only his or her death: one dies alone, even when surrounded by people. As Mbiti writes, the African philosophy is: "death is a monster before whom man is utterly helpless. Relatives watch a person die, and they cannot help him escape death. It is an individual affair [with] which nobody else can interfere or intervene" (*African*, 158). Thus, paradoxically, death both connects one to others at the most basic level of shared experience and yet is alienating and distancing because it is always experienced alone by the dying. By causing his wife to die for him, Edufa has not only disturbed the natural order of dying, he has also caused her to undergo an experience that was intended to be his. He mourns another instead of himself. A Ghanan audience would recognize the innate wrongness of what Edufa has done by making another, especially a loved one, die in his place.

At this point in the play Senchi, Edufa's happy-go-lucky friend who serves in the Heracles role, enters as the chorus is leaving. Edufa tries to disguise the situation to his friend, who is dressed in Western clothes and presenting a persona that suggests that he is thoroughly modernized and Westernized. Ironically, then, on the night his wife is to die, Edufa must throw a party in honor of the arrival of Senchi. Edufa enters in Western evening wear. Senchi is in a suit that does not fit because it has been borrowed from Edufa. Sutherland has crafted a powerful image: an African who is wearing borrowed Western clothes which do not fit him as well as the African garb he had on earlier. Senchi becomes a visual metaphor for the danger which Edufa has already fallen victim to: sometimes borrowed things don't fit. The whole household is in mourning for the imminent death of Ampoma, and thus the two men in their festive Western suits seem inappropriate and out of place, further evidence of Edufa's disconnection from tradition.

Edufa has bought both medicine and charms for his wife. He brings her medicine from modern doctors, but has also sent Sam, his servant, to a diviner to buy charms to ward off evil. The chorus of women arrive at the party, and Ampoma joins Edufa and the guests for the meal. She is distant and distracted throughout the party, but joins Edufa in a toast to their love. She makes a gift of waist beads to her husband and exits, falling three times on the way out. Martin Owusu claims in his analysis of the play that a Ghanan audience would recognize the gift of the beads as a form of curse which will "affect his manhood" (45). The beads are a woman's fertility charm, but on a man they cause impotence. In giving them as a gift to her husband, Ampoma's last action towards the man she is dying for is to remove his ability to be a husband or father to anyone else. Because he failed to carry out his duty to her as a husband, she ensures that he will never be able to do so. In doing so, the audience sees that "she possesses some of the wickedness which Edufa exhibits" (Owusu 45). Yet, her "wickedness" has been brought about by Edufa's failings. She curses him because he tricked her into making a declaration of love that resulted in her death, and he relied upon means to save her which he did not trust (modern medicine).

John S. Mbiti relates a Ghanan proverb: "A woman is a flower in a garden; her husband is the fence around it" (*Introduction*, 268). This proverb expresses the thought that it is the duty of a husband to protect his wife from all that could or would harm her. Another Ghanan proverb relates, "However kind a man is, he would never give his wife away as a gift to friends" (Mbiti, *Introduction*, 209). Not only does this proverb establish the importance and sacredness of the marital relationship, it also privileges the position of the wife over the husband's other relationships and duties. In traditional Ghanan society, a husband honors, protects, and supports his wife first. A Ghanan audience would see Edufa as having given away his wife as a gift to death for his own benefit. Edufa neither protected nor honored his wife. Instead, by his actions, he has brought about her death, which in Ghanan society shows him to be the opposite of everything he should be.

Ampoma dies offstage and Edufa cries out, "The last laugh will be mine when I bring her home again. I will bring Ampoma back" (61). Whereas Admetus believed he had lost his wife forever, Edufa intends to get her back. Yet his boast is that of a madman; Ampoma does not return. Senchi, ostensibly the Heracles figure, instead of going to the afterlife and bringing her back, simply remains confused by the situation, unaware of all that has transpired. The play ends with the weeping of the chorus and the descent into madness of Edufa over a still-dead Ampoma.

Sutherland has significantly changed many features of the play in adapting the story from the Greek original. Euripides's play is entitled after the wife, whereas Sutherland's is named for the husband. The father arrives before the death of the wife in Sutherland's play, while Euripides brings him in after her death. Senchi and Heracles are both comic figures who display a lust for life and a penchant for drunkenness. But Heracles can heroically bring the dead back to life. Senchi, however, is revealed as a shallow, hedonistic mortal whose company cannot avert death. As a symbol of the new, modern, urban, "hip" African, he is shown to be of no real value as a friend in facing a crisis. He is not even recognized by his host at the end of the play, as Edufa sinks into madness.

The structures of the plays differ slightly, as *Edufa* ends with the death of Ampoma, whereas the action continues in *Alcestis* with the return of Alcestis and the tricking of Admetus into accepting her as a "new" wife. In the original play, Alcestis's death is onstage, one of the few in extant Greek tragedies. In the adaptation, the death is offstage, thus out–Greek-ing the Greek original. The wife returns, albeit silently in *Alcestis*, while the silence of Ampoma is permanent for there is no resurrection. This change is the most significant which Sutherland has brought to the text. Ampoma dies and stays dead and the whole second half of the play is not adapted. By this, Sutherland adapted an "experimental" Greek play into a true tragedy. No one can escape the tragic fate which Edufa's *hamartia* has brought about.

It is this *hamartia* which gives the play its message and meaning. The tragedy is not that of the wife, but of the husband. Edufa is the tragic hero, not Ampoma. She loves him and she dies for it, but that is not a tragic action in the dramatic sense of the word. Edufa believes himself to be "emancipated" from tradition and "superstition." He believes himself to be thoroughly modern. Yet, when learning from a diviner that he would die soon, he buys a charm that will cause another to die in his place and then tricks his wife into volunteering. He sees the efficacy of traditional beliefs with his own eyes when Ampoma grows ill, and yet chooses to disbelieve again and place his faith in money and modern medicine to cure her. His is the tragedy of Oedipus: he ignores the information he already has, blindly believing that through his own actions he can make right what the oracles have told him is wrong. This idea is not present in the Euripidean original, but Sutherland places it at the heart of her adaptation.

Thus, Edufa's *hamartia* is that he believes in tradition and superstition enough to buy a charm that will cause his wife to die in his place, but not enough to solve this problem through traditional sacrifices. His fear of tradition and faith in modernity are both misplaced and unbalanced. Charles Angmor writes that Edufa is

> ...deracinated from his native traditions, he fails to respect its higher values (demonstrated in his lack of respect for his father) while at the same time he has not evolved any sane principle out of his Western education to be able to resist such a practice as witchcraft [63].

As Angmor correctly points out, Edufa's tragedy is based on the fact not that he ignores traditional belief or that he is not truly modern, but that he allows his fear to misplace his trust and his beliefs. Had he simply ignored superstition and never gone to a diviner and placed all his faith in modern medicine, he might be dead, but he would not suffer this tragic fate. Likewise, had he gone to a diviner and then performed the correct rituals without placing any faith in modern medicine, he likewise would have avoided a tragic fate.

Sutherland's play shows how the household suffers when traditional values are displaced entirely by modern values, but traditional superstition is still an active force in the household. The play is a cautionary tale, not against modernization, or even against superstition, but against not being able to strike the correct balance between traditional and modern values. Edufa was a successful businessman, but he allowed superstition to ruin his life. Had he found a balance between the two, and applied traditional solutions to traditional problems and modern solutions to modern problems, no tragedy would have or could have occurred. Like Oedipus, however, Edufa lacked true self-knowledge. He did not really know who he was until it was too late and Ampoma died because of it.

Of the three plays examined in this chapter, *Edufa* has arguably come under the greatest amount of criticism, both as an adaptation and as a piece of theatre in its own right. While *The Gods Are Not to Blame* has been deeply criticized as an adaptation, as noted above, it has nevertheless enjoyed much success and critical acclaim as a piece of theatre. *Edufa* has not been as fortunate. Charles Angmor claims that "as a work of art," Sutherland's play "is not convincing" linguistically, dramatically, or logically (76). Martin Banham dismisses the play as "rather static in construction and dialogue" (Banham and Wake, 53). Eliane Saint-Andre Utudjian observes that "The elements borrowed from Greek life and customs are particularly out of place in an African setting" (189). This last criticism, of course, is an indication that Sutherland's experiment is not considered a completely successful transculturation of the play into a

Ghanan context by all. The play does have dramaturgical problems, but one should bear in mind that Sutherland is working to develop a new form of drama, just as Aeschylus was as sophisticated a writer as Euripides because the form was still developing.

Yet, in comparing the play to its Greek predecessor, Sutherland has created a unique work in its own right, no longer Euripides's play, but something new. Devoid of the original messages and issues, Sutherland's play instead engages the issues relevant to an African society caught up in the thrills and dangers of independence and modernization. The voice of Efua Sutherland warns the polis of Ghana that there is tragic potential in the conflicts between tradition and modernity that must be intelligently and carefully negotiated. This voice tells the audience that to ignore tradition brings about not emancipation but tragedy, with similar results if one surrenders to superstition when a more modern answer is called for. The voice gives an important message, delivered to a nation still in its youth as an independent and self-governing entity. Tragedy is written as a lesson to the polis so that its citizens, individually and collectively, may learn from the mistakes that bring the people of myth to tragic ends.

South Africa as Tragic Protagonist: Demea

In the late 1950s, just after the passing of the Group Areas Act in South Africa, Guy Butler, a professor of English at Rhodes University and the founding president of the Shakespeare society of South Africa, wrote an adaptation of Euripides's *Medea*, which he set in South Africa and called *Demea*. For over 30 years the play was left in a desk drawer until the end of apartheid. Under the censorship laws of apartheid, the play, critical as it was of South African history and requiring a mixed-race cast, could neither be published nor performed. However, the play was eventually mounted in July 1990 in the Rhodes University Theatre at the Grahamstown National Arts Festival, followed by performances at the Arena State Theatre in Pretoria and the Alexander Theatre in Johannesburg for the next month and a half.

Butler recalls in his "Author's Note" in the published text of *Demea* that "In the late 1950s I came under the sway of the Greek dramatists" (v). In doing so he perceived a parallel between the situation of Medea as presented in Euripides's play and that of the indigenous people of South Africa under apartheid. Butler sees the theme of Euripides's play being "racial and cultural prejudice," and certainly much of Euripides's play focuses on the fact that Medea is a non–Greek foreigner living among the Greeks (v). Initially the Greeks welcomed Medea's assistance, when she betrayed her own family so that Jason might bring the Golden Fleece back to Greece. Then, after she had married Jason and borne him two sons, the Greeks feared and rejected Medea. At the behest of Creon, Jason divorced her, ordering her into exile.

It is this cycle of initial friendship and aid followed by betrayal and rejection that Butler sees as analogous to South African history. He writes, "It seemed that large numbers of English speakers (Jason = Jonas) were abandoning the cause of the coloured and black people (Medea = Demea) to vote for the racist Afrikaner nationalists (Creon = Kroon)" (vi). Butler has been criticized for this rather naïve over-simplification of the situation, reviewers calling it a "questionable notion" that "English speakers" were antiapartheid (see DeKock). Furthermore, in addition to oversimplifying his South African history, Butler might be accused, like Rotimi before him, of fitting the square peg of contemporary Africa into the round hole of Greek tragedy. In other words, critics claim that Butler misreads both South African history and Euripides's *Medea*.

Butler ignores the fact that Medea is a stranger in a strange land. As Page DuBois states, "Medea is not whole other culture, but the other within the city" (119). Medea is the alien living in someone else's land, as opposed to the situation in South Africa in which the Europeans were the invaders, aliens who came to take and rule land not theirs. Even the framing of Medea within the play is from outside her point of view, despite her sympathetic portrait. Nancy Sorkin Rabinowitz, in her feminist critique of Euripides, notes that Medea is not treated "as the representative of a full-blown culture of her own; she is, instead, presented wholly "within a Greek setting and point of view" (137). Indeed, Medea is completely an outsider living within the polis without being a member of it.

In contrast, the indigenous people of southern Africa were supplanted by European colonists. Their situation is not entirely akin to Medea's as they were still within the confines of their own land and culture. Medea was without her own people, without kin, without her own culture. Although the analogy is not entirely accurate, it should be noted that the process of apartheid is designed to make foreigners of the indigenous Africans within their own land. The active carrying out of the racist properties of apartheid, especially under the Group Areas Act, was designed to make those who had originally held the land aliens, foreigners, and disenfranchised outsiders. Those who once were the rulers of the land (let us remember, Medea was of the royal house of Colchis) are now powerless noncitizens. Apartheid makes Medeas, so to speak.

The play is set in the early 19th century during a Boer-led trek, a colonizing move to the lands inside South Africa. Butler points out in his note that "the Great Trek" was the "validating myth" of Afrikaner nationalism and apartheid (vi). According to this myth, the Afrikaners conquered the land and people, pioneering and settling the lands in the south of Africa and therefore ruling by right of conquest.

Medea is transformed into Demea, a Tembu princess. The Tembu are a house of the Xhosa, one of the indigenous nations of South Africa. It is worthwhile to note that Nelson Mandela is also of the royal house of Tembu. While this fact would not have mattered in the late 1950s when Butler wrote the play, in 1990 during its first production Mandela was a national figure and had been in prison for 27 years. He would have been in the front of many South African audience members' minds. An unintended, but very real effect of the play was therefore to remind the audience, in its initial run at least, of another royal Tembu who was victimized because of racism and apartheid.

Demea by Guy Butler, 1990 Grahamstown National Arts Festival. Nomsa Xaba as Demea, a Tembu Princess in traditional costume. *Photograph courtesy National English Literary Museum, Grahamstown, South Africa.*

Jason becomes Captain Jonas Barker, a former British officer in the peninsular wars who is married to Demea. They have two sons, Charlie and George. Their tutor is called Mr. Fitzwilliam, a British schoolteacher. Their nurse is Kantoni, Demea's Tembu handmaiden. Leading the Trek is Johannes Christiaan Kroon, the Creon-figure, a Boer with racist views and dreams of power. Instead of a chorus, various individual figures connected to the trek serve to comment on the principle characters and their actions.

Butler frames his drama with a scene of three figures

who will play many of the minor characters of color in the play. The first is a "traditionalist," the second is a mineworker who "knows about the freedom struggle," and the third is a colored man, thoroughly modern, listening to a radio (1). They climb upon a big rock both to dramatize the arrival of various peoples to the land (Khoi san, Tswana, Zulu, and, finally, the Boer), and to represent the changing fortunes of the indigenous. The scene reminds the audience that all peoples are ultimately migrants to the area, but the white man, last to arrive, changes everything that has come before.

The play proper begins with the tutor telling George and Charlie the story of Medea in rhymed verse. Jonas stole 100 sheep from the Tembu, we learn, and Demea saved the trek from their vengeance. Much like Medea saving Jason and the Argonauts from her own people, Demea has displayed both her resourcefulness and power and her loyalty to her husband over that of her loyalty to her people.

Jonas and Kroon debate the racial composition of the trek. Kroon wants to convert all indigenous people to Christianity, but insists on keeping them separate from whites. Jason believes "Mixture is inevitable" (11). Kroon instead announces that the trek is intended to found a land for whites only. Kroon does not respect anything indigenous, including the marriage of Jonas and Demea. The audience learns that the missionaries responsible for Demea's education asked Jonas to return her to her father's kraal when she refused baptism. Along the route the two fell in love, and Demea began wearing European clothes instead of tribal dress for Jonas's sake. Jonas gave Demea's uncle a hundred cattle in bride price, and, according to Tembu law, they were married. They had no formal wedding in the European sense, however, and Kroon uses this to force Jason to abandon Demea and marry a white woman.

Ironically, in the next scene, a couple seeks the help of Demea. Van Niekirk, a proud Boer, and his wife seek Demea's help because their newly born child is obviously colored, indicating that one of them has an indigenous grandparent. Choral figures comment on the situation:

> Fitzwilliam: …but now, suddenly, uninvited, you return.
> Van Niekirk: Until the third and the fourth generation.
> Mrs. Van Niekirk: And always upon the children [20].

The language is both Greek sounding and Biblical, speaking of a curse which echoes down generations. Having indigenous blood is seen as a curse. Yet the lines also serve to remind that the trek, as well as the nation of South Africa, is already more "mixed" than the members know or like. Demea agrees to take the child and raise it.

Jonas, converted by Kroon, however, announces that he will not lead a mixed-race trek. Butler uses much language that is Biblical sounding in the debates upon race. Cobus, a colored soldier, states that the people of South Africa want a land "Where thickness of lips and color of skin / Are not the same as original sin" (27). As the Boers frame their conquest of South Africa as a mission from God (Kroon, for example, wanting to convert the indigenous to Christianity, and historically the Boers promised to dedicate the nation to God if He would help them to wipe out the Zulu), the disenfranchised voices of the trek move to use the same language to create a counterdiscursive picture of the role of the divine and religion in the conquest of the land.

In following Euripides's basic structure, Kroon confronts Demea as Creon does Medea. Kroon tells Demea that her children will be raised by missionaries and she will return to her own people. He orders her to be gone an hour after dawn on the following day, as that is also the wedding day of Jonas and Kroon's daughter. Demea's reaction differs from Medea's. Demea threatens Kroon for his shortsightedness and selfishness. She calls his "white vision" of South Africa a "nightmare" for the indigenous people, and warns that "its pain may breed a vision in us that will be a nightmare to you" (37). Demea, and through her Butler, is addressing the great fear of many white South Africans during the apartheid years: that the backlash from apartheid would result in a huge indigenous insurrection. Like Kroon, white South Africa historically always attempted to oppress and crack down even harder when it feared resistance to apartheid was growing.

Jonas summons the members of the trek and divides the cattle and communal property. Rodney and Fitz, who are both white, decline Jonas's offer to join him and Kroon. Carollos, who is colored, wants to go, but is not allowed to join by Jonas. Cobus, another colored, remarks, "You're wasting your time. Will a man who throws away his own flesh and blood stop at his servants?" (46). It is clear that all members of Jonas's trek, including the white ones, believe he is making a mistake by joining Kroon on a "whites only" trek.

This mistake is further compounded by the arrival of the amaBena, a group whose antecedent in the Euripidean original is the Athenians. They are the representatives of Matiwane, king of the amaBena, who is the African version of Aegeus, king of Athens. "In contrast to the members of the trek, they look magnificently homogenous and heroic," writes Butler in a stage direction that ironically underscores the fact that it is the Europeans who have brought diversity and difference to the land. Visually, the myth of the noble *vortrekkers* is shattered by the truly heroic and culturally pure amaBena, who actually are what the Boers envision themselves to be.

The amaBena have been recently defeated by the amaTembu, Demea's people, who were given weapons and assistance by the English. The representatives of Matiwane ask Jonas for help, which he denies, having sold all of his guns and powder to Kroon's trek. As Jonas orders the former members of his trek to disband as he joins Kroon's, Demea instructs the amaBena to meet her at sundown.

Again, Demea confronts Jonas. She taunts him, saying, "Words are your undoing, Jonas," a direct reflection of the accusation Medea makes against Jason in the original (54). In Euripides's play, after Aegeus, king of Athens offers Medea his protection, she speaks to the chorus, saying:

> My mistake was made the time I left behind me
> My father's house, and trusted the words of a Greek,
> Who, with heaven's help, will pay me the price for that [800–2].

Medea states that it was Jason's words which first ensnared her, then promised her, then deceived her, and now dismiss her. Yet it is also his words that he will come to regret as she exacts her revenge. Demea, like her Greek forebear, warns her husband that his words will come back to haunt him, and that, as the saying goes, a man is only as good as his word and his words.

When Jonas tells Demea that she is getting the bulk of their shared property, she laughs at him, pointing out that her bride price was a hundred cattle, whereas the bride price for his new white wife was his guns and powder. Demea was valuable, but Jonas's white wife can only be bought with tools of destruction and conquest. There is no similar exchange in Euripides, and the point Demea makes is telling — whites do not value cattle or women as Africans do; they value only power, conquest, and destruction. After Jonas leaves, Demea orders Cobus to fill three empty barrels with sand.

In the next scene, Demea meets with Matiwane. The scene is unlike the exchange between Medea and Aegeus, as Demea promises to help the amaBena fight Kroon. Matiwane asks if she is willing to betray her husband and the whites. She responds, "They have betrayed me; worse, they have betrayed themselves," because they have abandoned their commitment to a mixed-race trek (63). Again, while not corresponding with any specific scene in the original, this exchange allows Butler to give voice to Demea's sense of betrayal, the amaBena serving as a choral body which can interrogate the protagonist about her motives and desires. It is arguably one of the most "Greek" scenes in the entire play. Matiwane agrees to Demea's plan to attack during Jonas wedding.

In the next scene, as in the original, Demea feigns resignation and defeat. Jonas, initially suspicious, allows himself to be convinced to send their two sons to Kroon's laager with the barrels of powder in the morning. He further accepts the gift of two karosses as a wedding gift for his bride, just as Medea sends a robe to Creon's daughter. Before he leaves, Jonas asks Demea how they lost their way. She refers to the Orpheus myth: "In one of Fitz's stories there is a man who, by looking back, sends his wife back into hell. The future, only the future" (73). She is, of course, attempting to distract him so that she might exact revenge, but her response is also very telling. The Greek myth is used to remind Jonas of the lessons of his own culture. The story of Orpheus and Eurydice is not a Tembu one, but European, one in which Eurydice is condemned to hell because of her husband's actions. It is an appropriate response to Jonas, but Butler also draws to the attention of the audience that they are watching an Africanized Greek tragedy, a Greek narrative placed into an African context. Demea's comment transforms the moment into a metatheatrical one as well.

Demea then changes out of European garb and into clothes that mark her as a member of the Tembu royal house — animal skins, bronze bracelets, and turban. The members of the trek begin to go their separate ways in small groups and Jonas must ride to his wedding alone. Demea cries out, "My sons! Why am I killing you? I break your father in pieces as a pot is broken" (80). Demea, like Medea, kills her sons to gain revenge on her husband. Unlike her predecessor, Demea does not wield the knife herself, but allows the boys to be placed into a position where they will be killed. The irony is, Kroon is the murderer of his future son-in-law's children. He had planned to sentence the sons to a living death of exile, but instead becomes the instrument of their death by bludgeoning them with a gun after they deliver sand instead of gunpowder. The overall effect is to remove the shock and horror of the death of the boys at their mother's hand, and place the actual murder weapon in the hands of the antagonist. Demea is more acceptable to an audience than Medea as she does not directly kill her children. Furthermore, the announcement by Fitzwilliam, the tutor, that the boys were beaten to death by Kroon would carry heavy resonance for its initial South African audience, where during the apartheid era blacks and coloreds were regularly beaten to death at the hands of the police, the army, and special forces. The play actually rings somewhat prophetic, as it was written before Sharpesville or Soweto, although no South African could watch the play after those events without hearing the echo of the beating of school children who would not learn in Afrikaans.

Jonas and Fitzwilliam, the only survivors of the "Zulu" attack which massacred Kroon's party, both accuse Demea of madness. Medea, too, was accused of having been mad. Medea, however, does not suffer from what Ruth Padel calls "tragic madness," defined as "an acute, temporary, visible event that results in recovery or destruction" (43). This type of madness is seen in such plays as *Ajax, The Bacchae,* or *The Madness of Heracles.* Rather, Padel argues, Medea suffers from what Hannah Arendt calls "world alienation," in which the tragic figure suffers "estrangement from the human world" (115). Padel claims that "Madness displaces: socially, geographically, internally. Self isolation is a sign of madness" (117). Yet, neither Demea nor Medea isolate themselves— they are exiled. They are driven out of society by the power of the state (Creon/Kroon) and by family (Jason/Jonas). Her isolation is not self-imposed, but imposed by decree from above: a ruler has exiled her and the man who agreed to protect her and her interests has agreed to this exile. Demea, and arguably Medea, suffer from a different kind of madness than even Padel argues, a form of self-displacement best described by Franz Fanon in *The Wretched of the Earth* in the chapter entitled "Colonial Wars and Mental Disorders."

Fanon presents a number of case studies of Algerians who were so profoundly affected by life under colonialism that they developed mental disorders, from reactionary paralysis to violent homicidal mania. He writes, "Because it is a systemic negation of the other person and a furious determination to deny the other person all attributes of humanity, colonialism forces the people it dominates to ask the question constantly, 'In reality, who am I?'" (250). The colonial subject begins to question not only his or her own humanity, but even his or her own identity. The self-displacement that colonialism engenders, argues Fanon, manifests itself as a violence towards others. A period of internal violence is supplanted by the outward direction of violence towards the colonial powers. The revolutionary conflict which thereby develops creates a tendency towards further violence in order to repay the hegemony for its oppression: "In reality, the soldier who is engaged in armed combat in a national war deliberately measures from day to day the sum of all the degradation inflicted upon man by colonial oppression" (250). The frustration over the colonial oppression which he or she endures moves the colonial subject to savage violence against both other colonial subjects as well as the oppressors. The violence and savagery of murder in Algeria, concludes Fanon, is "the direct product of the colonial situation" (309).

This idea is echoed in Bernard M.W. Knox's analysis of the Euripidean original:

> The energy [Medea] had wasted on Jason was tempered to a deadly instrument to destroy him. It became a *theos*, relentless, merciless force, the unspeakable violence of the oppressed and betrayed, which, because it had been so long pent up, carries everything before it to destruction, even if it destroys also what it loves most [292–3].

Medea's oppression by Jason and the Greeks leads to her unleashing "unspeakable violence" in order to free herself as well as avenge his betrayal and breaking of her trust, even to the point of killing her own sons. Demea's oppression by Jonas and the whites leads to her unleashing "unspeakable violence" in order to free herself as well as avenge his betrayal and breaking of her trust, even to the point of killing her own sons. This unleashed *theos* is the same force which caused both the murders in Algeria and the unrest in South African townships, including the practice of necklacing — placing a tire full of gasoline around the neck of a suspected collaborator and setting it on fire.

Fanon writes that liberation can only, indeed must, "be achieved with force," the realization of which results in violence (73). For Fanon, however, such violence is not revenge, but the only response to a situation created and perpetuated by violence in the first place. Colonialism is "violence in its natural state," and "it will only yield when confronted with greater violence" (61). Medea, Demea, and the colonized African peoples endure both violence and oppression, until ultimately the resistance to this oppression builds into a force which is unleashed in such a way as to overwhelm and destroy the oppressing agency. Knox and Fanon use the same terminology to describe Medea's revenge and the liberation of colonized people, which would seem to imply that Demea does not so much seek revenge as respond to the whites in the only way they know: with a greater force than theirs.

As in Greek tragedy, the death of Kroon and his daughter is not presented, but rather reported. Jonas himself tells Demea that Kroon's daughter was stabbed to death and Kroon was overwhelmed by the enemy: "For one moment his old white head was there among their neat black skulls, and then it was gone" (83). The image is an interesting and poetic one, appropriate for Greek tragedy, but also suggestive of a future overwhelming of the whites by an angry black uprising. Butler uses the Greek technique of painting a word picture of offstage action to remind the audience of their current reality.

In the final moments of the play Jonas realizes he was Demea's puppet for the unleashing of her fury against Kroon and himself. He has come to a point of recognition and reversal. In one sense, although the play is called *Demea* and focuses on her actions, the play is also, by Butler's own admission, about Jonas's tragic fall from accepting a multicultural, multi-ethnic, multiracial society in his youth to his rejection of this idea in exchange for Kroon's vision of white superiority. Jonas, as a symbol of the English-speaking whites, by his betrayal of Demea and his breaking of his promises to her, falls tragically.

Cobus has been making a bullwhip throughout the play and Jonas is now taken offstage and flogged. He is punished not only for his short-sightedness which has robbed him of his wife, his new bride, his sons, his people, and his power, but also for his helping to establish the new white order. He is punished by whipping, which once again places him on the level of the blacks and coloreds, who are punished by flogging in the world envisioned by Kroon. Punishment is one of two great equalizers in the world which Jonas has helped to bring about, death being the other. Kroon dies at the same time as Demea's sons, Kroon's daughter, many of his trek, and several amaBena warriors. Death defeats apartheid, as it is not for whites or blacks only.

As Demea and the women leave the stage, returning to the land of the Temba, the lights fade on an empty space. This ending suggests that neither Demea nor Jonas is the sole, true protagonist of the play. Instead, South Africa itself is the tragic hero. Its *hamartia*, its fatal missing of the target, is apartheid. Rule over a multicultural, multiethnic society cannot by achieved by decree and violent enforcement by one small group within that society. Herein lies Butler's message to the polis: unless South Africa ends the oppression of the majority by the minority, a tragic fate will befall the nation. Demea will exact a terrible revenge for the betrayal of colonialism. The only way to avert the tragic consequences of this fate is to end apartheid and extend full rights to all peoples and cultures.

The play was performed almost 40 years after it was written, and as a result, carried different associations from its initial writing. Furthermore, South Africa was in a period of transition in 1990, during which reforms had begun, and the oppressive policies of apartheid had been partly lifted, but the regime and legislations of apartheid were still in place, and many political prisoners were still being held in South Africa's prisons. The dismantling of apartheid had not yet begun in full when the play was first performed. Even as of this writing, under the auspices of a national government in which all citizens have the right to vote, the social, political, and economic forces which governed the lives of those who suffered under apartheid still exist, even if the policies of apartheid do not. Social systems and their economic effects change more slowly than the laws that ostensibly dictate them.

In this period of slow transition, reaction to the play was mixed. Some

Demea by Guy Butler, 1990, Grahamstown National Arts Festival. Nomsa Xaba as Demea and Graham Hopkins as Jonas. *Photograph courtesy National English Literary Museum, Grahamstown, South Africa.*

critics found the play to be slow, boring, and encumbered by either bad directing or bad acting or both (see Willoughby, Dekock, Elahi). Guy Willoughby of the *Financial Mail,* in a review entitled "One to Avoid," found the play "dull, dated, and embarrassing to watch" (74). Leon DeKock of *VryDag!* thought the text "reads better than it performs" (20). Other critics, however, found the play strong, well-performed and -directed, and relevant to the nation (see Michell, Mattera, Ronge, Accone). Barry Ronge of the *Sunday Times* felt the play provided a model for postapartheid South African drama, and said that the production gave "a sense of exactly where our drama should be at the moment" (14). John Michell wrote in *Business Day* that the play was even more relevant in 1990 than when it was written, and that all South Africans should see it (8).

Michell's point is essentially correct for the reason that between the writing of the play and its first public performance, almost 40 years of oppression under apartheid had proven Butler right. The atrocities committed against black South Africans individually and collectively were almost uncountable, and violent resistance to apartheid (as well as violent black-on-black crime) grew exponentially even during the State of Emergency of the late 1980s. Many whites did fear insurrection and Medealike revenge against the ruling minority. Butler's play is a warning to South Africa about its potential tragic fate as the nation stood at a crossroads. During the State of Emergency, a conflict between whites and those degraded by apartheid seemed inevitable. Butler's play was performed at a moment in history when that outcome was no longer certain.

To Butler's credit, the play has not only sparked criticism of the text and performances, but also caused the critics to engage both their own society and culture as well as the state of South African theatre. Darryl Accone, writing in the *Star Tonight,* asks "whether brutal hegemony gives way to the triumph of justice or the tyranny of retribution?" (5). He further argues that "the unjustifiable cruelty of oppression does not necessarily make of its victims better people," and that Demea's actions are just as brutal as those of Kroon and Jonas (5). Thabiso Leshoai of the *City Press* emphasizes the fact that issues of race and culture in South Africa are "usually" accompanied by violence (12). Whether or not one agrees with either Accone or Leshoai, the fact is that after four decades of censorship in which *Demea* could not be performed or published, the play and its messages were being debated by theatre reviewers. Butler's play raised political issues relevant to the community, which were then debated by that community, just as the Greek tragedians did 25 centuries before. The play is a voice of the polis, raised in warning to challenge the dominant discourse and engage in the political debates of the nation.

Albert Wertheim writes in his critical analysis of Butler's play that Demea's revenge is "political rather than personal," but this statement is not entirely accurate ("Euripides," 344). In apartheid South Africa, as was demonstrated again and again by those who resisted apartheid and became political prisoners, the personal is political and the political is personal. When the political process of the state determines one's own identity, when the Group Areas Act determines where one can live, work, even walk, the political is personal. Butler's play engages its subject in a manner similar to Euripides's original, as Medea was a woman and a barbarian living within the polis. She was disenfranchised and had no rights, and yet her actions gave voice to both of these groups. Butler, like Euripides, gives voice to those who cannot speak for themselves by law.

Herein lies the final connection between Butler's play and its source material, as well as the greatest of ironies. Both in ancient Greece and contemporary South Africa a white male citizen from the ruling class with full rights and protection of the law must counter the dominant discourse by becoming the voice, not of the polis, but of the voiceless within the polis. Both playwrights speak *for* those who cannot, and *against* the very system that allows the playwrights themselves the right and privilege of speaking.

ORESTES IN SOUTH AFRICA

"Justice has claimed her, but you have not worked in justice."
— Castor to Orestes, Euripides's *Elektra*, 1244
"I will pick the finest of my citizens and come back. They shall swear to make no judgement that is not just, and make clear where in this action the truth lies.
— Athena, Aeschylus's *Eumenidies*, 487–489
The Myth of Orestes

The Myth of Orestes

It is no coincidence that two incidents of terrorist bombings in South Africa, separated by 20 years and several hundred miles, would both inspire adaptations of the story of Orestes. Told in the *Libation Bearers* and *Eumenides* of Aeschylus and in the *Elektra* of Sophocles, and the *Orestes* and *Elektra* of Euripides, the story of Orestes concerns itself with violence, blood killings, revenge, and, ultimately, with justice. Orestes, with the aid of his sister Elektra, kills his mother Clytemnestra and her lover Aegisthus in order to avenge the death of his father Agamemnon. As a result, Orestes becomes deranged (from the Furies, claims Aeschylus; from his conscience, claims Euripides), is driven to flee his home to be put on trial (in Athens, claims Aeschylus; in Argos, claims Euripides), and is eventually acquitted, released to live the rest of his life free from fear of revenge (because of a jury trial and the wisdom of Athena, claims Aeschylus; because Menaleus talked him into marrying his hostage instead of killing her, claims Euripides).

The Orestes of Aeschylus is a tragic hero driven to kill his own mother by Apollo's command. The killing takes place near the tomb of Agamemnon, a reminder that it was Clytemnestra herself who killed Orestes's

143

father. When placed on trial, Orestes has Apollo for his defense attorney and Athena — who both puts together the first jury and then casts the deciding vote in Orestes's favor — as a fervent supporter. The trial takes place in Athens on the Acropolis, a site sacred to Athena. Orestes may have killed a blood relative, but the arguments of Apollo and the mitigating circumstances that surround the killing justify the homicide. Orestes is even presented in a positive light, as the hero who was the only one who could end the cycle of violence and revenge.

The Orestes of Euripides is a very different figure. Antiheroic and ironic, the son of Agamemnon is painted in a much more unflattering (and perhaps much more realistic) picture, contrasting the mythic and heroic stature found in Aeschylus's trilogy with the grim reality of the effects of violence. Euripides presents "a nervous homicide" (Grene and Lattimore, "Introduction," 182) in a play in which "the overall mood is savage" (Walton, *Sense*, 129). The world in which this Orestes lives is violent, and justice is little better than an unreachable ideal. Orestes is exhausted, deranged, cowardly, and cunning — a fugitive from justice who commits acts of desperation in order to save his own skin. We might term Euripides's play "Athens' Most Wanted": when it fits his interests, he takes hostages from the children of his hosts in Argos. The assembly in Argos is ready to stone him (and Elektra) for the killing of Clytemnestra. Only the interference of Apollo and the sudden (and seemingly senseless) change of mind by the chorus of Argive women saves their lives. As Apollo departs, he announces that Orestes will marry the woman he took as hostage and will rule as king in Argos.

The two dramatists present very different portraits of Orestes in terms of his motivations, his character, his demeanor, and his actions. Although the basic plot remains the same (boy kills mother, boy runs from furies, boy gets off on a technicality with some help from the gods), very different narratives with very different meanings are constructed. So it is with two very different plays — written over 20 years apart, and in response to two different "terrorist" bombings in South Africa — in which two different readings of the Orestes myth allow two different South African playwrights to examine the ideas of violence, justice, and revenge: Athol Fugard's *Orestes* and Tug Yourgrau's *The Song of Jacob Zulu*.

As in the adaptation of *Medea* in the previous chapter, the South African adaptations of the Orestes story concern themselves with cycles of violence, justice, and revenge. In the next chapter we will consider a South African *Antigone*, also concerned with the ideas of justice. Greek tragedy may have a particular appeal in South Africa as the ideas and themes that the writers explore are not simply ideas to the people living under apartheid, but part of an everyday reality in which justice seems impossible and violence is a fact of life. Thus, Greek tragedy has a particular appeal for exploring these issues.

The entire epic of the house of Atreus is a cycle of blood killings, familial murder and outright carnage in which, as Mary Karen Dahl observes, "private violence has public impact" (59). The two plays considered in this chapter use the Orestes narrative as a frame on which to construct and explore the reasons behind specific bombings in apartheid South Africa. Both, in a larger sense, examine the issue which Dahl claims is present in much modern political drama: "whether a single violent deed can have regenerative power for the community at large" (2). Both *Orestes* and *The Song of Jacob Zulu* present a single young man, white and black respectively, who chooses to plant a bomb in a crowded area (an act of violence) as a way to resist apartheid. As in the Greek tragedies, these two plays dramatize the trials of the Orestes figure in an attempt to generate both an explanation for the violent actions and a sense of justice for all. The story of Orestes is both personal and political, and both plays attempt to engage their human subjects as well as the larger issues. In both plays the specter of apartheid, like the Furies in Aeschylus, hangs over the proceedings, and must be somehow robbed of power, lest the cycle of violence and retribution continue unabated.

Orestes the Mother-Killer: Fugard's Orestes

On 24 July 1964, Frederick John Harris (a.k.a. John Harris), a 26-year-old white South African, filled a suitcase with dynamite and gasoline, wired the explosives to a timed fuse, and left the bomb next to a bench in a crowded Johannesburg railway station concourse. The bomb detonated, killing a young girl and badly burning an old woman. Harris was caught, stood trial, and was executed by hanging on 1 April 1965. Harris claimed that he carried out this "act of terrorism" as a protest against apartheid. Interestingly, although the African Resistance Movement ("a secret organization of your white liberals and others committed to the violent overthrow of the Afrikaner Nationalist government") carried out bombings both before and after this incident, John Harris remains the only white ever executed for "resistance to apartheid" through terrorism (Fredrickson, 298–9).

Harris's actions and trial stunned the nation. He claimed he did not know people were going to be hurt, but he did know that what he was doing "was right" (Fugard, "Reconstructed," 6). That a white South African could feel so strongly against apartheid, a system which, after all, benefited whites tremendously, and that he could carry out a bombing of other white civilians as a protest against that system, was incomprehensible to a nation that had come to see the ANC and other militant black organizations as the most violent threat to the stability of the daily life of white South Africans. Harris's act was not only incomprehensible, it represented a direct threat to the assertion that the apartheid system worked as the Nationalist government said it did.

In the decade following Harris's trial and execution, an increase in political and racial tensions occurred in South Africa. Likewise, the theatre in South Africa was also undergoing a change. The increased oppression from the Nationalist government and the concurrent increase in resistance to that government and its policies manifested itself in the increased politicization of the theatre. Mainstream theatre, including the latest hits from Broadway and the West End as well as revivals of Western classics, British sex farces, and the "harmless" tribal entertainments, continued on the stages of the large cities, but township theatre and political theatre created by mixed-race casts became more visible and vocal. Theatre resisted apartheid and the identities and images that the system attempted to create and maintain. Antiapartheid theatre was an alternative to the messages from the dominant culture. Gibson Kente, Workshop '71, and a veritable army of artists and actors began performing, both within and without the boundaries of the laws, plays which challenged the social order and presented the reality of life under apartheid, as opposed to the escapist fare offered by the mainstream theatre (see Graver and Kruger; Kavanagh, *People's*).

At this point in his career, Fugard had been directing plays for the Serpent Players and writing his own plays which attempted to present dramas of life in the townships, such as *Nongogo, No-Good Friday*, and *People Are Living There*. While not agitprop drama, these plays were political in that they presented a realistic portrait of life in the townships under an oppressive social and economic system — at least as Fugard imagined it to be. These plays, while well-intentioned and demonstrating many of the qualities which would make Fugard an internationally acclaimed playwright, are among the most criticized of his work, and are considered unrealistic and artificial. While sympathetic to his characters and their plight, Fugard was still a white man, argues his critics, who was speaking for the black man. This criticism aside, however, Fugard was praised for "developing an alternative theatre, less commercial and more thought provoking," than what was being offered on the other stages of the nation, as Kavanagh notes (xi). If Fugard were to be criticized for writing what he allegedly did not know about and as a white could never fully comprehend (i.e., the black South African experience), then perhaps *Orestes* can be regarded as one of Fugard's most honest and accurate plays, since the subject matter consists of the white liberal guilt response to life under apartheid.

The piece was experimental for Fugard, both in content and form. He had been "given the chance of working with three actors of my own choice with no strings attached.... It was in every sense a workshop scene," he noted to a friend in a letter, subsequently published in *Theatre Quarterly* (3). Gathering to him his longtime collaborator Yvonne Bryceland and Serpent Players Val Donald and Wilson Dunster, Fugard began working on a piece that would be "a valid theatrical experience using methods other than completed script, set rehearsal period, performance deadline, etc." (Fugard, "Reconstructed," 3). Fugard also wanted to "articulate, by way of dramatic metaphor, very primitive if not archetypal experiences" (4). He began working with the actors on a daily basis using the Greek material, developing a parallel between John Harris and Orestes. It was a process that Fugard would repeat with John Kani and Winston Ntshona with *Antigone*, deconstructing a Greek text and recontextualizing it within the world of apartheid, as will be considered in the next chapter.

Fugard's notebook entries for this project begin in August 1970. He first writes, "The Oresteian Trilogy as one of the projects for next year. Two questions: Clytemnestra? What is justice?" (Fugard, *Notebooks*, 187). It is worth noting both that Fugard sees Clytemnestra as a question and that his primary concern is justice. Also significant is the reference to the trilogy, obviously a nod to Aeschylus, although as the project developed Fugard would seem to echo more the Euripidean model than the Aeschylean one.

Fugard uses Euripides's version of the story, primarily for its realist portrayal of violence, but also because the threat of supernatural justice or revenge is removed. The Furies do not appear in Euripides, nor do the Eumenides, "the kindly ones." The Furies punish those who kill kin and the Eumenides protect and bless the city. In Euripides, these two forces are removed and the only supernatural aid comes in the form of a deus ex machina that is, at best, corrupt. J. Peter Euben argues that the play radiates "a sense of corruption," and the "resolution" proposed at the end comes from gods indifferent to mortal suffering but interested in preserving the status quo (229). Fugard, less interested in heroics than in, as Dennis Walder claims, "the effect of violence upon those who carry it out," would focus more on Euripides's version (13).

In September of that year Fugard returns to the project again in his notebook. This time, however, he reflects on the parallels between the John

Harris case, another case that he did not use in the final version (although it clearly influenced his thinking about the dramaturgy of the project), and the Greek material. Fugard writes:

> Oresteian Trilogy — John Harris — the bomb in the railway station in
>   Johannesburg. A cell? Madness?
> A modern Oresteian Electra — an ancient Clytemnestra. How to live now?
>   *Orestes*
> Sources: from Greek mythology — Aeschylus for Clytemnestra: Euripides
>   for Orestes and Electra.
> From our history, the image of John Harris and his suitcase
> [*Notebooks*, 188].

Fugard uses a variety of tragic sources along with the archetypal image of a traveler with a suitcase who is also a terrorist with a bomb. At this stage of development, it can be seen that Fugard was not interested in a straightforward adaptation, but rather a blending of different sources, both Aeschylus and Euripides. He is interested in violence, especially violence that results from injustice but paradoxically creates more injustice. These separate elements combine in Fugard's vision to ask not how justice is brought to terrorists, but how injustice makes terrorists out of those who would not otherwise be violent.

Further down in the same entry Fugard writes, "Very early on a sense that Harris stood in relation to society as Orestes did to Clytemnestra. An intolerable burden of guilt for the crimes committed — the act of violence an attempt to escape the burden of guilt" (*Notebooks*, 188). Fugard posits the white liberal (including Fugard!) in South Africa as Orestes: forced to respond to atrocities committed by his mother / the motherland. He must strike back against the thing that gave him life and raised him because that thing now acts destructively. Fanon would consider this an example of the mental disorders which colonization brings to all who live under it, whether colonized or colonizer. The neuroses that arise from guilt over benefiting from the oppression of another must inevitably result in a violent outburst again the cause of that oppression or a substitute for it. As Fanon before him, Fugard psychoanalyzes those who live in a colonial state in order to give explanation to violence.

Using a variety of texts, including transcripts from Harris's trial, Aeschylus, Euripides, and the writings of R. D. Laing, and the performance theories of Polish director Jerzy Grotowski, Fugard and his actors constructed a performance piece to explore the Clytemnestra-Orestes narrative and the John Harris story. The final result was a theatrical fusion unlike most of Fugard's other work. The final "script" of the performance exists only in three books, combining pictures and text for each of the three roles, and in Fugard's previously mentioned letter, describing the performance (Walder, 13). The piece was approximately 80 minutes long, consisting of a series of connected scenes in which the three actors (Dunster, Bryceland, and Donald) slid back and forth between playing archetypal roles (the boy, the mother, the girl, respectively), their characters in the myth (Orestes, Clytemnestra, and Electra), and the characters of John Harris and his two victims. The spoken text was only three hundred to four hundred words, and the entire project, for budgetary reasons, was performed only for a few weeks "for audiences no larger than seventy" (Vandenbroucke, 111).

Fugard explains that the "only external aid" was the following program note:

> From Greek mythology comes the story of Clytemnestra. Her husband was Agamemnon. She had two children, Electra and Orestes. Agamemnon sacrificed their third child, Iphigenia, so that the wind would turn and the Greek fleet could leave Aulis for the Trojan War. Agamemnon returned to Clytemnestra ten years later when she murdered him. Orestes and Electra avenged his death by killing their mother. From our history comes the image of a young man with a large brown suitcase on a bench in the Johannesburg station concourse. He was not travelling anywhere [Fugard, "Reconstructed," 3].

The audience would have immediately recognized the last paragraph as a reference to John Harris. The final lines, "He was not traveling anywhere," carries a powerful double meaning. Harris was at the station to carry out an act of terrorist sabotage, and thus not there to travel. Beyond this meaning, however, is the suggestion that his actions would not achieve anything other than wanton death and destruction. The exploding of Harris's bomb and the death of the girl changed nothing. Apartheid remained unchecked by these events. Harris became part of a continuing cycle of violence. As Orestes killed Clytemnestra to avenge the killing of Agamemnon, himself killed to avenge the death of Iphigenia, so Harris, too, does not travel anywhere but remains in a spiral of blood killing. We shall see below how this idea is perhaps the focal point of Fugard's marrying of Greek tragedy to South African politics.

The audience enters a large room "with a single row of chairs around the wall" (Fugard, "Reconstructed," 3). The actors join the audience in sitting until the performance begins. Initially the actors begin to notice each other and interact. The boy plays with a matchbox, the girl joins in and the two draw physically closer. They begin to play silent games under the watchful eye of the mother. The girl then speaks the first line of the play:

"Let's dream about the sea." The boy ignores her and continues to play. As the action proceeds, it becomes evident that they are playing on a beach, suggesting the importance of the sea to both ancient Greece and the Eastern Cape of South Africa. The girl then asks, "How do you spell 'Orestes'?" The girl and the boy continue playing on the beach, throwing sand at each other and making "sand bombs." The audience sees that even as children, the potential for violence is inherent; their games turn to play-violence and their toys are weapons.

The mother then gives birth to a child, who is identified as Iphigenia. Fugard instructed Bryceland to perform not only by miming birth with her body but also by giving birth to the name: "she took the name Iphigenia, broke it down into its elements—grunts, snarls, groans—and used these as her text. With great labor she put them together and the name Iphigenia was born (Fugard, "Reconstructed," 5). This performance has a twofold effect: first, it connects the physical process of birth with the creation of an identity, reminding the audience not only of the physical presence of the actor but also the identity that is born when an actor plays a role. Second, the "birth" of the word Iphigenia creates the person on stage, even though no such person exists physically. The power of naming is invoked by this act, an idea present both in Greek drama and South African politics (where names, identities, careers, places of residence, and races are determined by legislation such as the pass laws, the Group Areas Act, so on). To call something by a name is to identify it and make that name a reality.

Iphigenia is taken from Clytemnestra, for the woman who gave birth to Iphigenia must be Clytemnestra. A chair—the one in which the mother had been sitting—becomes Agamemnon. Slowly at first, and then in a fury, Clytemnestra destroys the chair, tearing the fabric and breaking the wood until it is in small pieces: "Every performance ... Clytemnestra destroyed one unique irreplaceable chair called Agamemnon. It was an awesome and chilling spectacle. You cannot destroy without being destroyed. As she went though the experience [Bryceland] wrecked her soul" (Fugard, "Reconstructed," 5). Clytemnestra, as she did in the Greek narrative, destroyed Agamemnon; but in doing so, she destroyed herself. Violence damages not only the victim but the perpetrator. The broken chair called Agamemnon also recalls the bench next to which John Harris left his suitcase. The wooden bench was destroyed in the explosion of Harris's bomb. The pile of chair remnants, left on stage for the duration of the show serves as a powerful visual reminder of both mythic and historic cycles of destruction whose effects are very real.

A further truism was represented on stage, as Fugard claims that

"You cannot witness destruction without being damaged" ("Recon-structed," 5). The boy and the girl stop playing their game and watch the death of Iphigenia, the destruction of the chair Agamemnon, and the haunting of Clytemnestra and they, too, are drawn into the cycle. The girl asks the boy a series of questions: "Who are you? What is your sex? What is your color? What is your nationality? Where are you?" He responds: "Me. Male. White. South African. Here" ("Reconstructed," 6). With this simple exchange Fugard creates the identity of the boy as John Harris, an identity confirmed when the girl hands the boy a suitcase. A second level of meaning is generated by this exchange as well, since, under South African law, identity is similarly constructed by the answers to the same questions: one's identity (and therefore one's place in South African soci-ety) is determined by one's color, one's nationality, one's gender, one's parents' races and nationality, which homeland one comes from, so on. Every aspect of life is controlled by the identity created for one under the South African legal system.

Such a system is rigidly oppressive in its construction of identity and the consequences of belonging to certain groups, and history bears out its destructive nature. John Harris, a member of the privileged elite, wit-nessed the effects of this system on those not born to the same group and it drove him to respond with violence. He responded to destruction with destruction. Like Orestes, commanded by the gods to kill his mother in revenge for the death of his father, Harris was driven to bomb whites in revenge for the oppression and destruction of those who live under apartheid.

Interestingly, under the Athenian constitution as reported by Aristo-tle, each candidate for the magistracies had to answer a remarkably simi-lar series of questions: "Who is your father, what deme [tribe] is he from? Who is your father's father? Who is your mother, your mother's father, and what is his deme?" (qtd. in Tyrrell and Brown, 134). Under the Athen-ian constitution, identity in the polis was determined by whether or not one was a citizen of Athens. One was a citizen by being born to two Athen-ian citizens. Thus, the identity of the individual was determined by the identity of the parents and by the social group to which they belonged. In both Athens and South Africa, whether or not one received the full benefits of citizenship depended on one's origins, one's homeland, one's parents, and one's ethnicity. An argument could be made that apartheid South Africa was a democracy truly modeled after the Greeks: political power and the right to vote existed only in the hands of very wealthy elite citi-zens from the right ethnic group.

At this point the action of the play shifts again and the two women sit down on a bench. The young man with the suitcase joins them. After sitting in silence for "what seems like an eternity," the young man opens the suitcase ("Reconstructed," 6). It contains newspapers, which the young man rolls into tubes resembling sticks of dynamite, a powerful image with numerous levels of meaning. Fugard seems to suggest that the news is both inspired by violence and inspires violence, that the everyday events occurring in South Africa as reported in the newspaper are the actual cause of both the violence in general and this act in particular. The image suggests a larger cause of violence than one man alone. There is also the suggestion that ideas and communication, as represented by the paper, are explosive. The more that people engage what is happening in South Africa and debate it, the more likely resistance to apartheid will grow. The audience is also reminded of the control that the South African government exerts over the press: the news is censored and approved by the government and only "official" news is released. Knowledge is regulated in South Africa, so that situations will not literally and metaphorically explode.

The exploding of the bomb is represented by the tearing up of the newspapers, adding to the very real physical acts of destruction performed on the chair. The performers then read three short pieces of text. The two female actors read passages from R.D. Laing's *The Divided Self* and *The Bird of Paradise* which suggest madness and a desire for change. The man reads from the trial testimony of John Harris, quoting:

> I knew that what I was doing was right. Later I heard that people had been hurt, but this did not make sense because I had known that people were not going to be hurt ["Reconstructed," 6].

Harris claimed he did not intend to hurt anyone, only protest the policies of apartheid. He felt driven to do this, and thus he knew that because it "was right" no harm would come to anyone innocent. The play, however, seems to hold to Nietzsche's famous dictum: "Beware when you battle monsters, lest you become a monster; for when you gaze into the abyss, the abyss gazes also into you." By fighting violence with violence John Harris became just like those whom he wanted to oppose: he caused destruction and took innocent lives. This cautionary warning seems to be the center of Fugard's play: the system creates and sustains violence, but those who battle the system with violence are also caught in the cycle and it is the innocent who suffer.

The critical response to this play has varied widely. Although initial reviews in local newspapers indicated that audiences did not know how to respond to what they were seeing (the head of the *Cape Times* review, dated 30 March 1971, is "Utter Bewilderment"!), critical evaluation of the production shifted as the play was a work in progress that changed with audience response. A later review by Daniel Raelord called it "dramatically pared down," indicating a production which not only changed, but which was significantly edited as a result of audience feedback (qtd. in Gray, *File*, 42).

The final result was a production that used Grotowskian performance techniques to filter recent events in South Africa through the archetypes of a Greek myth in order to address the larger issues of justice for those living under apartheid. Rather than simply focusing on a localized treatment of the Harris story, Fugard looked to the universal and timeless concerns. While the play was certainly topical, drawing, as it did, on recent history, Fugard sought to embody the basic impulses behind violence and explore not why John Harris killed, but why anyone might kill. The play is thus a fusion of both the topical and the universal; it distances the issues surrounding the violence of apartheid by filtering them through Greek tragedy, but, by distancing them, also presents them from a new and unique viewpoint. *Orestes*, while aiming for an "archetypal" theatre experience, still provides a critique of life under apartheid — less overtly so, perhaps, than *The Blood Knot* or *The Island*, but no less damning in its presentation and condemnation of the effects of a system which is sustained through violence on all the individuals living under it.

E.A. Mackay notes that Fugard does not interpret the Greek material, he "superimposed [it], like a double exposure in photography, so that one perceives two images which fused to form a new pattern" (32). Fugard can be said to bring the Orestes narrative full cycle. Euripides deconstructed Aeschylus, showing the reality of violence behind the heroic myth. Fugard, using Euripides for much of his source material, deconstructs the South African reality into myth, showing the audience the archetypal forces behind the violence of apartheid. No deus ex machina arrives at the end of Fugard's play, however. The audience is shown the problem of violence and the causes and effects of living under a system sustained by violence, but is not shown any pat, neat solutions. Instead, we are warned: as the house of Atreus demonstrates, violence begets violence; the hands of the children will be turned against their parents once they witness destruction; those who witness destruction are forever damaged by it; and those who destroy will themselves be destroyed.

Orestes on Trial: The Song of Jacob Zulu

The first half of the last decade of the 20th century witnessed incredible changes in the Republic of South Africa. Nelson Mandela, imprisoned for treason for 27 years, became the president of the country and shared a Nobel Peace Prize with F.W. DeKlerk, his predecessor in that office. Investigations into the behavior of the police and the army, as well as that of civilian officials, are being carried out (even as of this writing) by the Committee for Truth and Reconciliation, a government body designed to discover the truth about events during the apartheid years, as well as to promote healing between the racial groups. The republic now has a one person, one vote law, so that all citizens, not just the white minority, play a role in determining the government.

The African National Congress, for many years banned and labeled a terrorist organization, is now a legitimate political party, as are many other formerly banned groups. Changes have swept through South Africa at an amazing pace.

While these changes were occurring, playwright Tug Yourgrau, a South African by birth who had grown up in the United States, learned the story of Andrew Zondo. Zondo, the son of a Zulu Christian minister, escaped South Africa in order to avoid a prison sentence for his student activism, was trained as an ANC guerrilla in Angola, and returned to the country in December 1985 at the age of 18. In retribution for the murder of nine ANC refugees in Lesotho by the South African Defense Forces (SADF), Zondo was ordered to plant a bomb. He placed a limpet mine in a garbage can in a crowded mall a few days before Christmas, killing four and injuring dozens. Zondo was arrested by the police soon after. His accomplice, also caught, confessed and agreed to turn state's evidence and inform against Zondo in exchange for a lighter sentence. Zondo's trial lasted just over a week. He was found guilty on all counts and sentenced to death. He was hung in September 1986 along with two other ANC members.

This bombing and the trial and sentence which followed echo the John Harris case on some levels. The differences, however, are of greater significance. Harris was a white man working alone, whereas Zondo, a black, was a member of the ANC, whose military wing Umkoto We Sizwe ("Spear of the Nation") carried out many "military acts" against the South African state. From August to December 1985, the period when Zondo carried out his mission, 42 bombing incidents were recorded in South Africa, most of which were either ordered or sanctioned by the ANC (Clifford-Vaughn, 259). The bombing (included in this total) is an example of the use of violence in order to "destroy the existing political, economic, and social structure of South Africa by means of political subversion and propaganda and sabotage and terrorism" (Clifford-Vaughn, 254). In the late 1980s, however, the ANC began to distance itself from bomb attacks, particularly on "soft targets" for fear of losing Western support against the Nationalist government as well as the "moral high ground" (Clifford-Vaughn, 257). In short, the Zondo bombing occurred at the end of a significant campaign carried out by the ANC.

The ANC and similar organizations, however, claimed that the two most violent organizations operating within South Africa were the South African Defense Force (SADF) — the army — and the South African Police (SAP) — the police. As F.M. Clifford-Vaughn notes, the SAP is "a paramilitary gendarmerie which is legally the 'first line of defense' in the security of the republic ... [and] the force primarily responsible for combating terrorism" (253). The SADF's primary responsibility was defending the republic from external threats, including ANC members living in exile in neighboring countries such as Angola, Namibia, Swaziland, and Lesotho.

As part of the "first line of defense," the SAP was the group that quelled social unrest and political protests. From September 1984 to November 1987, over 2,600 people were killed during popular protests. One third of them died as a result of "black-on-black" violence during the protests. Two thirds, however, were killed directly by the SAP (see Herbst). In the 1986 Sharpesville Massacre alone, 31 blacks were shot dead by the SAP and over 300 were injured (Holland, 202). To say that most South Africans, especially black South Africans, lived in a violent world in which violent acts were used as a means to an end by both the government and the resistance is not an understatement.

This world is the one in which Andrew Zondo was moved to bomb a mall just before Christmas. After the fall of apartheid, Yourgrau resolved to develop this story for the stage:

> I decided to tell the story of a young man such as Andrew in the form of a Greek drama, but with an African twist: Aeschylus set in Zululand... I went back to the great Greek dramas, especially Aeschylus's *The Oresteia* and Sophocles's *Oedipus* cycle for inspiration and guidance [viii, x].

Yourgrau, like J.P. Clark, was inspired by the form and structure of Greek tragedy. Unlike Clark, though, Yourgrau drew heavily from a particular drama: *The Oresteia*. His borrowings include structure, use of a chorus, the religious context, and the presentation of character. Yourgrau's intent is also Aeschylean: *The Oresteia* celebrates the founding of the jury system in Athens and the end of blood vengeance; *The Song of Jacob Zulu* celebrates "the good news of the end of apartheid" (6).

Much like *The Eumenides*, *The Song of Jacob Zulu* begins after the violence has already occurred. The play opens with an ode, and the entrance of the chorus, which is atypical for Greek tragedy, and certainly does not occur in any of the trilogy, which begin with a watchman, Orestes, and the Pythia of Delphi respectively. Greek tragedy is structured to begin with the *prologos*, the dialogue or monologue that takes place before the first choral ode. In the typical Greek tragedy the chorus enters and sings only after the *prologos*. Yet Yourgrau frames his drama with choral odes.

One might note that the American musical comedy, a form pioneered by Broadway, and one with which traditional American audiences are comfortable and familiar, almost always begins with a choral piece which introduces some of the characters, sets the scene, and perhaps introduces the major themes of the play. Plays such as *Grease, Guys and Dolls, Cats*, and many others all begin with choral pieces. As *Jacob Zulu* was written in the United States for American audiences, even though the author and chorus itself (Ladysmith Black Mambazo) were South African, we might consider the play to be a true intercultural blend, mixing elements of South African, American, and Greek theatres.

The chorus enters singing "Lalelani," isiZulu for "Listen." Asking the audience to "open their hearts," the chorus then begins to relate the story of Jacob Zulu. The ode frames the personal, political, and theatrical contexts:

> Leader: This is the song of a young man called Jacob Zulu...
> Chorus: Zulu!
> Leader: Who suffered for the sins of South Africa...
> Chorus: South Africa!
> Leader: This is a song for whom the good news...
> Chorus: The good news, the good news, the good news!
> Leader: Of the end of apartheid...
> Chorus: If it really is the end... Amen.
> Leader: Comes too late [5–6].

Through this choral introduction, the audience becomes aware of the protagonist and his probable fate. It also locates the play at the end of the apartheid era, but not after it. Much like the original Greek tragedies, in which the story was known, the chorus "gives away" the ending. The audience therefore spends the drama not watching what happens, but rather how and why it happens. The repeated use of the word "song" refers not to the song the chorus is singing, but rather to the entire play, as the title *The Song of Jacob Zulu* suggests. The play is a song, possibly suggesting "goatsong," the origin of "tragedy." As in Clark's *Song of a Goat*, the title refers to tragic antecedents.

This opening passage is also suggestive of the choral ode at the beginning of the *Agamemnon*, in which the chorus sings of the tragedy of Iphigenia and the pain of Clytemnestra. Each section of the ode ends with the line, "Sing sorrow, sorrow; but good win out in the end" (1, 121, 139, 159). The choral ode that opens each play looks to the end, to the good that will arise out of the tragic events. In *Jacob Zulu* they sing of "the good news of the end of apartheid," although the events which are represented onstage after the ode occur before that end. Likewise, the chorus of *Agamemnon* display foreknowledge of the resolution of events that will be depicted after they sing. The ending is less important, being known, than the journey to that ending. The characters, chorus, and audience must "sing sorrow" in order to reach "the good news."

The repeated use of the phrase "good news" also invokes Christian imagery and ideas. Jacob's father is a minister. During the course of the drama the audience sees Jacob baptized. The suggestion that Jacob "suffered for the sins of South Africa" also posits Jacob as a Christlike figure, which is suggested again visually and textually in the closing scenes. Yourgrau blends the story of Andrew Zondo and the myth of Orestes with Christian iconography. Thus, in a single opening chorus, the play references Greek tragedy, American musical comedy, and the Christian gospels.

A radio announcer reports the bombing as the choral ode finishes and the first scene begins with Jacob, under arrest and being arraigned, detailing his injuries to the court. He has been beaten by the police. The scene is short and remains focused on a detailed description of Jacob's wounds. The audience is immediately connected with the physical body and the effect of violence (brought about through the policies of apartheid) upon it.

Through a flashback the audience is shown Jacob's baptism, which occurred when Jacob was 15 and was performed by his father, a minister. The chorus again sings, "Good news, good news, good news!" (12). In this context, the reference to the Gospel and to Christ is obvious. During the baptism, Jacob's uncle Mdishwa enters and places an *iskhumba sembuzi* on Jacob. The *iskhumba sembuzi* is a goatskin used by the amaZulu in a coming of age ceremony and is worn to please the *amaDlozi*, one's ancestors. Christianity and Zulu belief are thus both invoked in this scene and Jacob is shown accepting both.

This play does not present conflict between African ways and Western ways, between the ancestors and Christianity. In the very character of Jacob Zulu, both are fully embodied, making him even more of a Christlike figure. His very name refers both to the Biblical Jacob and, as his family name is Zulu, to the African people from whom he comes. At his baptism, Jacob Zulu becomes both follower of Christ, promising to "walk in His path, the path of peace, the path of righteousness everlasting," and a Zulu warrior, wearer of the *iskhumba sembuzi*, promising to bring peace and pride to the *amaDlozi* (913). He is Christian and Zulu warrior. The goatskin he wears comes from a sacrificed goat, offered up to the ancestors. This fact introduces the idea of sacrifice, but also refers again to the goatsong. The connection to Greek tragedy is reinforced again.

This flashback has introduced the first of two questions which the play poses: how does a young man who has accepted Christ and promised to walk in peace and serve his ancestors become a terrorist who kills innocent people with a bomb? Much like Fugard, Yourgrau is interested in the psychology behind the violence: how does a "good" person become a killer?

The next scene begins the trial with a choral strophe:

> Leader: Now begins the trial of Jacob Zulu.
>   Here there is no jury, no council of elders.
>   Only a judge in a robe of blood.
>   What can he know of a black man's life?
>   Can there be justice?
> Chorus: Can there be justice
>   For a black man
>   In a white man's court?
>   In South Africa?
>   The land of apartheid? [17].

Here the audience is introduced to the second question: can there be true justice for the black man in South Africa? This theme dictates the primary form of the play: a trial. The entire play consists of Jacob and the witnesses against him testifying and being cross-examined. The narratives they relate are enacted in the form of flashbacks performed in front of the courtroom set. This dramaturgy strengthens the connection to the Greek root of Yourgrau's drama. First, much of the action is not seen, but reported, as in a Greek tragedy. Second, Yourgrau's use of Sophocles and Aeschylus is demonstrated by the fact that the trial of Jacob Zulu shown to the audience is ultimately not concerned with the guilt or innocence of Jacob Zulu, but with the answers to the two questions posed above: what drives good men to violence and is justice possible within the South African system? The dramatization of a trial becomes a trial of the South African justice system under apartheid.

The next choral ode is also of particular significance:

> Leader: In South Africa
>   There has been a curse
>   A blood-red curse
>   The curse of revenge

The Song of Jacob Zulu by Tug Yourgrau. Orestes in the dock: the trial of Jacob Zulu (K. Todd Freeman) becomes a trial of apartheid and South Africa. *Photograph ©Jack Mitchell.*

> Since white fought black
> Two hundred years ago
> At blood river [22].

This ode refers to a very specific event in South Africa, the words "Blood River" being recognizable to any South African, much as reference to Athenian victories and defeats would be instantly recognizable to the original Greek audiences. On 16 December 1838 the Zulu were defeated by the *voortrekkers*, the Afrikaner pioneers, at a site near the Nkombe River in Natal. Five to seven wagons with 500 soldiers, armed with 500 guns and two small canon trekked through Zulu territory. At dawn on 16 December a Zulu army of approximately 10,000 warriors attacked the group, whose wagons had been lashed together to form a *laager*. Three thousand Zulu died, but not a single Boer lost his life. This famous event in South African history is known as the Battle of Blood River, and is viewed with great pride by Afrikaners, but viewed as a terrible event by indigenous South Africans. The Afrikaners also refer to this event as the Day of the Covenant, as the *voortrekkers* vowed to serve God and dedicate the nation to Him if He would grant them victory, thus giving the day not only civic and political connotations, but religious ones as well (Coplan, 356; Thompson, 91).

The reference to this event by a group of Zulu singers presents a very different set of associations than those of mainstream South African culture. By referring to the Battle of Blood River as the beginning of the curse of revenge, Yourgrau both establishes a blood feud between whites and blacks which is traced back to this event and associates that feud with the cycle of revenge presented in *The Oresteia*. The language suggests that the violent actions of the present are caused by a curse rooted in generations past. In *The Libation Bearers* the chorus sings of the curse on the house of Atreus:

> Here on this house of the kings the third
> Storm has broken, with wind
> From the inward race, and gone its course.
> The children were eaten: there was the first
> Affliction, the curse of Thyestes.
> Next came the royal death, when a man
> And lord of Achaean armies went down
> Killed in the bath. Third
> Is for the savior. He came. Shall I call
> It that, or death? Where
> Is the end? Where shall the fury of fate
> Be stilled to sleep, be done with? [1065–1076].

When one compares the two, similar language and similar ideas emerge. Yourgrau suggests that South Africa is cursed, as was the house of Atreus, for the misdeeds of ancestors. The curse is a violent cycle of retribution that will not end until someone comes forward to end it. That someone, the "savior" of *The Libation Bearers* is Orestes, embodied in South Africa by Jacob Zulu. Both play their role in the cycle of violent revenge, but by standing trial for their actions, they are able to break the curse. In both plays a cycle of revenge is transformed into a system of true justice through the sacrifice of a young man.

Jacob testifies, and the audience is shown through a flashback, that he was encouraged by other students to fight against the "Bantu education" policies enforced in their high school. When the teacher tries to teach the students, a riot breaks out and the police raid the school. Jacob is clubbed on the head by a policeman despite the fact that he is not participating in the riot. He learns the lesson of the use of indiscriminate violence as a way to obtain what one wants. In the next scene, we see Jacob's mother attending to his head wound.

Fatima Meer reports that Andrew Zondo testified that these events actually happened to him at Umzuwele High School (105). In fact, many of the lines in the play in the trial scenes are lifted verbatim from the trial transcripts as reported by Fatima Meer. For example, Andrew's accomplice testified, "When the bomb detonated people there were going to die and the building would collapse" (qtd. in Meer, 94). In the play, Mr. X, the witness based on the accomplice, states, "I thought that when this bomb exploded, the building would collapse and people would get killed" (29). Yourgrau uses the trial transcripts as source material, although no acknowledgment is made of this during the play or in the script. He therefore avoids making the play into a documentary piece, but the lines do add an element of verisimilitude to the play. The danger, of course, is that the real trial becomes material to be considered and used or discarded when constructing a fictional narrative. The real story becomes nothing more than potential source material, like Greek tragedy, or the form of musical comedy.

The last scenes of the first act are designed to further answer the question of how the good man becomes a terrorist. Jacob testifies, and we are shown that he joined an underground student organization after his brush with the police. He is given leaflets to hand out, but the police break into the Zulu household during dinner and arrest Jacob. Reverend Zulu, Jacob's father, secures Jacob's release from jail with the promise that his son will become a police informer. When Jacob is beaten by the police in front of other students a few days later he runs away, escaping over the border to train as an ANC guerrilla.

The second act begins with a choral ode. (Although Greek tragedies did not have an intermission, contemporary American audiences demand one, thus relying upon conventions of both ancient tragedy and contemporary American theatre.) The leader and the chorus detail the wandering of Jacob through the South African desert and over the river into Lesotho. The language and imagery are suggestive of both the wanderings of Orestes or other Greek characters such as Io in *Prometheus Bound* or Ajax in *Ajax* and, in keeping with the Biblical imagery employed throughout the drama, the wandering in the desert of both the Jews and Christ.

Jacob testifies that during his training the SAFD attacked their camp and several of his friends were killed. Realizing that nowhere was safe, Jacob made the decision to join Umkhonto We Sizwe and strike back at white South Africa. The scene is of particular significance for its demonstration of the regenerative power of political violence. In a violent system an individual is confronted by a choice, argues Mary Karen Dahl. Having been trained, Jacob may embrace violence or reject it. However, the choice is not merely one of action but also one of identity: "The fundamental choice is between becoming a victim or an executioner, inflicting or submitting to violence" (Dahl, 2). In other words, because apartheid is an inherently violent system, and because the Nationalist government chooses to maintain its hold on power through violent means, neither Jacob nor anyone living under apartheid has the first choice. Violence cannot be rejected, as it is part of the reality of the system. The true choice, according to Dahl, is whether or not to respond to that violence with violence or not. One can accept victim status, or one can become a fighter against the system. Jacob has continually displayed himself to be a victim, submitting to being the object of violence. Once his ANC friends are killed outside South Africa, however, he consciously chooses to become an executioner — inflicting violence in return for violence being the only active choice in a violent system.

During the night before the last day of the trial the chorus sings an ode in which the spirits of his ancestors appear to Jacob in his dreams. Jacob then awakes and tells the audience what he has not told in his trial: his younger brother Philip died many years previously when he became sick and the ambulance took several hours to arrive at the Zulu household. Jacob notes that the innocent suffer for no other reason than race in South Africa, and that had he been white, Philip would no doubt be alive today. While he feels remorse for having killed people, Jacob also realizes that under apartheid no one is innocent. Philip died because he was black; the people died at Shaka's Rock Mall because they were white — there is no difference. Jacob is guilty, but so is all of South Africa.

On the seventh day of the trial (the last scene of the play) the judge finds Jacob guilty on four counts of murder and sentences him to death on all four counts. The chorus sings a Zulu hymn as Jacob walks to the gallows. However, at the end of the scene, the gallows is revealed to be empty, an ambiguous visual image which suggests several possible meanings. The empty gallows suggests the empty tomb of Jesus, once again connecting Jacob Zulu to Christ and reminding the audience that he "died for the sins of South Africa."

Another interpretation of this final image is also possible. Mary Karen Dahl states that at the end of *The Eumenides*, the furies are incorporated into the polis as "the kindly ones," and yet they still retain their nature as furies. Orestes is acquitted, but the violence he has unleashed has been brought into the community in the physical form of these violent beings. Though subjugated, violence "still dominates human nature and social structures" (Dahl, 70). Likewise, while the empty gallows is a symbol of Jacob's sacrifice, the fact that there is a gallows on stage becomes a visual reminder of the subjugated violence carried out in the name of the state. Police torture, crowd-control techniques, execution, and military strikes into neighboring countries are all examples of state-sanctioned violence that is made manifest in the symbol of the gallows. The cycle of violence did not end with the death of Jacob Zulu; the gallows will claim more lives in the name of "justice."

Yet the gallows is empty. An empty gallows is a gallows not in use. The image is a paradoxical one, reminding the viewer both of the state-sanctioned violence of the past and of its absence in the present. The end of apartheid has brought about an end to this manifestation of state-sanctioned violence. An empty gallows is literally the presence of an absence — a reminder of what was and no longer is.

A final possible meaning draws us into the larger trial on stage. Jacob Zulu, on trial for the murder of four people, is sentenced to death. Yet the play is really a trial of South Africa and the apartheid system. The death of Philip and the dehumanization and degradation of Jacob at the hands of police and his own family made Jacob into a terrorist. He was a good man whom the system taught to be violent. If Jacob is guilty, then all South Africa is guilty. The gallows is not just for Jacob; it is empty because it represents the guilt of all South Africa — a South Africa ransomed from a potential death (i.e., violent revolution) by the sacrifice of Jacob Zulu, a Christlike figure who died so that the nation would not. His sacrifice helps to end apartheid and break the cycle of blood revenge begun at Blood River.

The chorus repeats the beginning ode at the end:

> This is the song of a young man
> Called Jacob Zulu,
> Who suffered for the sins of South Africa.
> This is the song for those whom
> The good news of the end of apartheid
> Comes too late [100].

They reacknowledge the Christlike role of Jacob, and return the audience to the beginning. The "good news of the end of apartheid" is the positive ending for the community which African tragedy demands, and Jacob Zulu is an African tragic hero as his suffering and death has helped to end the tragedy of apartheid. Jacob was a good man who, brutalized by the police, driven into exile, suffering the loss of friends and family, finally learned to use indiscriminate violence to fight the system. Though all South Africa is found guilty by the play, Jacob paid the price for it. Just as *The Oresteia*, for all its violence and terror, is a celebration of the Athenian justice system, so, too, is *Jacob Zulu* a celebration of the end of apartheid.

One cannot discuss *The Song of Jacob Zulu* without noting the profound significance of the chorus. Ladysmith Black Mambazo, the internationally acclaimed a capella *isicathamiya* singers do not simply play a chorus, they themselves represent the nation of South Africa emerging from apartheid. When they sing of the pains and trials of Jacob and South Africa, they know firsthand of these things: Andrew Zondo was the cousin of Joseph Shabalala, the founder and leader of Ladysmith Black Mambazo. The whole group grew up together in the townships of South Africa. Shabalala wrote the lyrics and music for *Jacob Zulu* with Yourgrau, and the songs are emblematic of the music of Ladysmith Black Mambazo.

Much like in the original Greek tragedies, Ladysmith Black Mambazo narrates the action, comments upon and contextualizes the events, and serves to link the audience to the action. Their voices sing as one, and yet, with Shabalala as leader, singing in a call and response style, the viewer is reminded of the origins of tragedy: an "answerer" stepped out of the chorus and dialogue was introduced into narrative chants. In many ways the use of Ladysmith Black Mambazo represents a return to a very Greek way of using the chorus, a way not found in many of the adaptations in this study.

The power of the chorus does not stem only from the manner in which it is used, but also from the tremendous power of Ladysmith Black Mambazo in live performance. Critics universally agreed that the chorus was, in large part, the reason for the play's success (see Kanfer, Kroll, Lahr, Torrens, Simon). Ladysmith sings in a form called *isicathamiya*, an a capella style whose name means "to walk like a cat." It developed in urban areas and mining centers where male choirs would complete with each other in unofficially organized contests. The form is based originally on Zulu war chants and marriage songs (see Erlmann, 7–9). Then, during the apartheid era, it became a way for miners, workers, and laborers to express discontent and dissent: "South Africa was then bubbling with discourses and practices that not only questioned the legitimacy of this order but also provided the imaginable with a form" (Erlmann, xx). In practice, the traditional songs of war and weddings were used to voice opposition to apartheid, safely performed in the guise of contests for workers in amateur singing groups.

Joseph Shabalala was one of the pioneers of this form. He was the first full-time professional composer and performer of *isicathamiya* (Erlmann, 93). He was also the first "to base his compositions on extended narrative sequences" (89). With *The Song of Jacob Zulu* he became the first to link *isicathamiya* with a dramatic narrative to form a modern Greek style of tragedy. Although in this essay the play has been called Yourgrau's, Sha-

The Song of Jacob Zulu by Tug Yourgrau. The use of Ladysmith Black Mambazo as chorus reinforcing a sense of Greek tragedy. K. Todd Freeman as Jacob Zulu, Joseph Shabalala as Chorus Leader. *Photograph © Jack Mitchell.*

balala and Ladysmith Black Mambazo deserve just as much credit for the Greek feel of the play and its overall structure and rhythm.

Shabalala himself discusses the unique tension that the presence of Ladysmith Black Mambazo and the use of *isicathamiya* in *Jacob Zulu* bring to the piece. In speaking of his work in general Shabalala says that *isicathamiya* is the "ritualized enactment of opposition and dissent which brings about 'mutual comprehension' and 'unity'" (qtd. in Erlmann, 287). In *Jacob Zulu*, the unity and mutual comprehension which occur (and, in fact, can only begin) with the end of apartheid can only come about after the "enactment of opposition" by Jacob Zulu. *Isicathamiya* is similar in principle to Aristotle's idea of catharsis: out of the ritual enactment of conflict comes a purging of the negative and a greater understanding and unity. The pleasure of *isicathamiya* comes only when a group of different voices come together and sing in unity. Only though resisting the order (or disorder) of apartheid can South African unity be achieved. The use of Ladysmith Black Mambazo is what makes *Jacob Zulu* arguably the closest transculturation of the actual Greek tragic form.

Through the use of the chorus, the achievement of catharsis, the blending of forms and structures, including Greek tragedy, the use of the myth of Orestes to interpret the actions of a good man who killed, and the celebration of the ultimate triumph of justice over a cycle of retributive violence, Yourgrau and Shambalala have crafted a true work of intercultural theatre which blends all of its elements into a modern African-Greek tragedy. This play is a model for further development of the form.

Changing Orestes, Changing South Africa

A comparison of these two treatments of the Orestes narrative in a South African milieu demonstrates the discontinuous path the Republic of South Africa and its people have taken, as well as the significant differences in concept, execution, and impact on these two plays— two plays, it might be added, that arrive at somewhat similar conclusions about the cycle of violence in South Africa.

Orestes, presented in Port Elizabeth in the Republic of South Africa during a little more than a few weeks in April 1971, was essentially a small production of very limited means. Performed in a small space with limited seating (only 70 people at a time could see the show), fewer than 700 people experienced the original (and, to this author's knowledge, the only) run of the show. The cast of three carried an 80-minute show with minimal costumes, setting, and properties. Most of the scholarship concerning the play (including this essay) is derived from Fugard's own account of the production and from the few reviews in local newspapers. Even within Fugard's own body of work, the play is not highly considered or often written about. Its significance lies in the fact that it was an important piece in the development of Fugard's ideas about theatre and acting.

The Song of Jacob Zulu, appearing in 1993, three years after the release of Nelson Mandela and one year before he was elected president of South Africa, was written and performed in the United States. Although the author, Tug Yourgrau, was born South African, his family came to the Unites States when he was ten years old. When the play was performed on Broadway it starred K. Todd Freeman (already known for his work in theatre and film), Zakes Mokae (who began his acting career almost 30 years before with Fugard, and has since starred in many films and plays, including several of Fugard's greatest plays such as *Master Harold ... and the Boys* and *The Blood Knot*), and Ladysmith Black Mambazo (now world famous from Paul Simon's *Graceland* album, Michael Jackson's movie *Smooth Criminal*, Spike Lee's documentary *Do It Acapella* [sic], recordings with Andreas Vollenweider and Black Foss, not to mention their own several dozen records and sell-out concerts [Erlmann, 307]). In short, the play featured famous stars and well-known actors. Thousands saw the show, including a number of people who did not regularly attend Broadway shows. In fact, record numbers of African-Americans saw the production, which was unique, as the *New York Times* reported on May 7, 1993: "The show had created an atypical audience with limited discretionary income [for whom] theatre tickets just weren't a high priority" (qtd. in Torrens, 18). Not only was the show a success on Broadway, but the cultural connection between and political interest by Africa-Americans and black South Africans became manifest. Broadway, primarily the (expensive) playground of the (most often white) middle class, discovered an African-American audience for this play.

Jacob Zulu had a cast of 26, fairly large, especially when compared with *Orestes*'s three, and ran just under three hours, nearly twice the length of its predecessor. *Orestes* focused on the cycle of violence from within. It was a play concerned about a contemporary reality. *Jacob Zulu* was a celebration of the ending of that cycle of violence that was a retrospective. It was a play concerned with history. Fugard focused on the mythic archetypes of the characters to give us a white Orestes and to consider why he became violent. Yourgrau and Shabalala used Greek structure and a chorus to give us a black Orestes and to consider why he became violent. Fugard relied on Euripides as his model, Yourgrau and Shabalala on Aeschylus.

Both plays are products of their political and theatrical environments. Both plays evidence conscious experimentation with form, character, and presentation. Both plays attempt to frame bombings and their aftermath with the story of Orestes in order to explore the violence of South Africa and why it drives good people to kill. Neither play is a direct adaptation of a Greek original, but both use specific Greek plays as models upon which to build. Both present an Orestes for their respective times, just as Aeschylus and Euripides did in fifth-century Athens.

Both plays are African tragedies inasmuch as they concern African subject matter, were written by African writers, and contained performances by African actors (and singers). *The Song of Jacob Zulu* is an Americanized, Broadway extravaganza that nevertheless is arguably one of the most transcultural pieces considered in this survey. It combines elements of Athenian, South African, and North American cultures in order to address questions about apartheid. Like all other African tragedies, its concern is the community, and, as noted above, the audience community drew heavily from the African-American population. Ironically, the play actually performed in South Africa, *Orestes*, is less concerned with the community than it is with the effects of apartheid on the individual, and, in particular, the individual white citizen who does not agree with apartheid.

What is interesting about the use of the Orestes tragedies to explore South Africa is that the story ends positively. Aeschylus's play is a celebration of justice and the community. Euripides, Fugard's model, wrote a darker version of the story, but the ending is still positive. Both playwrights construct stories in which violent beginnings meet positive resolutions contradictory to the present reality of the play. Fugard, writing in the heart of apartheid, still used a model that presented hope for a bloodless resolution. The violence of apartheid, seemingly running full tilt toward mutual annihilation and endless destruction might end positively with a union, no matter how improbable it may seem — this is what Fugard suggested by the choice of *Orestes*. It turns out he was right, as *The Song of Jacob Zulu* was able to celebrate a quarter century later.

AFRICAN ANTIGONES

"Antigone is the perfect tragedy. It defines what tragedy is and should be."

> The Joy of Reading
> Charles van Doren

Antigone in Africa

George Steiner, whose *The Death of Tragedy* was decried by many African critics for hailing only the death of European tragedy, while African tragedy is alive and well and growing, also wrote a survey of adaptations of Sophocles's *Antigone* entitled *Antigones*. Steiner tells us that Romantic and 19th-century Europe admired Sophocles first among the Athenian tragedians and that *Antigone* was the perfect tragedy, an intellectual heritage that continues well into the present day, as van Doren's epigraph above demonstrates (3). The play was first translated and adapted in Europe in the 1530s, claims Steiner, and there have been thousands of adaptations since. To name just a few of the more recent versions, I could cite adaptations by Brecht, Anouilh, or Hölderin. Arthur Honegger and Carl Orff both adapted the story into operas, while Mikis Theodorakis created a ballet version. George Tsavellas made a filmed version in 1961. The adaptations of Sophocles are not limited to Europe: there are South American, Japanese, Chinese, Indian, Arabic, and Australian adaptations. In 1973, Kemal Demirel set the play in his native Turkey. In short, the play has been adapted in many cultures in many eras, and might even be considered the "most transcultured / most transculturable" tragedy.

As Steiner then argues, why "a sequence of recapitulations of the classical?; why a hundred *Antigones* after Sophocles? (121). Indeed, while all the plays considered in this survey are recapitulations of the classical, *Antigone*, more than any other, is adapted, deconstructed, reconstructed, recapitulated, and presented in new contexts. Steiner offers a few reasons for the play's popularity: its themes, its structure, which has "built into [it] the tensions between organic collectivity and the aloneness of the individual" (277), the presence of all five "conflicts in the condition of man" (man versus woman, young versus old, individual versus group, living versus dead, mortal versus immortal) (231), and the simple fact that the story presents the audience, as do so many Greek tragedies based on myth, with a "universal" archetype true to the human condition. "We have added very few indeed," Steiner concludes, "to the seminal presences given us by the Helles" (129).

While all of these reasons are certainly true, and the sheer number and variety of the adaptations speak to a universal quality of the play, there are certain qualities and aspects of the tragedy which have suited the play for adaptation in a variety of cultures in the 20th and 21st centuries. The two greatest factors are that *Antigone* is essentially a play about the aftermath of war and the attempt to ensure order after that war, and that the tragedy's main conflict concerns the rule of law versus the dictates of both personal belief and traditional religious codes. From 1814 to 1844 in Europe, Steiner reports, there were a number of Napoleonic *Antigones* (139). Walter Hasenclever's 1917 adaptation corresponds to conditions in Germany during the First World War (142). In her 1936 adaptation, Marguerite Yourcenar's seemingly prophetic *Feux* featured a contemporary mise en scène in which "the streets of Thebes are shaken by the passage of tanks," (Steiner, 142). Brecht's version features a fascistic Creon and a Gestapo-like secret police. Jean Anouilh's famous and influential adaptation is the product of an occupied France, in which Creon is presented somewhat sympathetically as trying to quell the resistance movement of which Antigone is a part.

Steiner records the use of Greek tragedy during the latter half of the 20th century, equating the burning of cities from 1939 to 1945 with the fall of Troy. Sartre and the Living Theatre, "during the wars in Algeria and Vietnam," turned to the Greek archetypes to express outrage and identification with human and colonial struggles (285). *Antigone* might be perceived as the ultimate protest play, a matrix for interpretation and a model upon which we can frame the "tragic politics," to borrow Steiner's term, of our era (285). *Antigone* can be adapted into any situation in which a group is oppressed, or in which, in the aftermath of struggle, the forces of communal and social order come into conflict with the forces of personal liberty.

Antigone can also be an activist play depending on the answer to the question: for what does Antigone die? For what convictions and causes does she perform a forbidden action? The play is both personal and political. It gives voice to the voiceless: the dead (Polynices, after all, cannot speak on his own behalf of the right to be buried), women, and those outside the civic law. Ober and Strauss, in their essay on political rhetoric and Athenian democracy, argue that in Athens, "the citizenry remained hierarchically stratified in terms of class and status, and the interests of elite citizens were sometimes at odds with those of the mass of ordinary citizens" (237). *Antigone* demonstrates the disenfranchised speaking out against the powerful whose interest is the preservation of power, not necessarily doing what is right or just.

Lane and Lane also see the play as a political statement, claiming that Antigone is "the epitome of responsible citizenship" (182). Antigone acts according to tradition and community values, and she justifies her actions not only by citing her obedience to the laws of the gods (see lines 494–503, 570, 978–982), and her obedience to tradition ("I gave reverence to what claims reverence" [1001]), but also by appealing to her fellow citizens of Thebes and citing her Theban heritage; "You see, you people of my country..." (870) and "O my father's city, in Theban land..." (995). She uses what S.C. Humphries calls "the language of patriotism," and she "calls on the polis and its citizens to witness her fate" (74). Antigone makes her actions publicly known and insists on trial and sentence in public. She is led off to her imprisonment and death in front of the citizens of the city, thus "performing" civil disobedience. Antigone takes on the identity of the dutiful family member, the obedient mortal, the keeper of tradition and community, and thus the good citizen.

Thus, the appeal to African theatre artists and audiences of this text includes the inherent conflicts between the disfranchised and the ruling elite which the text presents, the opportunity to explore the idea of what makes a "good citizen" and what is "good citizenship," the theme of resistance to oppression, oppression in the form of the governing power represented as a single powerful individual, the theme of resistance to power and its capricious display through unjust laws, the theme of conflict between divine law and tradition on the one hand and political policy and man-made law on the other, and, lastly, the sense of community which rallies behind Antigone in her resistance, although that community may be afraid to act on its own.

Antigone, therefore, as the tragedy whose tragic hero acts for the good of the community, may be the perfect Greek drama for adaptation into an African tragic mode.

Scott Kennedy, in his personal account concerning working as a theatre artist in West Africa, *In Search of African Theatre*, describes a production of the Sophoclean original on 14 February 1968 at the Seventh Annual Festival of the Arts at the Cultural Center in Kumasi, Ghana. He notes that Dr. A.A.Y. Kyerematen, Director of the Cultural Arts Center, directed the play, having also translated the play into Twi, the Ashanti language. Kennedy writes, "All through the play, music, drumming, dance, and mime have been interwoven with the basic actions and characterizations in the play, making for the total creation or celebration of life experience" (157). Kyerematen added much traditional African performance forms to the story of Sophocles in order to present a Greek tragedy made African. Kennedy exults: "They've opened up the play and really made it African. In fact, it is possible that *Antigone* plays even better in Twi than many of the English versions which I have seen" (157). While Kennedy's criticism is admittedly biased, we can discern the point that the use of traditional performance forms enable the Greek classic, whose translations into English can seem formal, stilted, and distant, to become a live, thrilling event. Kennedy's enthusiasm for the Africanization of European classics also bears witness to the special place occupied by Greek culture in postcolonial African culture, as well as to the popularity of *Antigone*.

Popular and "universal" as *Antigone* is, playwrights use one of two strategies to adapt the play to an African context. The first play I shall examine, Edward Kamau Brathwaite's *Odale's Choice*, is a straightforward adaptation, setting Sophocles's plot and characters in an African setting. Femi Osofisan's *Tegonni* also adapts the story of *Antigone* to an African setting, but it also introduces the character of Antigone from the Greek original, thus adding a metatheatrical element to the play that is the other strategy for adaptation. Interestingly, both of these plays were written while the authors were "in exile": Brathwaite writing his play in Ghana, away from his native Caribbean, and Osofisan writing in the United States, away from his native Nigeria. Fugard, Kani, and Ntshona and Sylvain Bemba wrote *The Island* and *Black Wedding Candles for Blessed Antigone* respectively, and offer critical, metatheatrical explorations of Africans presenting *Antigone* and the effect the play has on their lives.

Before examining these individual tragedies, it is first necessary to survey Athenian and African beliefs, rituals, and attitudes towards death, burial, the afterlife, the bodies of the dead, and the proper way to respect and obey the laws of the gods. This comparison serves to locate useful commonalities that may help explain the popularity of *Antigone* in Africa.

African and Greek Attitudes to Death, Burial, and the Gods

There exists a remarkable similarity between ancient Greek and traditional African attitudes toward the dead and the processes of dying and burial. The burial practices in ancient Greece were fairly straightforward, and, as Walter Burkert notes in his study of Greek religion, "burial customs and beliefs about the dead have always gone hand in hand...." (190). In other words, the way in which a body is handled after death indicates much about the culture's beliefs about death and the afterlife. Conversely, the beliefs about death and an afterlife will dictate ways in which the body must be handled and prepared.

In Greece, after the death of a family member, the family would take the body to the home where the women would prepare the corpse for burial. Thus when Antigone claims it is her responsibility to prepare her brother's body for burial, it is not only because the gods have dictated that she do so, but by tradition it is her duty as the closest female relative. Mary Lefkowitz states, "Sophocles' audience would have seen Antigone's action as ... certainly within the bounds of acceptable female behavior" ("Influential," 52). In another article, Lefkowitz points out that Antigone would be seen as fulfilling her proper familial and societal role: as a woman, she is to "prepare the bodies for burial and sing laments over the body" (*Women*, 81). The ritual tasks of preparing the body that must be performed by the female relatives of the deceased included washing the body, anointing it with oil, dressing the body, "crowning it," "adorning the body with flowers," and then wrapping it in a shroud for burial (Rehm, 7). The body, adorned with flowers and crowned with a wreath, would then be presented at the funeral proper that would take place at the home. The funeral was a public presentation, any member of the polis could attend, and as there was no priests or set funeral service, the family would run the funeral and the banquet that followed (Bukert, *Religion*, 192; Rehm, 7). Therefore, when Antigone buries Polynices, she is performing the duties required of her in Greek culture.

During the funeral, the female relatives would wail and sing dirges. Grief was publicly performed. The body was then carried to the grave, and then the family performed sacrifices, buried the body, and held a funeral banquet, which could go on for several days depending on the wealth and status of the deceased. Libations would be poured out and offerings made for the dead. The rituals that marked death were both community-oriented and designed to perform the acts of mourning in public.

In Greek belief, death literally changes everything. According to Jon

D. Mikalson, there are a "new set of rules" for the deceased, and the "justice of the living" no longer matters (140). One receives a "new set of gods" at death; the Olympian gods no longer mattered to the dead — only Hades and his cohorts (140). The living must perform burial practices, but the dead are beyond help or need, and these practices do not matter to them (194). The banquets held at the tombs of the deceased, carried out on the third, ninth, and 13th days after burial are "an important family obligation"; they are important because of their value to the community, but are of no real value to the dead (122). The dead are "nothing ... inaccessible to prayer and ritual and may not even perceive their own funerals" (121). Mikalson demonstrates that Greek funeral practice is carried out for the living, the mourning, the community and not for the dead, who neither require them, nor are affected by them. S.C. Humphreys describes how funerary vases, "convey the sense of a personal relationship between the dead and the mourner ... who comes to care for the tomb.... At the same time, however, the vases clearly separate the dead from the living" (106). The dead are forever cut off from the living and the relationship between the two can only be continued from the side of the living.

It is the memory of the deceased that keeps them connected to the living. The family still considers the deceased a member of the family. Burkert observes, "the burial place still proclaims the unity of the family" (191). In fact, though the dead are removed and remote, they are very important to the identity to the living. The ancestors are very important in Greek culture. Burkert notes, "The cult of the dead remains the foundation and expression of family identity: the honour accorded to forbears is expected from descendants: from the remembrance of the dead grows the will to continue" (194). Honor accorded the ancestors is part of one's own sense of continuity: we descend from the ancestors, whom we will some day join in death; we shall also create our own descendants who will duly pay honor to us, then join us in death. Paying tribute to the ancestors both acknowledges one's place within the community and also creates unity and continuity within life, even though it is of no benefit to the dead. The benefit of funerals and of tributes to the dead, according to the Greeks, was to the living.

African burial practices vary widely, although there are some factors and practices that seem more common than others. The preparation of the body is quick; because of the tropical heat of much of sub–Saharan Africa, decay begins quickly, and burial is the preferred form of disposal (Mbiti, *Introduction*, 120). In many ethnic groups, the female relatives of the deceased, or the women of the village, prepare the corpse and are expected to "wail and weep, lamenting the departure of the dead person..." (Mbiti,

121). The mourners then fast for a day or two and the family offers communal feasting (Mbiti, 121). Food and drink, similar to libations, are left out for the dead (Mbiti, 129).

Many of the practices of African cultures bear surface similarities to Greek practice. Unlike the Greek funeral, however, which is for the living, most African cultures recognize the continuance between the living and the dead, which influences burial practices. John Eberebulam Njoku reports that "Africa recognizes two burials. The first burial is the burial of the body and the second burial is the burial of the Spirit. The important obligation that the living owes the dead is a good burial" (1). Unlike the Greek dead, the African dead are aware of their own funeral rites and how well or poorly they are executed. The spirit must be protected from evil, including the powers of witches, sorcerers, and evil spirits, and thus the need for a funeral which will "bury the spirit." This second burial is an obligation of the highest importance of the relatives of the deceased: "The living must help the spirit of the dead to make an uninterrupted journey to his or her maker" (Njoku, 1). In other words, the obligation upon family members is not for their sake alone, or for the sake of the community, but for the sake of the deceased, whose continued survival and status after death depends on the actions of the living.

The common belief in Africa is in a highly active and interactive afterlife that is not divorced from the world of the living, as in Greek thought. John S. Mbiti reports that the hereafter is "invisible but very close to that of the living" (*Introduction*, 122). The worlds of the living and the dead connect, and traffic and communication run both ways. The dead can both influence and be influenced by the living, and the proper relationship with the dead must be maintained because they are not cut off, as the Greek dead are, but a present and powerful reality.

The ancestors are extremely important in most African societies therefore, not only for continuity and family unity and the will to continue, as in Greece, although those factors certainly matter. The African ancestors are beings who are in contact with the gods, who can influence events and destinies, and who have power over their living descendants. The dead are treated very carefully for this reason. African ancestors are powerful, and their will is efficacious. As Njoku reports, "No one talks ill of one's dead relatives. It is a duty bound for one to accord one's dead relatives the last honor" (1). The ancestors are a real presence in the everyday life of Africans, and honor and respect are their due. Regular sacrifice and rituals are performed, not just for the sake of the living, but to keep the ancestors safe, happy, and bestowing their support and good will on the living.

Significant differences exist between the reasoning behind Greek and

African burial practices, although the outer forms of those burials are similar: female members of the deceased prepare the body, the same then mourn the deceased, and the body is buried in the ground with attendant sacrifices and rituals, followed by communal banqueting and feasting. The dead are accorded honor and respect, and the ancestors remain an important part of the family in both cultures, although the actual relationship to the dead differs.

In almost any cultural context, whether ancient Greek or contemporary African, nonburial is considered a bad thing. To not bury a dead relative, to fail to carry out the traditional rites, rituals, and sacrifices following death is especially heinous, as well as an offense to the gods, the dead, and the ancestors. Nonburial in most African cultures punishes both the dead, who in some cultures are denied access to the realm of the ancestors if not buried properly, and the living, who are haunted by the unburied. Thus, in many cultures to which the play has been adapted, Creon's decree that Polynices remain unburied is not only an insult, but literally a sentence to a fate worse than death.

In burying a dead relative, even one who is an enemy of the state, Antigone has acted in accordance with and preserved tradition, the community, and the laws of the gods. This sense of piety and communal / familial preservation easily finds its cultural echo in almost every African society. The laws of man may never go against the laws of the gods. John S. Mbiti reminds us that "the moral demands of human conduct," according to African philosophy, require obedience to the gods, ancestors, and tradition (*Introduction*, 179).

The similarities between cultural beliefs about the burial of the dead, pious behavior, obedience to the gods, the ancestors, and tradition, and giving honor to the ancestors allow for fairly easy adaptation to a variety of African settings without the conceptual difficulties faced by *Oedipus Rex* or *Medea*. The Greek concepts of burial as expressed in *Antigone* shift much more easily into an African context due to similar belief structures in African cultures.

Antigone in Exile 1: Odale's Choice

Edward Kamau Brathwaite is a writer and scholar who straddles the borders of many cultures. He is a Caribbean writer by birth who worked and taught for many years in Ghana in the late 1950s and early 1960s. Brathwaite wrote and directed his adaptation of *Antigone*, *Odale's Choice*, while living in Ghana. A student cast first performed it in June of 1962 at Mfantsiman Secondary School in Saltpond.

In the "Production Note," Brathwaite claims his adaptation is *Antigone* "modernized (though to an indefinite period) and made to apply to an African country, but no country in particular" (3). In other words, Brathwaite removes the Greco-Theban setting of the play, but does not transculturate the original into a specific African culture, instead choosing to create and maintain what Gilbert and Tompkins call "geographic vagueness," as well as temporal vagueness (42). They trace this choice of nonspecific contextualization to Brathwaite's own Caribbean heritage, noting that in his work Brathwaite is on a "mission to find in Africa an 'authentic' ancestral homeland for West Indians of African origin…" (42). As most West Indians of African origin cannot claim a specific homeland or specific culture, ethnic group, or nation within Africa, all of Africa then becomes the homeland. An absence of a real, traceable, historic connection results in the creation of a connection to the whole and the creation of an artificial, perhaps idealized, "Africa" which contains elements of real African cultures, but recontextualizes them as part of a much larger set of cultural forms. Brathwaite has written a Creole *Antigone* set in what Said would call the "imaginary geography of Afric," an African homeland for the Caribbean dispossessed who acknowledge several general roots (African, Amerind, European), but none specific (*Orientalism*, 49). Brathwaite uses a European text set in "Africa" in order to explore the moral issue of choice. *Odale's Choice* is arguably just as much a Caribbean play as it is an African one, if not more so.

Brathwaite claims a "timeless" theme: "the defiance of tyranny," tyranny being identified with the reign of Creon. Brathwaite Africanizes the names: Antigone becomes Akwele, known as Odale, Ismene becomes Akwuokor, also called Leicho, and the soldier who guards the body is given a name: Musa. The sole exception to this Africanization of identity is Creon, who remains Creon. The character who embodies tyranny, the character responsible for the personal tragedies of the other characters retains a European name. Creon, the symbol of misguided power and ego-centrism, remains European in name, although his character is obviously African.

The play is titled *Odale's Choice* to further reflect on Brathwaite's theme. While many critics feel that the Sophoclean original is weighted evenly between Antigone and Creon in terms of focus and tragic status, Brathwaite's title suggests that his adaptation rests solely on the Antigone figure. Odale's choice is not whether or not to bury her brother against her uncle's orders, but whether or not to resist oppression, to fight for justice.

The play begins with Odale dancing at a festival. Leicho enters and tells Odale that their brother Tawia (Polynices) was captured in a battle outside the town. A chorus of women then enter, lamenting, "Creon your uncle has killed him" (8). Brathwaite eliminates the Eteocles character and has Creon kill Antigone's brother. Brathwaite thus oversimplifies the play, removing much of the original's moral complexity and ambiguity. When both of Antigone's brothers kill each other, one of Creon's primary arguments against Antigone is that by honoring one brother she has insulted the other. Likewise, Creon's position becomes much more simple and negative: he himself is the murderer who killed the man who now cannot be buried. Gone is the Sophoclean character who tries to maintain order after a war, replaced with an obvious, murderous tyrant. Leicho does not mourn Tawia, saying, "He left of his own free will to join the enemy. He left of his own free will to fight against his own uncle. He knew what he was doing..." (8). The battle for Thebes in Brathwaite's world is no longer brother against brother, but nephew against uncle. Creon is unambiguously the villain of the piece because of Brathwaite's alterations.

But Brathwaite has also introduced his main theme, both with Leicho's line and with his simplification of the relationships: fighting against a tyrant is an act of free will which one must consciously choose. Leicho dismisses her brother's death, blaming him for choosing to fight in the first place. She represents one choice: accepting the status quo and blaming those who act for their own fates. Odale, however, calls out, "That man is a tyrant! Creon! He's cruel" (8). Odale recognizes Creon's tyranny for what it is and does not accept it. Brathwaite thus gives the audience two possible choices to tyranny: acceptance or resistance.

Tawia's body is thrown down by soldiers as Creon proclaims, "I, Creon, have spoken. Who disturbs this place or approaches the body will die" (9). Guards then remain to watch the body and a sergeant tells the others that Odale's father was "foolish and proud," thus leaving a curse on the family (12). This line marks the only reference Brathwaite makes to the Oedipus story. Also, it is the only acknowledgment of any kind of "tragic flaw," supposing Odale were like her father. The guards sleep and Odale and Leicho argue about what course of action to pursue. Leicho exits fearfully after begging Odale not to do anything, but Odale responds, "What has he done to deserve this? What horrible crime has he committed? Following his own mind? Fighting for his ideals? Is that wrong? Is that a crime? Is that a sin?" (16). Odale then "buries" Tawia by arranging the body, covering it with a cloth, and placing flowers on it, in keeping with both traditional African and ancient Greek practice.

Odale then asks Tawia's body to forgive the women of the city. She alone has done her womanly duty: "We are women. We bring you into the world and we bear you out again. We weep at your birth and mourn at your death. That at least is our duty; that alone we can do" (16). Odale makes acknowledgment of the fact, as noted above, that it is the duty of women in both African and Greek societies to prepare the corpse for burial and mourn it. She alone has obeyed the gods. Brathwaite, however, is less interested in correct piety than in the fact that Odale does not obey the orders of a tyrant. She does what she knows is right.

Upon awakening, the guards do not recognize Odale, and so arrest her and take her to Creon. The Sergeant tells Creon a fabricated narrative, eliminating many details of the real events and implying that he and his men are heroes. Brathwaite here uses an archetypal figure from West African drama: the lazy, braggart trickster, seen in other plays such as Soyinka's "Jero" plays, or Femi Osofisan's *Once Upon Four Robbers*. The story is comic relief, but also demonstrates the corruption and incompetence of the administration and the military in Creon's city.

Creon asks Odale what happened and she tells him simply that she buried her brother, which the soldiers resolutely deny. Creon and Odale debate the law:

> Creon: Do you not know the law?
> Odale: Which law, my lord and uncle?
> Creon: I mean the law of the land, my law.
> Odale: And what is your law, my lord and uncle?
> Creon: That whoever buries that boy on the hillside, be it my own
>   daughter, will die.
> Odale: My lord, I have broken your law [27–8].

Odale calls it "your law," distinguishing the dictates of a tyrant from true law. Furthermore, she initially calls him "uncle" until he acknowledges that anyone, even a relative, will be put to death for breaking the law. Then she simply calls him "my lord," as he denies their familial relationship in favor of their relationship as tyrant and subject.

Odale then continues, as in the Sophoclean original, to argue that she has followed a truer law, that of the gods. She argues that her actions, though illegal by his proclamation, are, in fact, the just and correct thing to do:

> Odale: We must bury our dead when they die.
> Creon: My law says you shall not!
> Odale: But a man is a man and a god is a god.
> Man's laws are not god's [28].

Odale's argument, after Antigone's, is that the laws proclaimed by men never supersede the laws given by the gods. When Creon's laws are in opposition to the dictates of the gods, it is the gods who must be obeyed.

Odale's actions and arguments are directly contrasted by the chorus of women and Leicho, who beg Creon to pardon and forgive Odale:

> Our Lord and master, great one, wise one…
> Lender, protector, you who watch over us,
> Our life is in your hands; our hearts
> Are in your hands; our children nestle safely
> In your arms. Help us, help us, protect us,
> For we are weak, weak, poor, weak and inadequate
> Vessels and we need you, need you, need you to help
> Us and save us [29].

They sing in supplication using language reserved for prayer, for begging the gods. On the one hand, such an action further adds to Creon's blasphemy. He gives laws in opposition to those of the gods and must be addressed as a god himself. The chorus ascribes to him all power over life and death. He is the father; they are his children. Though their intention is good—they wish to save Odale from execution—their pleas are ultimately a capitulation to Creon's tyranny, a contrast to Odale's respectful yet resistant exchanges with Creon. While the chorus makes a god of Creon, Odale reminds him that "a man is a man and a god is a god." They accept his tyranny and the powerful role he has assumed in their lives, while Odale chooses to defy him.

Creon announces that because of the chorus's supplication he will be merciful. Odale is to be banished and he denies all relationship to her any more, but she will not be executed. Odale then asks for permission to properly bury Tawia, which Creon refuses. She takes his pardon and "throw[s] it back in your face," refusing to be banished until her brother is buried (31). Creon orders her killed and her body thrown next to her brother's. She says goodbye cheerfully to the chorus and her sister and as the soldiers move to take her she pulls away from them, proclaiming, "Don't touch me! Of my own free will, I will go!" (32). This exclamation echoes Leicho's earlier dismissal of Tawia: of her own free will Odale chooses to die, recognizing that by dying she is resisting oppression, but by accepting the pardon she would be given into tyranny. The play ends with Odale exiting triumphantly to her death, which differs significantly from the original in which the play continues through Creon's tragic fall.

Again, Brathwaite's adaptation places the focus entirely on the Antigone figure. Creon's actions do not matter, as the actions of oppressors do not matter as much as the resistance to their oppression. The title

of the play, the actions of the characters, and the alterations to the original which Brathwaite has made reflect his belief that one must choose to
resist tyranny and oppression, that of one's own free will one can and must
choose not to participate in a system which oppresses. *Odale's Choice*,
though not at all Brechtian in performance style, is a Greco-African
Lehrstück: an example of political theatre in which the audience is shown
a situation and then instructed in the correct choice of action.

The choice not to transculturate the play into a specific culture while
relying upon the performance codes of Anglophone Africa (i.e., using both
English and African performance techniques) creates a unique piece which
is equally reflective of both Brathwaite as a Caribbean playwright and
Ghana as a newly independent nation when the play was first performed.
Brathwaite is both outsider, having come to Ghana from the Caribbean,
and insider, serving as a teacher in the new nation that was attempting to
create its own new national identity. Brathwaite, likewise, was attempting
to connect to his African heritage, from which he, as someone born to the
African diaspora, was historically disconnected. As such, the European
influence is present and strong, both in his heritage, and in the memory
of a nation just recently a colonial state. Brathwaite's adaptation is a play
that both instructs its audience to make the choice to resist oppression,
and celebrates the choice to actively resist in a country newly independent
and free from colonial domination yet still not secure in its infancy as a
nation-state.

Antigone in Exile 2: Tegonni

Femi Osofisan is a very prolific playwright with a rather large output
whose plays are among the most frequently produced in his native Nigeria (Dunton, 67). He is "a poet, theatre director, university professor, literary theorist and newspaper columnist" (Richards, *Ancient*, xv). Born
Babafemi Adeyemi Osofisan in 1946 in Erunwon village in western Nigeria, he came of age in a very turbulent time in Africa. The year that the
Nigerian civil war began, Osofisan began studying at the University of
Dakar in Senegal and with the Daniel Sornno Theatre Company under the
direction of Maurice Senghor (Richards, *Ancient*, xix–xx). He went on to
study under Wole Soyinka at Ibadan and in France and England.

Chris Dunton cites two major features present in all of Osofisan's
work: first, framing devices, plays within plays, disjointed flow and other
Brechtian techniques used to generate a sense of metatheatricality, through
which Osofisan always reminds the audience of the presence and power
of theatre; second, the relentless probing of Nigerian society and culture

to find the causes and solutions of economic injustice (67). Osofisan, a committed Marxist, is concerned with corruption within the system, the exploitation of the workers, and the betrayal of the people by those who would rule over them. Richards also observes that Osofisan "manipulates his Yoruba and western heritages to speak directly of sociopolitical challenges facing his society and to scrutinize art as a (counter) hegemonic practice" (vii). Osofisan uses theatre to critique society, but he also uses theatre to critique theatre. Many of Osofisan's plays are responses to other playwrights, either in the form of rebuttals or in the form of adaptations. His play *No More the Wasted Breed* is a critique of Wole Soyinka's *The Strong Breed*, in which Osofisan not only "debunks the oppressive class in the person of the priests and acolytes" (Ibitokun, 161), but also criticizes the Yoruba pantheon (and ostensibly Soyinka for his acknowledgment of them) for "a historical failure on the part of the gods to intercede to prevent colonial domination" (Dunton, 87–88). Osofisan's play *Another Raft* is a critique of J.P. Clark's *The Raft. The Oriki of a Grasshopper* is Osofisan's variation on Beckett's *Waiting for Godot. Who's Afraid of Solarin?* is Gogol's *The Inspector General* reset in contemporary Nigeria. Osofisan uses both western and African plays as source material to construct his dramatic examinations of the values of the West and the sociopolitical realities of Nigeria.

Osofisan has no objection to the use of gods, spirits or other metaphysical beings in his plays. He is not rooted in social realism; rather, in engaging Nigerian society on its own terms and through familiar metaphors and materials he attempts to demonstrate the underlying power relationships in society. Richards argues, "The Yoruba pantheon, then, offers the artist a vast panoply of metaphorical constructs that are not only familiar to his audience but also may be reinterpreted to advance social progress" (119). In other words, Osofisan uses the gods of the Yoruba to stand for a wide variety of referents: the West, individuals and groups within Nigeria, the working class, historic forces, capitalism, the will of the people, so on. His plays then use Nigerian culture to offer a radical critique of both society and the socioeconomic and political realities of the current regime.

Due to the current climate in Nigeria, as of this writing, many of the most vocal critics of the government have been forced to live in exile or face arrest, imprisonment, and even execution. Osofisan has been living in exile from Nigeria, including a period of teaching at Emory University in the United States, where *Tegonni* "was inspired" (*Tegonni*, 1). In addition to the familiar Nigerian elements in the play, Osofisan turned once again to a preexisting drama in order to frame his play: *Antigone*, a play no doubt familiar to his American university audience. The play was work-shopped at Theater Emory in 1994 with a student cast and remains, as of this writing, unpublished. As Osofisan wrote to the author, "it is still very much a working script" (letter to the author, 15 November 1994). The final version of this play, if such a thing can ever be, may differ considerably from this early version.

The play is an adaptation of Sophocles's play, set in the town of Aiye-san, "an imaginary town in northern Yorubaland, in Nigeria," taking place "towards the end of the 19th century" (2). Osofisan adds, "The story may or may not have happened, none of us was there," both putting the play in the realm of "just-so" fables, a tale told for its moral truth rather than the historic truth of its narrative, and also rooting the play within a realm of revisionist history — a reevaluation of colonial Nigeria.

Osofisan's target is the colonial exploitation of Africa by Europe during this period, and he takes aim at such issues as Empire-building, racism, wealth transfer, and colonial interference in indigenous political and social struggle. These issues all develop the main dialectical battle between tyranny (in the form of colonial powers) and the oppressed individuals who choose to resist that tyranny. Osofisan also raises the specter of the role of slavery both in the New World and in Africa, which also might have been inspired by the locale of the production — in Atlanta, Georgia — in the heart of the former slave-owning South.

Before the main action of the play, a silent prologue is performed in which Yemoja (the Yoruba water goddess) is rowed in on a platform, attended by female servants who carry mirrors. Yemoja, also known as Yemaya, is the "Mother of the Sea ... the Womb of Creation. She is the Mother of Dreams, the Mother of Secrets ... intelligence beyond human comprehension" (Jones, *Development*, 282–3). The goddess is a metaphor for creation and intelligence. She is the embodiment of motherhood. Her entrance is silent, and it is like seeing it through a window of thick glass, writes Osofisan (3). We are able to see clearly, and yet are distanced from the action. Her presence is an invocation to creation, yet as water goddess, she is also responsible for sea journeys. Her being rowed silently across the stage connects the Old World and the New, the mythos of the Yoruba with the reality of the Middle Passage. She is a Yoruba goddess and a future slave.

The play begins in the public square of Aiyesan on the wedding day of Tegonni, daughter of the late local king, and Captain Herman Price, the British District Officer. Tegonni's father died in the period before the play begins and her brother, Oyekunle, was the appointed heir. Adeloro, Oyekunle and Tegonni's brother, wishing to usurp his older brother, went to the British and received their endorsement for the throne. The two brothers went to war.

In the opening scene, two drummers Oje and Kekere are talking about the return of the soldiers from war. As they drum for Tegonni's sisters and friends, a group of people enters. They are Greeks, led by Antigone, who tells Oje she has come for the play: "I heard you were acting my story, and I was so excited I decided to come and participate" (9). Osofisan thus engages his traditional metatheatrical presentation very early in the drama, calling attention to the fact that the audience is watching a play based upon another play. The unique effect in this play is that the original character has arrived to watch the adaptation, thus providing a visual metaphor for the comparison of adaptation with original. Antigone herself will judge how well the story is adapted. Osofisan even refers to the numerous other adaptations: when Tegonni's sister explains that the play is about Tegonni, not Antigone, Antigone insists that the story is the same, despite cosmetic differences: "I've traveled the same route before" (10). Osofisan presents us with the first self-aware personified archetype in Greco-African tragedy.

By adding the character of Antigone, Osofisan historicizes and trans-historicizes his adaptation, locating it in a specific time and place but allowing for comments by a character from an earlier era. Antigone tells the gathered guests to celebrate the wedding: "Sing! And dance! But that's the story of our lives, we Greeks! With it we built an empire, once. And lost it all again, dancing and singing!" (10). Osofisan engages in the reality of Athenian history and, by virtue of his locale, a British colony in Africa, draws a connection between singing and dancing (read: theatre) and empire-building. Even as those who build an empire celebrate it, the machinery of history will tear the empire apart again even as they celebrate.

Osofisan, student of Brecht that he is, has his characters reveal themselves as constructions. Antigone tells the gathering that she and her companions are metaphors, "capable of endless metamorphosis" (10). The actors are metaphors, representing something on stage that they are, in and of themselves, not, with the potential to play anything. But the characters are also metaphors, representing a variety of concepts and people, also with the potential to represent anything.

Morenike, Tegonni's friend, gives the men accompanying Antigone black masks and tells them they are now in the Hausa constabulary, in the service of Lt. General Carter-Ross. When they protest she tells them, "Theatrical illusion: Now you're no longer Greek, but African soldiers. Mercenaries in the pay of the British" (11). Simultaneously the audience is reminded of the theatrical illusion, that the people onstage are actors playing roles, and also of the historical reality, that the actors represent real people in real situations. In particular attention is called to the reality of life for the African under British domination: the colonizer assigned roles and instructed the indigenous to play them: worker, soldier, teacher, servant. Four Greeks become three African mercenaries and the corpse of Oyekunle, Tegonni's brother.

Governor Carter-Ross has ordered Oyekunle's body placed on display in the market square, and Tegonni's bridal party is told by the soldiers that they may not pass through the square on the way to the wedding as no one may approach the corpse. The soldiers explain that the display is a warning and a lesson to those who would revolt against the British. Upon learning the corpse is her brother, Tegonni returns to her home instead of going to the home of her husband-to-be.

Price waits for his new bride at his home with the Reverend Bayo Campbell, a minister in the Southern Baptist Church who escaped from slavery in the United States and returned to Nigeria. This revelation reminds the audience of the first major relationship between Africa and the New World: the slave trade. The Reverend Campbell's history serves to both bridge the gap between Georgia and Africa, as well as connect the colonial exploits of England in Africa with the buying and selling of Africans in the United States. Both practices are examples of the eco-

Tegonni; An African Antigone by Femi Osofisan, Theater Emory 1994. Communal tragedy: Tegonni surrounded by the chorus. Back row: Leah Burnette, Christina Robertson, Bimpe Oyelami, Maia Knispel. Front row: Leigh Davis, Kenya Scott (Tegonni), Gina Brady, Ifeoma Obianwu. *Photograph by Annemarie Poyo.* © *Emory University Photography.*

nomically dominant West exploiting Africa and Africans for personal and economic gain.

Price receives a telegram from the Governor General stating that both indigenous princes are dead. Adeloro is to be buried with honors; Oyekunle is to be "made an example" by displaying his body in the square (33). Anyone who attempts to bury Oyekunle is to be executed without trial. Price, as District Officer, is ordered to enforce the decree. In this scene Osofisan does two important things. The telegram demonstrates Fanon's contention that only violence can keep colonialism in power: the colonizer must make a public display of his violence to keep the colonized in place. Osofisan also presents a character from the colonizing culture who is faced with a choice. Price is one of the "good" British — he is marrying an African, his sympathies are clearly with the people he rules over — and yet he is still part of a system based on and built upon economic and colonial oppression. Osofisan does not reject the British; he rejects that one can be a part of the system and not perpetuate it. As Tegonni mourns her brother, she is also bitter that her husband-to-be will not do what is right.

Captain Price, who is the Haemon figure in this adaptation, is different from his Greek forebear. Haemon reject's Creon's sentence and kills himself. Price, a British officer, attempts to reason with his superior. Carter-Ross tells Price that many of the British believe that he is betraying England and the empire by marrying a "nigger," a term which would certainly carry emotional and political resonances in contemporary Georgia, where the play was first staged. The Governor General also states that he is opposed to the wedding as the Africans will think it places them on an equal footing to the British. His racism and commitment to the empire confirm the character as the embodiment of all that is wrong with the West in its relationship with Africa. Carter-Ross does not see Africa as a tabula rasa but as a thing to be conquered and exploited. He is imperialism and aggressive capitalism personified. When Price asks that Oyekunle be buried, the Governor not only refuses the request but announces that according to the Empire code no British officer may take a native to wife; thus Price is ordered to cancel the wedding. Not only does this scene echo the scene between Haemon and Creon in *Antigone* in which Haemon's betrothal to Antigone is canceled by Creon, but the lack of mention of the "Empire code" until Price's request for burial indicates that Carter-Ross changes or follows the rules when it benefits him to do so. He wields authority as a dictator, enforcing his beliefs in particular when they are challenged.

Tegonni is dragged into the office by the soldiers during this conference. They claim she covered her brother's body with a cloth, closed his eyes and threw dust on him, thus "burying" him. The first act closes as the Governor orders her imprisoned and preparations be made for her execution.

The second half of the play opens with the three soldiers building a stake for a firing squad. They are interrupted by a group of masked *Egungun* approaching. *Egungun* is a masked "ancestral masquerade" in which the participants are informed with the power and the presence of the ancestors (Banham, Hill, and Woodyard, 4). *Egungun* is a secret society, open to initiates only, and different groups of *Egungun* (the words refers to both the dancers and the performance) worship different ancestors and even compete in festival contests (see Ukpokodu, 252). The *Egungun* are very powerful, and their approach is not to be taken lightly. The soldiers flee and the *Egungun* smash the stake and burn it. Removing their masks, we learn the men are led by Oje the drummer, who announces his intention to free Tegonni.

Banham, Hill, and Woodyard observe that "*Egungun* is given a complex metaphysical significance by the playwright Wole Soyinka" in his plays (69). Osofisan, however, demonstrates the political and human reality behind the *Egungun*: Tegonni is freed because of their power, but not the metaphysical, transformative power ascribed to them by Soyinka, but rather the very real political and psychological power of a group of armed, masked men. When Oje removes his mask, he literally reveals the face of human political machinations behind the metaphysical mask. The power of *Egungun* is not only metaphysical, it is social and political and lies in the fear and respect accorded this secret society by those who are not members.

As David Kerr argues in *African Popular Theatre*, *Egungun* is a "lineage-based cult," and thus "the class origins of cults were preserved for centuries" (11). Different *Egungun* existed for the elite and for the workers, and secret societies based in the worship of common ancestors ensured that class boundaries would be strictly enforced by membership within *Egungun*. Interestingly, Osofisan does not show this political reality, that traditional society can be a double-edged sword. While the traditions of the Yoruba can be used to combat and resist colonialism, they also contain the seeds of class conflict and social hierarchy. Osofisan has often criticized traditional institutions that preserve an indigenous class system, yet in this play the need to combat imperialism from without is prioritized. First, the colonial yoke must be resisted and ultimately removed, after that traditional structures and hegemonies may be engaged and removed.

Price, who has been under house arrest, learns that Tegonni is to be executed. Carter-Ross explains that the wedding of Price to Tegonni would undo years of work that he, Carter-Ross, has done in "civilizing" the indigenous peoples of Nigeria and teaching them their place. Price realizes that Carter-Ross ordered the corpse displayed knowing it would be buried, and thus serve as a pretext to stop the wedding. Carter-Ross schemes to prevent Western and African from negotiating and engaging on a level playing field. Interestingly, Osofisan's is the only play in which this charge against the Creon figure is leveled, although it is possible in all versions. In other words, as Antigone and Ismene are the ones who by tradition would bury Polynices's body, Creon's declaration that he not be buried is therefore at least in part aimed directly at them.

Osofisan also again reveals the political machinations below the surface actions. Carter-Ross does not care very deeply about Oyekunle or Adeloro and whether or not they were buried. The only manner in which they matter is that Adeloro was the British choice for local ruler, and Britain's rule (in the person of Carter-Ross) must be respected and obeyed. But the two Africans as individuals did not matter. Carter-Ross used the corpse to stop the wedding in order to preserve British power and the image of the British both in their own eyes and the eyes of the indigenous. The Governor is a racist, ethnocentrist, classist aristocrat of the "white man's burden" school, who insists that nothing be allowed to occur which might encourage "the niggers" to believe themselves the equal of their British overlords (2:7). He argues that the white men are masters, needed in Africa to "build order from chaos" (2:7). The Governor firmly believes in the myth of black inferiority.

Bayo and a disguised Morenike meet, and Bayo informs her that the elders are pleading Tegonni's case to the Governor. The three soldiers then enter and tell Morenike they want new roles. They do not like being soldiers, carrying out unpleasant duties, guarding corpses, terrorizing people, preparing for executions, molesting women, and collecting bribes. Again, Osofisan invokes a metatheatrical discourse which both reminds the audience of the theatre which frames this experience and also depicts those who serve colonial masters as performers who are playing at something they are not. These men represent those who, but for the British, would not be part of the colonialist oppression of their own people. Morenike's initial response is to tell them, "our soldiers are trained to look upon their own people as enemies" (2:12). The British (like all imperialists) select a group of indigenous people and give them power over the others. They are, as Osofisan has constructed, instructed to maintain an adversarial relationship with their own people to the advantage of the British, which carries over into the postcolonial era.

The Nigerian military consists of approximately 160,000 soldiers

Tegonni; An African Antigone by Femi Osofisan, Theater Emory, 1994. Tegonni meets a colonialist Creon. (l. to r.): Adam Richman, Gina Brady, Rick Vigo, Leigh Davis, Kenya Scott (Tegonni), Eric Carston, Brian Kimmel. *Photograph by Annemarie Poyo.* © *Emory University Photography.*

(Haygood, 19). The military has controlled Nigeria for 28 of the first 38 years of its independence (Marriott, 47). General Ibrahim Babangida, having held power since 1985, held elections in 1993, which Moshood Abiola won. The military declared the election invalid and General Sani Abacha took power in 1993. Abiola was imprisoned and subsequently died while in captivity. For over the past decade, Nigeria has been run by what Wil Haygood calls "military gangsterism and killings" (18). Even after the colonial presence has left, the legacy of a military set against its own people continues into the present day.

The problems with military rule and the military's adversarial relationship with the civilian population begin at the top and go all the way down to the common soldier. The Provisional Ruling Council, a military junta which controls the nation, suppressed prodemocracy movements and political opponents, closed down independent newspapers, and declared martial law (White, "When," 39). On the local level, individual soldiers enjoy a reputation for being corrupt and violent. Innocent, unarmed civilians are killed on a regular basis by the police and the military, and corruption and demands for bribes are widespread (Abiola, 40; Haygood, 18; Soyinka, *Continent*, 5). Soyinka even reports that the armed mobile police force in urban Nigeria has acquired the sobriquet "Kill-and-Go" as a direct result of their public actions (*Continent*, 54). Osofisan's play questions the role of the military and the police collectively, but also, and perhaps more importantly, individually in the oppression of Nigeria's people.

When the men persist in changing roles, Morenike tells them to find Bayo who will let them play elders in the next scene. Such a response maintains the flux and flow of theatrical performance, in which the reality of performing a play becomes a metaphor for existence in a colonial state, which would seem to be confirmed by Fanon's writings. The fact that they will next play elders is not coincidence either. Osofisan seems to suggest that when given a choice, most would rather exchange the role of colonial policeman for wise, indigenous government. In another world those who supported the system might have been good leaders themselves. Similar to *Odale's Choice*, there is also an element of *Lehrstück* in Osofisan's metatheatrical demonstration: one can choose not to remain part of a corrupt system.

The next scene is set in the sacred forest, where Tegonni is in hiding with her friends. She wants to give herself up to Price, but Oje warns against the British: "The foreigner, in the end, thinks only of his own interest" (17). Not only does Oje set up a difference between the selfish individuals from Europe and the communal nature of the Africans, who work together as a group, but he also indicates that the problems of the community cannot be solved from without. Those who would help Nigeria from without ultimately have their own agenda, which they prioritize first. The community which does not help itself ultimately surrenders to rule from outside.

Bayo tells Tegonni that the Governor will pardon her if she renounces her actions and publicly apologizes. The Governor was deaf to pleas of clemency because of Tegonni's youth, Bayo explains, but Tegonni's death would mean martyrdom and resistance when an apology would restore British hegemony in the eyes of the people. The Governor is disgusted by the situation and yearns for a time when "you always knew you were right, because you were white" (2:29). The Governor agrees to grant clemency in exchange for an apology, but adds a stipulation: Price must also renounce Tegonni. If he does, she will be spared and he reinstated to his position. Because it will save her life, Price agrees.

In the next scene it is revealed than Morenike is the daughter of Orunmila and Tegonni is the daughter of Yemoja. As Shango and Ogun are the focus of Soyinka's cosmology, Orunmila and Eshu the trickster are Osofisan's patrons. Orunmila is the god of divination, who can see the future. Orunmila "assists Olodumare [God] with matters of insight and wisdom" (Jones, *Development*, 281). Orunmila is a metaphor for intelligent action in the name of human progress; Orunmila's children can see the future and use their wisdom to guide the community wisely. Morenike is therefore another metaphor, the hand of the playwright (she assigned characters to the Greeks, after all). She creates the drama, casts it, forces the issues and guides the characters (and audience) to a better future.

Tegonni, however, is also Antigone. As Antigone herself says, "Anywhere there is tyranny and oppression, there you will always find one Antigone rising up to challenge the tyrant and reduce his terrible power to dust" (34). Only by accepting the system can the system continue. Antigone provides a model for the resistance of tyranny, and there is always an Antigone figure where oppression exists. The opposite of Antigone lies not merely in accepting an oppressive system, but actively working in the system to help oppress one's own people. Just as the soldiers were required to carry out the orders of the Governor, just as the current military of Nigeria works to oppress its own people, so, too, there are always those who instead of resisting oppression support it for personal gain. Oje observes that the Europeans did not conquer Africa because of their weapons or numbers. The white man conquered because there were those in Africa willing to help the Europeans in exchange for a share of the profits and power. Blacks captured other blacks to sell into slavery in the New World. Oje asks, "Why did so many of our people team up with the invader when he came?" (37). The answer: economic and political gain.

Tegonni asks Antigone why she has not helped them. Antigone claims that she cannot interfere as she herself is white: "From Greece, from among the white races" (2:40). The trap which Antigone has just set for Tegonni encourages the Africans to reject Antigone and her help because she is white. As the previous debate shows, the whites have historically led Africans astray into betraying their own people. The argument which follows is Osofisan at his most dialectical: Antigone and her African alter ego, Tegonni, debate the best course of action in the face of tyranny, especially tyranny that is based in supposed racial superiority. Antigone argues, "Men throw off their yokes only for themselves to turn into oppressors. They struggle valiantly for freedom, and in the process acquire the terrible knowledge of how to deny it to others" (40). Antigone offers an explanation as to why cycles of oppression continue: once power is achieved, it is always abused and then the freedom fighters are more concerned about holding on to power than to achieving true freedom. Power corrupts. In Osofisan's view, this is a false argument, as the history of class struggle is not cyclical but linear. Struggle is a process rooted in the idea of progress. Once the bonds of oppression are truly broken for all, argues Marxism at its most basic, then they will not reform, they will dissolve forever.

Tegonni; An African Antigone by Femi Osofisan, Theater Emory, 1994. Foreground, (l. to r.): Antwan Mills, Kenya Scott (Tegonni), Leah Burnette, Chuma Hunter-Gault. Background, (l. to r.): Ifeoma Obianwu, Maia Knispel (Antigone). *Photograph by Annemarie Poyo. © Emory University Photography.*

Tegonni, realizing the trap in Antigone's argument, decides that she will not apologize but will die for freedom. Antigone embraces her, calling her "Sister" and proudly declaring, "Oppression can never last" (41). The two then recite Shelley's "Ozymandias," ironically using a British poem to point out the limits of power, empire, and tyranny: "Look upon my works ye mighty, and despair." The poem is a warning against hubris, but is also a tribute to the inevitable passage of time and the progress of history that symbolically and literally wears down oppression and tyranny. Osofisan has very consciously and deliberately inserted one canonical Western work inside another canonical Western work in order to prove that the colonial oppression of Africa by the West cannot last.

In the public square, Tegonni apologizes to the crowd for their oppression, but announces that she will not apologize for resisting the British. She further states that in her eyes she is married to Price. He agrees with her, which causes Carter-Ross to have a stroke. As he collapses, however, he orders Price court-martialed and Tegonni sold into slavery. The walling up of Antigone, isolating her from the community and sentencing her to a slow death in the Greek original is transculturated into an isolation from Africa and a slow death through slavery. The epilogue, however, reveals Antigone as Yemoja. Although Antigone accepts her fate onboard a slave ship, she is rewarded by dying and joining her mother. Price kills himself that he might join her. The play ends with their two intertwined corpses in the public square.

The play differs in numerous ways from the Greek original, but these differences are not mere transculturations or alterations, but conscious changes by Osofisan to reveal the political reality underlying the actions of the characters. Carter-Ross is not committed to the law as Creon is, but rather to the preservation of the Empire, the preservation of white economic and political hegemony, and to acquiring a knighthood for himself. He is a racist, remaining firm in his convictions even as he drops from a stroke and must be helped by those he despises. Osofisan demonstrates the failure in his way of thinking. If empires are destined to fall and class struggle to end, then to dedicate one's life to preserving empire and class will ultimately result in failure. One can only prolong the inevitable. The alternative action, to resist oppression and stand up against tyranny will result in eventual success, even if one should lose one's life in the struggle.

The play also considers the results of British imperialism and Western exploitation of Africa in terms of the consequences for the Africans brought to the United States. Osofisan's play demonstrates a sense of pan–Africanism: both Africans and African-Americans suffered because of the colonial system. Thus, both groups must not only work actively to oppose tyranny, but work together so that the West cannot exploit Africa and its people any further.

Aside from this historical reality, however, Osofisan encourages moving past race as the sole focus of conflict. Oje points out that both blacks and whites were involved in the slave trade. Antigone demonstrates that though she is white and European, she is involved in the struggle against imperialism. Even Price redeems himself at the end, joining Tegonni at the cost of his own life. The struggle is not white versus black but oppressors versus those who would overcome oppression.

The saying, "Love knows no color," has become a popular phrase at the beginning of the 21st century. Osofisan's play displays the idea that oppression and tyranny know no color as well. Osofisan uses a European play, *Antigone*, set in Africa to interrogate the behavior of people living in an oppressive system. The choices are resistance, submission, and participation, none of which are racially-based. Osofisan attempts to move beyond colonialism and slavery into the realm of social and economic justice for all in a system that is currently unjust. Individuals must work for communal freedom rather than individual profit. Oppression will eventually fail, so long as there are those who will publicly oppose it.

Antigone Under Apartheid: The Island

The Island by Athol Fugard, John Kani and Winston Ntshona may be the most written about play in this study. Much ink has been spilled about its meaning, its significance as a work of theatre, and the roles of its three authors in its creation. Steiner even writes of it: "Fugard's is the satyr play to all preceding *Antigone*s," implying that the play comments not only on the Greek original, but on all adaptations which came before it (144). For the purposes of this study what is unique about *The Island* is the interplay between its narrative and the original Greek text, as will be explored below, as well as the metatheatrical exploration of the power of the Greek myth, and its fulfilling of the dictates of African tragedy.

Fugard has come under criticism for his free use of Greek mythology. Stephen Gray calls him an "irresponsible scholar of the Greeks," using only the material he wants and changing it freely ("Chair," 23). Fugard has used Greek dramaturgy and structure in his early plays. Gray cites "Greek thinking" in *No-Good Friday* and *Nongogo*, two of Fugard's earliest works, specifically in the use of choral figures to both participate in and comment on the action (20). Gray also argues that Fugard returns to the theme of fate in plays such as *The Blood Knot, Hello and Goodbye, Boesman and Lena*, and *People Are Living There* (21). Fugard has certainly acknowledged his interest in things Greek. In fact, one of his first onstage roles was playing the herdsman in Andre Huguenet's *Oedipus Rex*, while his soon-to-be wife Sheila played one of Jocasta's handmaidens (Gray, "Chair," 20). Fugard was very familiar and even partial to Greek material when he began his collaboration with Kani and Ntshona.

Albert Wertheim, in his analysis of *The Island*, finds a much stronger Greek presence in the play than simply the story of *Antigone*. He argues that "The essence of *The Island* is contained between its Sisyphian beginning and its Sophoclean end; and it is concerned with the way in which the plight of Sisyphus can be connected with and transformed into the power of Antigone" (246). The play begins with Winston and John, two prisoners on Robben Island, miming the digging of holes in sand at the beach, and then using wheelbarrows to dump one's sand into the other's hole, thereby filling it back in. The play begins, therefore, with the two doomed to a meaningless, unfinishable task whereby each is the cause of the other's woe. The play ends with the two performing an adaptation of *Antigone* for the guards and other prisoners. Wertheim's argument is an interesting one, demonstrating the play's thematic links to Greek culture.

Deborah Foster, on the other hand, emphasizes the rhythm and structure of the play as owing something to Greek antecedents. She argues that the play follows an episode/stasimon structure from the opening scene through Winston's final words (9–10). It should be noted, however, that Foster views the play as an "anti-tragedy" which demonstrates not the falling of a great man due to *hamartia*, but rather that catastrophe is "the result of social phenomenon" (18). As argued in the second chapter of this survey, however, if Foster's theory is true, the play is not "anti-tragedy," but a form of African tragedy, as the community is at the root of the tragedy still.

The play has its origins in two productions of *Antigone*. In July 1965, the Serpent Players decided to present Sophocles's play as part of "a series of suitable adapted productions of 'classical' works" (Walder, 79). They rehearsed in a classroom at the Moslem Institute and were going to perform in St. Stephen's Church Hall in New Brighton, Port Elizabeth. Antigone was played by Nomhle Nkonyeni, Creon by Georges Mnci, and Haemon by John Kani, his first speaking role, which he was given because the original actor had been arrested. Norman Ntshinga, playing a supporting role, was also arrested before the show could be performed and was found guilty of "petty offenses" (Vandenbroucke, 100). He was sentenced to several years' imprisonment in Robben Island, the prison where most political prisoners of apartheid were kept.

Ntshinga "entertained his cellmates by acting out the production he had been rehearsing when arrested —*Antigone*," which made for the second production of the play from which *The Island* would be crafted (Vandenbroucke, 116). After his release, Ntshinga shared the story of the prison cell play with Fugard, Kani, and Ntshona. While his notebooks show that Fugard was already thinking about a project based on Robben Island, it was only when he began working with Kani and Ntshona that such a play began to take shape.

First performed at The Space on 2 July 1973, the play was originally called *Die Hodoshe Span*, after the never seen yet always present "Hodoshe," a Xhosa word meaning "carrion fly" that was the nickname of an infamous senior guard at Robben Island, well known for his cruelty (Gray, *File*, 49). Hodoshe remains ever the absent presence: though he never appears onstage, his oppressive and threatening presence is always felt. John and Winston threaten each other with calling Hodoshe when they argue. They are beaten by him, respectfully respond to him when spoken to, and curse him when left alone in their cell. Hodoshe is the third character in the play, and a real presence. The name of the play, however, was changed to reflect the reality of Robben island, a place which Fugard observes is a present absence in all South African lives, in as much as it is real, it is visibly present in the ocean just off Capetown, and yet they may never speak openly of it (Vandenbroucke, 126).

The plot is remarkably simple, as Michael Etherton notes, consisting of only two events: John is told of the reduction of his sentence, and the two men rehearse and perform the trial scene from *Antigone* (128). What is so powerful in the play is not the events themselves, but the way in which the events resonate deeper meanings about life under and the struggle against apartheid.

John and Winston collapse in their cell at the beginning of the play, after a long day of digging in the sand and filling in each other's holes. In six days the prison is having a variety show of sorts. Other cell blocks are singing or dancing, but John wants to perform an adaptation of *Antigone*. Winston does not. He does not even remember the plot or the characters' relationships. John reviews the plot for Winston, and his plot summary and character descriptions reveal as much about their own experiences under apartheid as they do about *Antigone*.

John does not have the text. He remembers the New Brighton production which the Serpent Players had performed years before and recreates the play from that memory. John reviews the steps of Antigone's trial for Winston, which they have based on the South African legal system: Antigone is the Accused, King Creon is the State. Winston confuses the brothers and John erupts, crying out, "I told you, man, Antigone buried Polynices. The traitor! The one who I said was on our side. Right?" (52). John's outburst reveals much about the understanding of the myth of Antigone that he has. Polynices, a traitor, is on the side of the men on the island, who are themselves in prison for traitorous crimes under apartheid: burning their pass books, demonstrating against apartheid, belonging to seditious organizations, so on. Polynices is identified with the struggle against apartheid. As the sister who tried to bury him, Antigone is also therefore identified with the struggle.

The two men list the stages of the trial. After the state lays its charges against the accused, Antigone is to plead. Winston thinks Antigone should plead "Not Guilty"; then John explains that Antigone pleads guilty because she did, in fact, do what she is accused of: she did bury her brother. Winston responds, "To hell with the play! Antigone had every right to bury her brother" (52). The play is important to John, who grows angry at Winston's frustration, but Winston is frustrated by a legal system that does not make sense. Winston distinguishes between right and wrong, not between legal and illegal, which can often be two very different things. The comments Winston makes about *Antigone* tell us just as much about Winston and his attitude towards his situation as they do about the play. *The Island* also posits the very postmodern idea that all texts are interpreted through the life experiences of the reader or viewer. Winston's *Antigone* is not the *Antigone* of a British classroom or of Femi Osofisan. Winston's *Antigone* is the product of living under the apartheid system.

As Winston studies the outline of the trial, John reminisces about the New Brighton production, mentioning the actors by name: "Georgie was Creon," and "Nomhle played Antigone" (53; 54). While the actors drew on the real life experience of Norman Ntshinga (who is also present in the play as the man in the next cell, just offstage — "Norman" is frequently spoken to during the course of the play), and remember an actual performance, the use of these events and their real names turn the entire play into a metaphor for South Africa (Wertheim, "Political," 251).

"John" and "Winston," political prisoners, are really John and Winston, South African citizens imprisoned in the reality of apartheid and in danger of actually being sent to Robben Island should they violate any of the many laws regarding theatre, performance, and race in South Africa. Theatre becomes a form of resistance, not just by the playing out of *Antigone*, but by "performing" in their everyday life. Joanne Tompkins writes of the irony of their situation in the play: "The best the two prisoners can hope for is to be released from a maximum security prison into apartheid South Africa" (43). The island is a prison. The nation is a larger prison. The actors are playing themselves, both in a cell on the island, but also in the larger prison of the nation in which their identities are just as constructed as those of the characters they are playing. Martin Orkin argues that *The Island* is "powerfully constructed to show in what ways the oppressed subject is structured and constructed by the apartheid state" (*Drama*, 159). If one's identity is fluid and unstable because of the political reality under which one lives, then identity is performed every day, and performance becomes identity.

As the two prisoners prepare to sleep they perform a telephone conversation to their friends in New Brighton. The scene is justifiably famous for its imaginative power. Benedict M. Ibitokun calls the telephone conversation "wholesome othering for self catharsis." In it, John splits himself into self and the voice on the other end to which he responds. Later on in the play, when Winston objects to playing a woman in *Antigone*,

John points out this "othering," in which one is recognized as both the thing one is playing and one's self: "They will know it's really you" (62). Winston is afraid the others will laugh at him cross-dressed as Antigone. John tells him they will laugh when they see him, but when they hear him they will stop laughing, and "that is the time when our Antigone hits them with her words" (61). By making believe, we can achieve a release from our suffering, as in the telephone conversation. But also by making believe, we can convince those who oppress us that we have given in to them when we are actually resisting them and their attempts to destroy our identities, as when John and Winston perform *Antigone*.

Winston also objects to the play on the grounds that it is not real as he understands reality:

> Only last night you tell me that this Antigone is a bloody…what you call it…legend! A Greek one at that. Bloody thing never even happened. Not even history! Look, brother, I got no time for bullshit. Fuck legends. Me? I live my life here! I know why I'm here and it's history, not legends [62].

The Island by Athol Fugard, John Kani, and Winston Ntshona. Market Theatre Production Publicity Photograph, South Africa, 1977. Winston and John on the phone to New Brighton. © *Market Theatre, used with permission.*

Winston does not want to do the show because he feels it's not real and therefore has nothing to do with him and the struggle against apartheid. John must convince him that *Antigone*, while a legend, actually demonstrates a greater truth about their reality. Also, by presenting history in the guise of legend, they may continue to resist without seeming to.

While they argue, the guards come for John. After a meeting with the warden, John returns to tell Winston that his sentence has been reduced and that he will be released in three months. They react to this news and reminisce about their arrival on the island. Winston, realizing John is to be released while he will be there for life, grows depressed and resentful. Winston asks John, "Why am I here?" (72). John explains that they were fighting for freedom and their children's future. Winston

The Island by Athol Fugard, John Kani, and Winston Ntshona. University of Pittsburgh Production, 1997, directed by the author. Same scene as the previous photograph, Derrick L. Sanders as John and Javon Johnson as Winston. *Photograph by Ashley Wells.*

responds that none of that matters to him anymore. John again relies upon Antigone as an example: like her, Winston is imprisoned until he dies for doing the right thing in the face of oppression. As Osofisan indicates, Creon's law is aimed directly at Antigone, for she is the one who would bury Polynices. Likewise, the laws that have imprisoned Winston are aimed specifically at blacks. Whites were not imprisoned for burning passbooks, violating the Group Areas Act, or moving their residence to a new area without permission. The pass laws resulted in huge numbers of arrests and imprisonment, all in the name of the law and the state, all in the name of keeping order. For example, for a 12-month period from 1972 to 1973, an average of 1,413 trials for pass law violations were held every day, including Sunday, and yet this still marked a "significant decrease" from the previous year (Orkin, *Drama*, 165). Just as Antigone was trapped by a decree aimed at her, so, too, were black South Africans trapped by pass laws.

In the final scene of the play within the play (which also is the final scene of

The Island by Athol Fugard, John Kani, and Winston Ntshona. University of Pittsburgh Production, 1997, directed by the author. Javon Johnson as Winston playing Antigone. *Photograph by Ashley Wells.*

the play), John, as Creon, tells the audience, "There was a law. The law was broken. The law stipulated its penalty. My hands are tied" (77). One can hear the echo of the magistrates at the 1,413 daily pass law trials in these lines. Fugard even reports in his notebooks that the prosecutor who tried Norman Ntshinga and saw him sentenced to five years at Robben Island for pass law violations visited Norman in his cell after sentencing. Fugard reports that the prosecutor said, "Norman must not think he [the prosecutor] wanted it that way [five years]. He was only doing his duty. He *had* to" (126). The irony, of course, is that those responsible for the system and who benefit most from the system blame the system when it punishes individuals. Those who control the system argue that the system is beyond their control; they must obey its dictates. The white participants in the South African judicial system are all Creons, claiming the force of law dictates their action when they themselves made the law.

This irony is the lesson of the performance of *Antigone* given in the prison. The actual audience for *The Island* becomes the audience of prisoners and guards for *Antigone*. This convention continues the metaphor of South Africa as prison (the play was, after all, devised to be performed in South Africa), and reminds us that the prison is also a prison for the guards as well. So long as one group is oppressed, the other group must remain constantly vigilant and active in quashing any signs of resistance. South Africa traps all: whites, blacks, everyone. Lastly, the use of the real audience for the stage audience is a magnificent metatheatrical convention that serves to remind the audience of the power of theatre.

John, after giving a brief introduction and plot summary, then reenters as Creon. He speaks of the prosperity of the citizens and calls himself the servant of the people. He notes, however, that the king is also a servant of the law. The law is a shield "to defend" and a sword "to strike" (74). As Antigone has broken the law, she must be tried and the sword of the law must come into play. Just as in *The Song of Jacob Zulu*, by staging a trial, John and Winston have put the law on trial.

Fugard writes in his notebook of Norman Ntshinga's trial and the role of law in his imprisonment:

> If there was evil and wrong in that courtroom, where was it? The hearts of a few men — Magistrate, Prosecutor, Special Branch? Or in the Law? If it was the latter, what morality, what moral dimension was there to those who execute it? The real stink of that courtroom — the surrender of conscience? [126–7].

It is in these lines that we find the heart of *The Island*, which also reflects, in part, Osofisan's contention: one must resist a corrupt system of oppression, as too many others will simply become a part of the system and thereby surrender and perpetuate the system. These individuals will argue, as did Ntshinga's prosecutor, as does Creon, that the system is to blame, and yet none will resist the system. If the law is unjust, then resisting the law, opposing the law, is a just and good act. But by doing so, one is punished under the law and imprisoned. In the face of this cycle, how could and why should one resist? How does one resist the reality of the injustice of apartheid? How does one resist the Island?

The play's answer to this problem lies in Winston's response as Antigone to his/her sentence. Creon decrees, "Take her from where she stands, straight to the Island. There wall her up in a cell for life with enough food to acquit ourselves with the taint of her blood" (77). Not only does this sentence echo the original Creon's, the mention of the Island reminds the prisoners (and the audience) of their own fate, remarkably similar to Antigone's. Society believes itself free of "the taint of [their] blood" because they are fed and sheltered in prison. Yet to be on the Island is to be sentenced to living death. Winston responds to this sentence by crying out: "Brothers and sisters of the land! I go now on my last journey. I must leave the light of day forever for the Island, strange and cold, to be lost between life and death. So, to my grave, my everlasting prison, condemned alive

The Island by Athol Fugard, John Kani, and Winston Ntshona. University of Pittsburgh Production, 1997, directed by the author. Accusation and defiance through metatheatre: Derrick L. Sanders as John playing Creon in the play within the play; Javon Johnson as Winston playing Antigone. *Photograph by Ashley Wells.*

to solitary death" (77). Winston, although performing *Antigone*, is speaking no longer as Antigone but as himself. He is describing his own reality. For the last lines of his speech (and of the play), he removes his wig and directly addresses the audience as himself: "Gods of our Fathers! My Land! My Home! Time waits no longer. I go now to my living death because I honored those things to which honor belongs" (77). These lines are almost a direct quotation of the Sophoclean original's last words of Antigone, yet they reflect Winston's position in a much more real way. Like Antigone, his choice of action, honoring that to which honor belongs, will result in his imprisonment and death. Yet, as in Osofisan, to resist oppression, and even die while doing so, is its own reward. One dies knowing one did the right thing. At the end of the play, John and Winston begin running again, as they did at the beginning of the play. Even John, due to be released in three months, will never really be released from oppression so long as he lives under apartheid.

This ending is different from Sophocles's, and Deborah D. Foster argues that unlike the original, "the opposition between the State and the accused is never resolved, nor is it dissolved" (16). Creon never achieves recognition and reversal as he does in the original. But the original, as Winston would point out, is a legend. The unresolved tensions of *The Island* are reflective of the historical reality of South Africa in 1973, in which the tension between the apartheid system and those oppressed under it were not and could not be resolved.

The ending also demonstrates the difference between *The Island* and other adaptations of *Antigone*. Actor Danny K. Moleko, who played John in the 1998 Northwest Arts Drama Company production of *The Island*, observed that performing *Antigone* in prison was a way to remind the inmates that "They are inside here and that the struggle hasn't stopped just because you are inside" (interview). Everyday the political prisoners must continue to resist and struggle against apartheid. Each day they must again be Antigone, must again continue to resist a system bent on erasing their identities, oppressing them, and removing their humanity. Whereas Odale and Tegonni go to their deaths victorious, having won their struggles, Winston must continue to be Antigone every day of his living death. His Antigone's "death" does not end the struggle — every day one must resist anew.

At the 1995 National Festival of the Arts in Grahamstown, Fugard, Kani and Ntshona reunited for a 20th anniversary revival of *The Island*, and then toured the production throughout South Africa. Albert Wertheim, in his review of the festival, notes three ways in which the play continues to generate meaning after the fall of apartheid. First, the production serves as a reminder of a not too distant past, still in the living memory of most audience members. Second, the audience "recognize the power of theatre and what plays and players like these had done during the struggle" (75). Third, the show allows for comparison between 1975 South Africa and 1995 South Africa, demonstrating, as did *Orestes*, a better society now than the one which created this play. *The Island* has moved from a play protesting present tyranny to a play celebrating the overcoming of that tyranny, much as *Demea* did. The theatre is recognized as being a valuable part of the struggle; the playing of *Antigone* is an acting out of the message of *Antigone*: do what is right and resist injustice and oppression.

As if to prove these celebratory points, *The Island* is still frequently mounted in South Africa. At the 1998 National Arts Festival in Grahamstown, just three years after the anniversary production, the Northwest Arts Drama Company presented a production of the play that was a critical and popular success. *Cue*, the festival newspaper, gave the production a strong review, stating, "All South Africans should take time to experience this piece" (Breytenbach, 9). South Africa is not alone in its admiration of the play. There have been German, French, Turkish, American, British, and Eastern European productions. The play, despite being located in apartheid South Africa, is universal enough to be transplanted to any place in which the oppressed do what is right and pay the price for it. Just as *The Island* follows from *Antigone*, non–South African adaptations of *The Island* demonstrate the continued power of Fugard, Kani, and Ntshona's vision.

Life Mirrors Art: Black Wedding Candles for Blessed Antigone

In 1910, the area now known as the Republic of the Congo was officially made part of French Equatorial Africa; it later achieved independence from France in 1960. In 1963 the National Revolutionary Movement took over the government, which moved to the left. In 1968 the military under the leadership of Marien Ngouabi seized control, and the nation became a one-party socialist state run by the Congolese Workers' Party. In 1969, the name of the country was changed to the People's Republic of the Congo and ties to the Soviet Union and communist China were strengthened, although, interestingly, the primary trading partner of the PRC, both economically and culturally, remained France (Ramsay, 82). In fact, until 1994 France retained an "economic hegemony" in its former colony, especially in the oil industry and the production and gathering of natural resources (Masland, 39). The French did not actively bring drama to the Congo as the English did in West Africa, and the introduction of Western drama and theatre occurred relatively late in the Congo, thus making for a more recent start to indigenous contemporary drama. By the end of the 1960s three theatre companies were active in the Congo, and writers in other mediums began to try their hands at playwriting.

Sylvain Bemba, "usually considered the Congo's most important dramatist," according to Oscar Brockett, was born in 1934 in the Congolese city of Sibiti (657). In 1953 he became a sportswriter, quickly becoming an editor and professional writer by 1955. He then worked for the government after independence, holding an administrative position in the Ministry of Information (Bemba, iv). He began writing sketches for radio, a script for a short film, and "a pageant" on the Congo's colonial experience (Banham, Hill, and Woodyard, 25). Bemba also wrote novels and remained an active journalist, even while serving in other positions.

In 1968, eight years after the Congo's independence, at the height of the conflict which led to the military takeover of the government, Bemba wrote *L'Enfer C'Est Orfeo* (*Hell Is Orfeo*), his first theatrical play, which was published a few years later and became what Banham, Hill, and Woodyard call an instant "political classic," known for its "preoccupation with social and economic injustices" (25–6). Over the next decade, several more plays followed: *The Man Who Killed the Crocodile* (1972), *Black Tarantula and White Devil* (1976), *A Rotten World for an Over-Honest Laundryman* (1979), and a few others. During this period Bemba also served in the government in various capacities as director of the Congo's radio and television industries, as Director of Information Services, as head of the Brazzaville University Library, and in various roles in the Ministry of Culture. In 1988 he wrote *Noces Posthumes de Santigone*, which roughly translates as "The Posthumous Marriage of Santigone," but which was published in English in Townsend Brewster's translation as *Black Wedding Candles for Blessed Antigone*, subtitled "A Drama in Three Acts and Fourteen Tableaux Inspired by Sophocles' *Antigone*." In 1990 he again began working for the government, running the cultural division of the Department of Education. Bemba died 8 July 1995 in Paris, leaving a long legacy of service to the people and culture of the Congo.

The action of *Black Wedding Candles for Blessed Antigone* takes place in England and in the city of Vangu, fictitious capital of the fictitious country of Amandla, a word which means "Power is ours" or "Power to the people," used often as a freedom cry during the apartheid years in South Africa. The name is ironic as the regime is corrupt, and freedom and justice, while given lip service, are nonexistent. Bemba describes the country as "a former British colony, which is one of the poorest nations on Earth," thus firmly setting the play in the postcolonial, postindependence troubled political and economic situation in which many African nations have found themselves (44). The prologue is spoken by a griot who "may wear a mask to help differentiate him" from the other actors, and speaks of "a memory of forgotten pain" (1). Bemba's use of a griot not only frames the story with the device of a traditional African storyteller, with all the cultural resonances which that implies, but also offers a counterpoint to the ostensibly more Western-style, realistic characters. The griot gives the audience a familiar figure to narrate the story, yet also provides commentary and serves to anchor the play very firmly in indigenous culture, despite being an adaptation of a Western classic.

The first act introduces Dorothy and Margaret, two university students in their dormitory room in Birmingham, England, which is decorated with a British flag, a poster of Michael Jackson, batik artwork, and an African doll collection. The images of the room provide a counterpoint to the traditional Africa of the griot; the two women come from modern Africa: a mixture of world culture in which traditional African arts are blended with American popular culture and British national culture. Margaret, having played numerous other roles, including Saint Joan, Juliet, and Mother Courage, feels that she should play Antigone in the university's production, a role that has gone to rival Melissa. Immediately one notices that all the African women have European names, and that the roles which Margaret has played are all European classics. In the conversation which ensues between the two and John Abiola, a fellow Amandlan, the audience learns that their country is experiencing unrest, and the present regime is threatened.

Melissa's triumph as Antigone is spoken of in the next scene, and the audience further learns that Amandla is a new name — until two years ago the country was called "Gold Nugget," on account of the gold which the European colonizers found there. It is also revealed that Melissa is the fiancée of President Titus Saint Just Bund, the newly elected leader of Amandla, whose personal motto is "Strive for justice through just means" (12). His name suggests Roman glory, the French revolutionary, and the German word for nation or federation. He is a mixture of classical glory, revolution and nationalism, as well as European influences.

The second act begins backstage at "The Pure Speech Society's production of the *Antigone* of Sophocles, tragedy in five acts. Directed by Sir Richard Cooper, First Citizen of Birmingham" (20). The name of the producing organization suggests the linguistic debate outlined in the second chapter of this study, in which language can be a tool through which colonial domination is achieved. A stagehand preparing for the show refers to Melissa as "a black ball of fire endowed with a diamond tongue" (21). As in the first act, Melissa's praises are sung, but those who compliment her all focus on her race: "young black actress," "black ball of fire," so on. Her nationality and ethnicity distinguish her in the United Kingdom. As Erika Munk notes in the preface to *Black Wedding Candles*, the play begins with the Greek tragedy and is "narrating it through the silenced voices of women or black people, viewing the dominant culture through the eyes of those it has dominated" (viii). Melissa is a black African woman living in Europe, learning to act through European classics. In many ways, as demonstrated by the setting of the first scene, the Amandlans have assimilated into the multicultural cosmopolitan world of European university, despite the fact that they are recognized as different, as the compliments Melissa received demonstrate. The experience of playing Antigone, however, transforms Melissa into a voice for justice and peace. The mask and voice she has been given to play the role become her real voice and face.

John Abiola visits Melissa backstage, impressed by her performance. He tells her, "You're Antigone." She responds, "Not quite. There are centuries between the two of us. In the past few months, I've embarked upon a long journey in search of her. Moving towards her isn't enough. We must intermesh. The audience must feel what's taking place on stage is a current event" (23). Like Osofisan and Fugard, Kani and Ntshona, Bemba uses metatheatricality to express to the audience the power of theatre. Melissa wants to "intermesh" with Antigone. Present in these lines is a desire to supersede mere acting and to embody the character in a real and efficacious manner. Furthermore, in the desire to cause the audience to encounter the Greek tragedy as a current event, Melissa foreshadows her own involvement in the performance of politics. Ancient theatre as current event is perhaps another name for transculturation: the playwright adapts an ancient play to a modern context in order to explore a current event or political situation.

The action switches to Vangu in the next scene, where a besieged President Bund and his few remaining supporters are seen fighting for their lives against a military coup. Titus admits to his cohorts that he made mistakes during his reign. A malaria epidemic decimated the population and "another unidentified plague is doubling the infant mortality" of the country (29). The situation in Amandla is representative of the real health care problem in many of Africa's poorer nations, some of which have a population almost 50 percent HIV positive. By 1983 the Centers for Disease Control "established that HIV was widely spread throughout central Africa" (McCormick and Fisher-Hoch, 187). By 1988, when Bemba wrote the play, both Western officials and African leaders were concerned about the economic and social impact of AIDS on Africa's development (Garrett, 477). More recent studies have borne those fears out, with over ten million orphans from AIDS alone by 1999, 45,000 of them in the Congo (Bartholet, 37). Even more frightening was evidence of "other disease emergence" which would "synergize" with AIDS and become even more threatening than they had been in the past due to poor health conditions (Garrett, 497). Instances of dengue fever, hepatitis, tuberculosis, and drug-resistant forms of both malaria and cholera were on the increase in the 1970s and 1980s (Garrett, 497). More exotic and even more deadly diseases such as ebola and lassa are beginning to become more common, the latter being particularly active in West Africa while the worst outbreak of the former took place just across the border from the Congo in then–Zaïre (McCormick and Fisher-Hoch, 55). A current high infant mortality rate combined with AIDS and the associate lowering of life expectancy has resulted in negative population growth despite a very high birth rate in some nations (Garrett, 485). Thus the "unidentified plague" which troubled Bund's presidency was a current event in much of Africa in 1988. An unidentified plague is also a plot device from Greek tragedy, perhaps the best-known instance being the plague ravaging Thebes at the beginning of *Oedipus Rex*. The play connects the current events that Melissa desires the audience to perceive with the dramatic events onstage and with the elements of Greek tragedy. Life mirrors art, but the horrors which serve as entertainment in Europe are the reality in poor African nations.

Bemba stages the battle through the use of music and sound until the climax of the scene in which the palace is destroyed and Titus is killed. As the bombs fall, he tells the audience, "I don't give a damn for what they'll do with my body because they'll never be able to shit on my spirit" (31). Bemba draws a parallel between the Greek tragedy of *Antigone*, in which a body is ordered to be defiled and left unburied, and events in recent African history, in which the body of an overthrown ruler or rebel leader is defiled and mutilated by those who defeated him, such as was seen recently in the civil wars in Rwanda, Burundi, and Zaïre. Greek tragedy and African reality parallel each other.

The play's coup is not unfamiliar to those aware of African history. In the Congo Marien Ngouabi was assassinated in 1977 and replaced by Colonel Yhombi-Opango. For two decades the Congo was ruled as "a self-proclaimed Marxist-Leninist one-party state," which did not assure stability, political or otherwise, but conversely promoted instability within the nation (Ramsay, 81–2). Bemba focuses on the social and political realities of central Africa and how *Antigone* both reflects the horror of living in such a world and provides an example of how to respond.

When Melissa sees Titus in her dressing room, she cries out, "The President is dead!" (33). She begins to speak to herself, saying, "Polynices will die twice today. Once in Vangu this afternoon and once again this evening before the play begins" (33). She draws the parallel between her husband-to-be and Polynices (although her betrothed would have been the Haemon character, Bemba combines brother and future spouse into a single character), as both were killed in battle attempting to hold onto power, and both lie in the battlefield, unmourned. As the make-up woman prepares Melissa for her performance as Antigone, Melissa tells her:

> I must go on to join forces with the men and women who for more than twenty-three hundred years have pointed the road to high standards by way of dignity and honor in the face of direct adversity [33].

Like Tegonni, Melissa views herself as part of a larger group who follow the ideal of Antigone. Melissa is now "intermeshed" with the Antigone spirit. As the Amandlan situation finds its reflection in the Greek play, so, too, does Melissa become a living Antigone. Like Antigone, she will defy those who now rule her country and bury the body of the man she loved.

The next scene is taken directly from *Antigone*, as Bemba shows the audience Melissa playing the role onstage. Melissa and the two actors playing Creon and the sentry perform the scene in which Antigone admits to burying the body. Antigone claims the moral high ground, believing her actions to be right and just, but the last line is Creon's: "But while I live, no woman shall prevail" (34). We are reminded of Antigone's strength and courage, of the original Greek narrative, and of Melissa's situation as a woman and an expatriate, returning to an African country in the throes of revolution in order to bury the body of her betrothed, the president who was killed in the coup. During the curtain call for *Antigone*, she appears onstage wearing a black veil, thus casting herself in the role of widow, though she was not Titus's wife. Though not wedded to him in this world, she will wed herself to his ideals: "Strive for justice through just means."

Melissa returns to Africa a celebrity, landing at an airport outside her own country. The griot tells the audience, "This African woman of Amandla burns with the flame of all our unsatisfied demands and embodies the brutalized conscience of her country" (38). In a war-torn land, Melissa will speak for justice. Amandla has been in a state of constant turmoil. The name change two years ago did not bring about an end to the problems which colonialism and its abrupt end created. Amandla, a poor, strife-ridden nation is unstable, and the recent coup has left the country in the hands of various military factions. The people want freedom, health care, opportunity, development, but these are denied them because of political, economic, and social instability. Melissa returns to her country in order to change it, by acting as Antigone did. She has received special permission to marry Titus posthumously, so that she will legally become his widow.

When she arrives she is introduced as "Mrs. Melissa Antigone Bund," her identity now firmly intermeshed with both the character she plays and the former president. She is called "the female Billy Graham," which she denies on the ground that he fights for souls in the name of Jesus, whereas she "[is] fighting in the name of a mere man who loved Africa, who loved his country, who loved freedom" (39). The current regime has called out for her to stop speaking publicly against the government, but she announces that she will never renounce her citizenship or cease her fight. Instead, she wants a passport, "in order to return to Vangu to insure my husband's decent burial. I know that you love freedom. Help me; help your Antigone to attain hers in her native land" (39). Melissa has adopted the persona of Antigone entirely. Not simply Antigone, but *your* Antigone. Melissa has recognized the power of symbols and the greater reality that she has come to embody. Like Tegonni, she is now a metaphor. Like Antigone, she presents herself as the model of responsible citizenship.

When Melissa and the other Amandlans arrive in Vangu they are informed of a new law which prohibits even saying the name of Titus Bund aloud. A number of books are also forbidden, including the works of Sophocles and any book which analyzes Greek tragedy, as "Antigone" has become a symbol of antigovernment sentiment because of Melissa. At the end of the list of forbidden things, the griot remarks ironically, "Wisdom, when it's African, is prodigious" (45).

The four returnees are detained and questioned by the Amandlan police. Melissa then meets with the "New Leader," as he is termed. The audience is never told his name or how he became the ruler of Amandla. She is informed that when she began speaking out against the new regime he ordered her family imprisoned, resulting in the death of her younger brother. Her family has been tortured, though she herself has not been harmed for fear of international repercussions. He orders her imprisoned and she, in response, demands the burial of her husband's body. The New Leader says, "Let the dead bury the dead" (53). He then reveals that a group of former Bund supporters have seized the army's main ammunition dump in Vangu and he asks her as the respected and beloved widow of their former commander to ask them to surrender. He asks her to help create peace rather than continue civil war. He appeals to her desire to stabilize the nation. His request has similar overtones to the offer Carter-Ross makes Tegonni—her willingness to cooperate with the regime will lend it legitimacy and restore a social hierarchy. Melissa reproaches him: "Your words are of our country, but my loyalty is to our native soil. I am, I remain, I shall die an Amandlan" (56).

Melissa believes that a citizen demonstrates loyalty to the nation by showing respect to the dead, by showing honor to those who deserve it, by genuinely committing to real peace in the land, rather than accepting peace on the terms of those who acquired and hold on to power through violence and force. The New Leader holds no such ideals: might makes right and he is leader because his faction defeated the elected president and took hold of the capital city. Force is his mandate; his authority lacks legitimacy, but as power is his goal, he is not concerned.

Melissa announces her intention to see the Archbishop to arrange for a funeral for her husband. Her Antigone does not steal down at night to throw dust on a corpse. She publicly announces her plan to bury her husband and will carry it out as a state funeral in public as well. She has found Titus's copy of Thomas More's *Utopia*, stained in his blood. The offstage crowd chants, "The Blood of Titus Saint Just Bund," and the New Leader collapses physically. Soldiers enter and threaten Melissa who has by now completely abandoned her old identity. She cries out, "Hands off! No one lays a hand on Antigone!" (58). She instructs the soldiers to tell the New Leader when he recovers, "from Antigone that these words completely comprise my strength: 'My ways are those of love and not of hate'" (58). She is quoting from Sophocles, when Creon tells Antigone that an enemy is an enemy, even in death, and that she should hate one brother and love the other. Antigone responds, "My nature is to join in love, not hate" (576). The audience has heard the line before, when Bemba presented a scene from *Antigone*. Thus, life has fully imitated art. As the soldiers lead her off, she claims that she has responded to the selfishness of the new regime with love: love of country, love of her husband, love of justice, and love of Africa. She is escorted out to her imprisonment. The final moment of the play shows the mask-wearing griot playing a tape of Melissa reciting a speech from Antigone. He continues the monologue as the tape ends and then claims, "the memory of the people will one day rise again" (59).

Bemba's play demonstrates the dangers of instability and the selfishness of those who would rule for personal gain. Melissa/Antigone serves as a model for good citizenship. She loves her country and she loves justice. She returns to a hostile environment in order to improve the lot of her countrymen. Melissa's "intermeshing" with Antigone is characteristic of Bemba's work.

Hal Wylie, whose "The Dancing Masks of Sylvain Bemba," argues that the predilection for masks in Bemba's work demonstrates that masks "are less a disguise or protection than a symbol, a projection of the self, a label, an 'identity'..." (20). The role of Antigone is a mask for Melissa, at first worn in the world of Europe where it is a theatrical mask, one that does not yet reflect her inner truth. As she is subjected to the tragedy of Amandla and President Bund, she is transformed into Antigone: the wearer becomes the mask.

Wylie observes, "the mask game is a game of identities and identification in which the wearer of the mask chooses to imitate another person, or an already standardized role" (21–2). Melissa chooses to imitate Antigone, slowly becomes identified with her, and then finally is identified as her. She becomes "the conscience of the people of the nation," and the "hope of unsatisfied demands." Even with the main characters all imprisoned or killed in battle, the tape-recording reminds us that the Antigone identity lives on. The voice of the people, the conscience of the nation, will rise again and again.

Titus and the New Leader are also stock characters, identities who have standardized roles. Democratically elected leaders who fail to provide overnight miracles in the face of overwhelming difficulties become the victims of coups with alarming frequency. Likewise, the New Leader does not even need a name — he is a type more than a real identity. He is a military strongman who will hold power through force for as long as he can until he is replaced with another military officer just like him. The traditional masks of Africa are replaced with personas which reflect the political instability of central Africa, itself caused by the legacy of colonialism and the continued oppressive policies of the West towards Africa. In the 1970s and 1980s, many African nations built up massive international debt through loans from the First World, the International Monetary Fund, and the World Bank (Khapoya, 211). By 1990, two years after Bemba's play, the total international debt of African nations was 260 billion dollars, which, according to Vincent Khapoya, is a "substantial burden, considering the weakness of African economies" (211). The legacy of colonialism is crippled economies, crushing debt, and political instability. Rather than blaming the colonial powers, Bemba's play questions the cyclical nature of African politics and advocates working for the advancement of the nation, rather than a faction or regime or individual. Only by breaking the cycle of power struggles will Amandla be able to escape being torn apart. Melissa/Antigone provides a model of behavior for how the individual citizen might work for justice.

All four adaptations of *Antigone* considered in this chapter use Sophocles's play to explore larger political issues within specific contexts. The primary political issue in all four plays, regardless of specific context, is the need to resist tyranny and oppression and to work for justice. All but *Odale's Choice* are also metatheatrical: plays which demonstrate the power of theatre. Any *Antigone* adaptation will engage the idea of power, but these three adaptations in particular link political power with theatrical power and with the power of the people to resist leaders who are unjust.

All four plays also suggest a connection between the Greek original and the "new" Antigone. Odale, Tegonni, Winston, and Melissa all embody "Antigoneness" in their stand against oppression. They form a special group of those who resist, who do not accept the unacceptable. It is as Osofisan's Antigone remarks: "Anywhere there is tyranny and oppression, there you will always find one Antigone." African Antigones are an enduring sign of the power of the individual citizen against an unjust state. African Antigones, it might be said, are all Amandlan: power is theirs.

CONCLUSION: AFRICAN THEATRE IN A POSTCULTURAL WORLD

At the 1998 Standard Bank National Arts Festival in Grahamstown, South Africa, the University of Witwatersrand presented an adaptation of Euripides' *Hippolytus*, directed by Gina Holloway and Catherine Duncan, two fourth-year drama students. The presentation deconstructed and commented on the original Greek text by adding dance, narration, other pieces of text, presenting scenes out of sequence, and eliminating certain characters and events altogether. The set consisted of four cloth panels on which was written in English the story of Hippolytus and Phaedra and two outer panels with puppet figures of a man and woman on them. Four actors, two men and two women, dressed entirely in black, entered and silently read the panels. They then performed the story.

Any theatre training program in the world could have created this production. There was nothing inherently African about the presentation or performances. Except, at one point, the actress playing Phaedra, Esther Mugambi, who was a person of color, stepped out of the story and remarked to the audience, "Early on in the rehearsal process the directors told us to visualize our characters. I saw her as being tall, willowy, with long blond hair." The action onstage then stopped as the other actors looked at her looking at the audience. It was a very telling moment in an otherwise ordinary student production of a Greek play.

The production was clearly part of a university assignment, training a new generation of South African actors and directors for the challenges of postapartheid theatre. Peter Larlham, in his article "Theatre in Transition:

The Cultural Struggle in South Africa," lists five "definite characteristics of current South African theatre," one of which defines it as "an eclectic intercultural theatre that integrates performance conventions and acting styles from different cultures" (210). The Witwatersrand *Hippolytus* was certainly intercultural, although, arguably, more use could have been made of indigenous performance styles and less use of European dance and realism.

Another of Larlham's characteristics is that the theatre of today's South Africa is one of "playmaking, rather than working from preexisting scripts" (210). Again, *Hippolytus* took the original text and deconstructed it using the actors' own experiences, resulting in a play which both told the story of Hippolytus and Phaedra and commented on that story from a South African point of view.

Finally, Larlham observes that the theatre of South Africa must "record the cultural history of people, [and] that assists in reeducation after the long period of enforced censorship and disinformation" (210). While a production of a Greek tragedy does not inherently "record the cultural history" of South Africa or shed light on the apartheid era in a manner like that of a play by Maishe Maponya or Athol Fugard, it can be used to analyze how South Africans regard European culture and theatre. When the actress playing Phaedra described her character as having blonde hair, she revealed her own moment of discovering her prejudicial thought pattern which South African culture had imprinted upon her. The moment was truly powerful because the African actress exposed her own Eurocentric proclivity — she saw a mythological character as inherently white and blonde, in short, European. This revelation onstage challenged the audience to reexamine how they approached and viewed the original play and their preconceptions about Greek mythology, tragedy, and culture. The actress's identity at that moment consisted of both the African actress and the character that the actress admitted to seeing as being a member of a completely different ethnic group. This action challenged the play, the audience, and the performers to reengage South Africa's Europe-oriented culture from a different, "outsider" standpoint.

University theatre programs can afford to be experimental in a way in which commercial theatre cannot; thus it is not unusual that this production came from a university. *Hippolytus* is a hybrid; it explored a variety of cultural forms and theatrical performance styles. Students of different ethnic and economic backgrounds had worked together to create a piece of theatre based on a classical text. Larlham's characteristics of new South African theatre also apply, as we have seen, to African approaches to productions of classical texts: multicultural, multimedia, multiperformance style, and multiple viewpoints generate not only new plays, but also new ways to interpret, view, and convey the meaning of preexisting texts.

The resulting performances that are now being created not only in South Africa but all across the continent are hybrids of hybrids of hybrids. The transcultural generation of culture never ends: theatre artists continually appropriate and reappropriate from different cultures and transform their borrowings into elements and forms more emblematic of their own culture. As Afrocentric classicism is largely an African-American enterprise, post–Afrocentrism affects not only African writers and theatre artists, but writers and artists in the African diaspora, and even Euro-American and European theatre artists. Meeting as equals, cultures can blend and their elements transculturate in a way impossible in the colonial era. In the exchange of cultures and ideas, African theories of tragedy and theatre will continue to develop in their own right, yet will both influence and be influenced by intellectual developments in the West and, for that matter, the East. The concept of the "Global Village" is not limited to the simple binary of Western, non–Western, but rather represents the acknowledgment of a pluralistic humanity, all culturally equal.

There will be resistance to the blending of cultures, to the cultural borrowing which is called for by it, and even to the mutually appreciative coexistence of cultures from all sides of the cultural debate, as observed in the first chapter, in which various groups try to either appropriate, claim, devalue, or ignore the classical canon. Sue Ellen Case and Janelle Reinelt, reporting at a 1990 conference in San Diego on the subject of "The Classics in the Contemporary Theatre," note that two University of California at San Diego professors of color "spoke up about their disinterest in the classics in light of the pressing need to foster and produce new writings based in the lived experiences of ethnic communities" (xvii–xviii). While it is certainly true that new writing based on the lived experience of all communities needs to be fostered, supported, and developed, this fact in no way invalidates the classics as both important texts which speak to the audiences and readers and as raw material for adaptation by contemporary playwrights and theatre artists to connect the lived experiences of present day communities with the lived experiences of historical communities. It is not hard to argue that *The Island* or *Edufa* speaks more readily to and generates more meaning and resonance with its original audience than a straightforward production of a Greek play would to a middle-class, Euro-American audience. Multiculturalism does not exclude the classics simply because of their age or European origin. Instead, the temple doors are flung wide open so that there is room for all texts, experiences, and voices.

In *Yoruba Drama in English*, J.B. Alston states that the "primary aim of this [his] study is demystification and the eventual production of the plays..." (24). His goal as a scholar examining African plays is not only to uncover meaning or share his research, but also to connect the plays both to the reader and to those who might ultimately mount productions of these plays. The raison d'être for drama, one might argue, is performance: plays exist to be performed. I share Alston's belief and see production as another form of research as well, a way of studying the play from within, so to speak. Many of the plays in this volume have been mounted several times in different places. The plays of Soyinka and Fugard are mounted regularly in Europe, Africa, and America by professional, academic, and community theatres. Many of the other plays in this survey are produced much less, but have unique performance histories. Femi Osofisan's play, for example, as of this writing, has never been produced in Nigeria, but was originally mounted at Emory University in the United States. *The Song of Jacob Zulu* ran on Broadway, but only a few hundred saw Fugard's *Orestes*. Production and performance, both as tools of research and as tools by which cultural borders may be crossed so that understanding between peoples and cultures may occur, should thus be encouraged and engaged. All of the plays surveyed in this study would and should be welcome additions to the professional and academic canons, not just in Africa abut around the world. Let production thrive!

The current popular term to describe the state of the world, as mentioned above, is "the global village"; that is, the world is shrinking due to technology, and the ease and inexpense of communication across the continents indicates that the cultures of the world will become increasingly intercultural. We are now in an age of "postculturalism," claims Christopher Clausen, in which "culture" is both consciously and subconsciously invented, constructed, appropriated, and equated with race and ethnic origin: "Many black Americans exaggerate and sentimentalize their connection to a homeland across the sea — Kwanzaa, after all, was invented in Los Angeles — but Italian Americans and Irish Americans do exactly the same thing" (4). Our "culture" becomes, rightly or wrongly, whatever we deem it to be. As Clausen's statement demonstrates, there is feedback in the loop: what is supposed to be an African celebration was invented in America. Conversely, travel anywhere in Africa and you will meet individuals wearing Italian suits, or drinking Coke and Pepsi, wearing Nike, or watching American and European films and television shows while sporting baseball caps, enjoying Chinese food or pizza.

The cultural borders are notoriously difficult to patrol, and cultures cannot always control what is appropriated from them and what they appropriate. No one can guarantee authenticity of culture or the material of culture. Like tourists in a foreign marketplace, the appropriators of culture are not certain if they are acquiring a genuine artifact or something else. Nor is there any guarantee that the appropriator will then use those parts of culture in the manner in which they are used in the originating culture.

Interestingly, this phenomenon makes little difference in the end for two reasons. First, the item, once safely ensconced back in the home culture, becomes authentic anyway, simply by virtue of having come from somewhere else, regardless of actual origin. Intercultural theatre may be the equivalent of souvenirs of New York City made in China and purchased by tourists from Taiwan. The second reason is that the appropriated culture becomes so quickly assimilated that it is identified more with the appropriating culture than with the originating culture. For example, pasta is inherently Italian, although noodles came to Italy by way of China. No one would call spaghetti or vermicelli Chinese by virtue of the fact that noodles were assimilated and transformed by Italian culture. These two possibilities are the inevitable consequences of transculturalism — either way cultural authenticity is continually established and maintained, regardless of origins.

African theatre (and by extension, all theatre) is therefore moving into a postcultural, post–Afrocentric, and postmodern realm in which all culture is not only acknowledged as hybrid, but is also "up for grabs" by any artist, author, actor, or playwright who wishes to appropriate ideas and techniques and texts and transculturate them into his or her own culture. To do so is to break down artificial barriers and boundaries between cultures and societies and to acknowledge all history and culture as one's heritage. African adaptations of Greek tragedy provide a model for not only African theatre artists, but also for the world.

> *Humani nihil alienum.*
> (Nothing human is alien to me.)
> — Terence

> Humanity is my tribe.
> — Ola Rotimi

BIBLIOGRAPHY

Abah, Oga S. "Perspectives in Popular Theatre: Orality as a Definition of New Realities." Breitinger 79–100.

Abiola, Hafsat. "A Daughter's Demands." *Newsweek* June 22, 1998: 40.

Accone, Darryl. "Reible Faithful to Butler's Tale of Revenge." *Star Tonight* July 30, 1990: 5.

Ackerman, Robert. *The Myth and Ritual School.* New York: Garland, 1991.

Adejumo, Debo. "Myth and Drama: Modern Adaptations of Classical Tragedies." *Critical Theory and African Literature.* Eds. R. Vanamali, E. Oko, and A. Iloeje. Ibadan: Heinemann, 1987: 55–68.

Alston, J.B. *Yoruba Drama in English.* Lewiston: Edward Mellen, 1989.

Amankulor, James Ndukaku. "The Concept and Practice of the Traditional African Festival Theatre." Diss. U California Los Angeles, 1977.

Angmor, Charles. "Drama in Ghana." Ogunba and Irele 55–72.

Apollodorus. *Gods and Heroes of the Greeks: The Library of Apollodorus.* Ed. Trans. Michael Simpson. Amherst: U Massachusettes P, 1976.

Aristotle. *Poetics.* Tr. Kenneth Telford. Chicago: H. Regnery, 1961.

Armstrong, Robert Plant. "Tragedy: Greek and Yoruba: A Cross Cultural Perspective." *Research in African Literatures* 7.1 (1976): 23–43.

Ashcroft, Bill, Gareth Griffiths and Helen Tiffin. *The Empire Writes Back.* London: Routledge, 1989.

Baldry, H.C. *Ancient Greek Literature in Its Living Context.* New York: McGraw Hill, 1968.

Bamikunle, Aderemi. "Nigerian Playwrights and Nigerian Myths: A Look at Soyinka's, Osofisan's and Sowunde's Plays." *Critical Theory and African Literature.* Eds. R. Vanamali, E. Oko, A. Iloeje. Ibadan: Heinemann, 1987: 126–131.

Banham, Martin. "Nigerian Dramatists." *Journal of Commonwealth Literature* 7 (1969): 132–6.

_____. "Ola Rotimi: 'Humanity as My Tribesmen.'" *Modern Drama* 33.1 (1990): 67–81.

Banham, Martin, and Clive Wake. *African Theatre Today.* New York: Pitman, 1976.

Banham, Martin, Errol Hill, and George Woodyard, eds. *The Cambridge Guide to African and Carribean Theatre*. Cambridge: Cambridge UP, 1992.

Barnes, Sandra T., ed. *Africa's Ogun: Old World and New*. 2nd ed. Bloomington: Indiana UP, 1997.

_____. "The Many Faces of Ogun." Barnes, *Africa's* 1–26.

Bartholet, Jeffrey. "The Plague Years." *Newsweek* January 17, 2000: 32–37.

Bearsley, Grace. *The Negro in Greek and Roman Civilization*. New York: Russell and Russell, 1967.

Beik, Janet. *Hausa Theatre in Niger*. New York: Garland, 1987.

Bell, Robert E. *Women of Classical Mythology*. Oxford: Oxford UP, 1991.

Bemba, Sylvain. *Black Wedding Candles for Blessed Antigone*. Trans. Townsend Brewster. *Theatre and Politics*. New York: Ubu Repertory, 1990.

Bernal, Martin. *Black Athena: Volume I: The Fabrication of Ancient Greece 1785–1985*. London: Free Association, 1987.

_____. *Black Athena: Volume II: The Archeological and Documentary Evidence*. New Brunswick: Rutgers UP, 1991.

Bhabha, Homi. "The Other Question: Difference, Discrimination, and the Discourse of Colonialism." *Literature, Politics and Theory*. Eds. Francis Barker, Peter Hulme, Margaret Iversen, and Diana Loxley. New York: Methuen, 1986. 148–172.

The Bhagavad Gita. Trans. Barbara Stoler Miller. New York: Bantam Books, 1986.

Bishop, Norma. "A Nigerian Version of a Greek Classic: Soyinka's Transformation of *The Bacchae*." Gibbs and Lindfors 115–126.

Boas, George. "The Evolution of the Tragic Hero." *Carleton Drama Review* (1955–6): 5–21. Rpt in *Tragedy: Vision and Form*. Ed. Robert W. Corrigan. San Francisco: Chandler, 1965: 143–154.

Boehmer, Elleke. *Colonial and Postcolonial Literature*. New York: Oxford UP, 1995.

Bohannon, Paul. "Patterns or Murder and Suicide." *African Homicide and Suicide*. Ed. Paul Bohannon. Princeton: Princeton UP, 1960: 230–266.

Brathwaite, Edward Kamau. *Odale's Choice*. London: Evans Brothers, 1983.

Breitinger, Eckhard, ed. *Theatre and Performance in Africa*. Bayreuth: Bayreuth African Studies, 1994.

Brenner, Leslie. "Playing Jacob Zulu's Song." *New York Magazine* April 12, 1993: 26.

Breytenbach, Willem. "Life's No Beach on *The Island*." *Cue* 3 July 1998: 9.

Brockett, Oscar. *History of the Theatre*. 7th ed. Boston: Allyn and Bacon, 1995.

Burkert, Walter. *Greek Religion*. Trans. John Raffan. Cambridge: Basil Blackwell, 1985.

_____. *Homo Necans: The Anthropology of Ancient Greek Sacrificial Ritual and Myth*. Trans. Peter Bing. Berkeley: California UP, 1983.

Butler, Guy. *Demea*. Capetown: David Philip, 1990.

Cartledge, Paul. "Classical Studies." *Encyclopedia of Social and Cultural Anthropology*. Eds. Alan Barnard and Jonathan Spencer. New York: Routledge, 1996. 100–102.

Case, Sue-Ellen, and Janelle Reinelt, eds. *The Performance of Power: Theatrical Discourse and Politics*. Iowa City: U Iowa P, 1991.

Clark, J.P. *The Example of Shakespeare*. Evanston: Northwestern UP, 1970.

_____. *Three Plays*. Oxford: Oxford UP, 1964.

Clark-Bekederemo, J.P. *Collected Plays and Poems 1958–1988*. Washington: Howard University Press, 1991.

Clausen, Christopher. "Welcome to Postculturalism." *The Key Reporter* 62.1 (1996): 1–6.

Clifford-Vaughn, F.M. "Terrorism and Insurgency in South Africa." Crenshaw 253–270.

Coker, Adeniyi, Jr. "The Context and Development of Ola Rotimi at the Ori Olokun Theatre." *Journal of Black Studies* 23.1 (1992): 60–74.

Conradie, P.J. "Debates Surrounding an Approach to African Tragedy." *South African Theatre Journal* 10.1 (1996): 25–34.

Conteh-Morgan, John. *Theatre and Drama in Francophone Africa.* Cambridge: Cambridge UP, 1994.

Coplan, David. "A Terrible Commitment: Balancing the Tribes in South African National Culture." *Perilous States.* Ed. George E. Marcus. Chicago: U Chicago P, 1993. 305–358.

Cosentino, Donald J. "Repossession: Ogun in Folklore and Literature." Barnes, *Africa's* 290–314.

Crenshaw, Martha, ed. *Terrorism in Africa.* New York: G.K. Hall, 1994.

Crow, Brian, and Chris Banfield. *An Introduction to Post-Colonial Theatre.* Cambridge: Cambridge UP, 1996.

Dahl, Mary Karen. *Political Violence in Drama: Classical Models, Contemporary Variations.* Ann Arbor: U Michigan P, 1987.

Dallmayr, Fred. "Modes of Cross-Cultural Encounter." *Cross-Cultural Conversation.* Ed. Anindita Niyogi Balslev. Atlanta: Scholar's Press, 1996. 211–236.

Davidson, Basil. *The African Genius.* Boston: Little, Brown, 1969.

_____. *Modern Africa.* 3rd ed. New York: Longman, 1994.

Dei-Anang, Michael. "My Africa." *Poems from Black Africa.* Ed. Langston Hughes. Bloomington: U Indiana P, 1963: 74.

DeKock, Leon. "Players battle valiantly with Butlerism and red sand." *Vry Dag!* 3 August 1990: 20.

Diop, Cheikh Anta. *Civilization and Barbarism.* Trans. Yaa Lengi Meema Ngemi. Eds. Harold J. Salemson and Marjolijn de Jager. New York: Lawrence Hill, 1991.

Doughery, Carol. *The Poetics of Colonization.* Oxford: Oxford UP, 1993.

Dowden, Ken. *The Uses of Greek Mythology.* New York: Routledge, 1992.

Drewal, Margaret Thompson. *Yoruba Ritual: Performers, Play, Agency.* Bloomington: Indiana UP, 1992.

DuBois, Page. *Centaurs and Amazons.* Ann Arbor: U Michigan P, 1982.

DuBois, W.E.B. *The Souls of Black Folk.* New York: The Modern Library, 1996.

Dunton, Chris. *Make Man Talk True: Nigerian Drama in English Since 1970.* London: Hans Zell, 1992.

Durant, Will. *The Life of Greece.* New York: Simon and Schuster, 1966.

Elahi, Nushin. "An African Magic." *The Citizen* 1 August 1990: 19.

Eliade, Mircea, ed. *The Encyclopedia of Religion.* 16 vols. New York: Macmillan, 1987.

Erlmann, Veit. *Nightsong: Performance, Power, and Practice in South Africa.* Chicago: Chicago UP, 1996.

Etherton, Michael. *The Development of African Drama.* New York: Africana Publishing, 1982.

Euben, J. Peter, ed. *Greek Tragedy and Political Theory.* Berkeley: U California P, 1986.

Fanon, Frantz. *The Wretched of the Earth.* Trans. Constance Farrington. New York: Grove, 1963.

Finnegan, Ruth H. *Oral Literature in Africa*. London: Clarendon, 1970.

Fortes, Meyer. *Oedipus and Job in West African Religion*. Cambridge: Cambridge UP, 1983.

Fortier, Mark. *Theory/Theatre: An Introduction*. New York: Routledge, 1997.

Foster, Deborah D. *Blood Knot and the Island as Anti-Tragedy*. Madison: African Studies, 1977.

Frazer, James George. *The Golden Bough: A Study of Magic and Religion*. Ed. Robert Fraser. Oxford: Oxford UP, 1994.

Fredrickson, George M. *Black Liberation: A Comparative History of Black Ideologies in the United States and South Africa*. New York: Oxford UP, 1995.

Fuchs, Anne. *Playing the Market: The Market Theatre Johannesburg 1976–1986*. New York: Harwood, 1990.

Fugard, Athol. *Notebooks 1960—1977*. New York: TCG, 1983.

_____. "*Orestes* Reconstructed: A Letter to an American Friend." *Theatre Quarterly* 8.32 (1979): 3–6.

Fugard, Athol, John Kani and Winston Ntshona. *Statements: Three Plays*. Oxford: Oxford UP, 1974.

Gannon, Martin J., et al. *Understanding Global Cultures*. Thousand Oaks: Sage, 1994.

Garland, Robert. *Introducing New Gods: The Politics of Athenian Religion*. Ithica: Cornell UP, 1994.

Garrett, Laurie. *The Coming Plague*. New York: Penguin, 1994.

Gaster, Theodor H. *Thespis: Ritual, Myth and Drama in the Ancient Near East*. New York: Henry Schuman, 1950.

Gibbs, James. "The Masks Hatched Out." Gibbs and Lindfors 51–80.

Gibbs, James, and Bernth Lindfors, eds. *Research on Wole Soyinka*. Trenton: Africa World Press, 1993.

Gilbert, Helen, and Joanne Tompkins. *Post-Colonial Drama*. New York: Routledge 1996.

Girard, René. *Violence and the Sacred*. Trans. Patrick Gregory. Baltimore: Johns Hopkins UP, 1977.

Goldhill, Simon. *Reading Greek Tragedy*. Cambridge: Cambridge UP, 1986.

Götrick, Kacke. "The Actor, the Art of Acting, and Liminality." *Culture in Africa*. Ed. Raoul Granquist. Uppsala: Scandinavian Institute of African Studies, 1993: 145–171.

Graver, David, and Loren Kruger. "South Africa's National Theatre: The Market or the Street." *New Theatre Quarterly* 5.19 (1989): 272–281.

Gray, Stephen. "A Chair Called Agamemnon: Athol Fugard's Use of Greek Dramatic Myths." *Standpunte* 184 39:4 (August 1986): 19–27.

_____, ed. *File on Fugard*. London: Methuen, 1991.

Gregory, Justina. *Euripides and the Instruction of the Athenians*. Ann Arbor: U Michigan P, 1991.

Grene, David, and Richmond Lattimore. *The Complete Greek Tragedies*. 1960. 2nd ed. 9 vols. Chicago: Chicago UP, 1991.

_____ and _____. "Introduction." *Greek Tragedies Volume 2*. Chicago: U Chicago P, 1960.

Gunner, Liz. ed. *Politics and Performance: Theatre, Poetry, and Song in Southern Africa*. Johannesburg: U Witwatersrand P, 1994.

Gurr, Andrew. "Third World Drama: Soyinka and Tragedy." *Critical Perspectives on Wole Soyinka.* Ed. James Gibbs. Washington, D.C.: Three Continents, 1980. 139–146.

Hamliton, Edith. *Mythology.* New York: New American Library, 1940.

Hanno. *The Periplus of Hanno.* Trans. Wilfred H. Schoff. Philadelphia: Commercial Museum, 1912.

Harrison, Jane Ellen. *Themis.* Cambridge, Cambridge UP, 1912.

Havelock, Eric A. *The Literate Revolution in Greece and Its Cultural Consequences.* Princeton: Princeton UP, 1982.

Haygood, Wil. "Nigeria on Trial." *Boston Sunday Globe* April 7, 1996: 1, 18–19.

Henninger, Joseph. "Sacrifice." Trans. Matthew J. O'Connell. Eliade 12: 455– 557.

Herbst, Jeffrey. "Prospects for Revolution in South Africa." Crenshaw 375–396.

Heusch, Luc de. *Sacrifice in Africa.* Trans. Linda O'Brien and Alice Morton. Bloomington: Indiana UP, 1985.

Holland, Heidi. *The Struggle: A History of the African National Congress.* New York: George Braziller, 1989.

Hubert, Henri, and Marcel Mauss. *Sacrifice: Its Nature and Function.* 1898. Trans. W.D. Halls. Chicago: Chicago UP, 1964.

Humphreys, S.C. *The Family, Women, and Death: Comparative Studies.* London: Routledge, 1988.

Ibitokun, Benedict M. *African Drama and the Yoruba World View.* Ibadan: Ibadan UP, 1995.

Irele, Abiola. *The African Experience in Literature and Ideology.* London: Heinemann, 1981.

Jeyifo, Biodun. "Introduction: Wole Soyinka and the Tropes of Disalienation." Soyinka, *Art* viii-xxxii.

_____."The Reinvention of the Theatrical Tradition." *The Intercultural Performance Reader.* Ed. Patrice Pavis. New York: Routledge, 1996.

_____. *The Truthful Lie.* London: New Beacon, 1985.

Johnson, John William. "Yes, Virginia, There Is an Epic in Africa." *Research in African Literatures* 11:3 (1980): 308–326.

Johnson, John William, Thomas A. Hale, and Stephen Belcher, eds. *Oral Epics from Africa.* Bloomington: Indiana UP, 1997.

Jones, Edward L. *Black Zeus: African Mythology and History.* Seattle: Edward L. Jones, 1972.

Jones, Eldred D. "African Literature 1966–1967." *African Forum* 3.1 (1967): 5.

Jones, Joni Lee. "The Development of an African-Based Dramatic Structure." Diss. New York U, 1993.

Kanfer, Stefan. "On Stage: The Trivial, the Traumatic, the Truly Bad." *The New Leader* April 5, 1993: 22–4.

Katrak, Ketu H. *Wole Soyinka and Modern Tragedy.* Westport: Greenwood, 1986.

Kavanagh, Robert, ed. *South African People's Plays.* London: Heineman, 1976.

_____. *Theatre and Cultural Struggle in South Africa.* London: Zed, 1985.

Kennedy, Scott. *In Search of African Theatre.* New York: Charles Scribner's Sons, 1973.

Kerr, David. *African Popular Theatre.* Portsmouth: Heinemann, 1995.

_____. "African Theories of African Theatre." *South African Theatre Journal* 10.1 (1996): 3–23.

Khapoya, Vincent B. *The African Experience: An Introduction.* 2nd ed. Upper Saddle River: Prentice Hall, 1998.

Knox, Bernard M.W. "The *Medea* of Euripides." *Oxford Readings in Greek Tragedy.* Ed. Erich Segal. Oxford: Oxford UP, 1983: 272–293.

Kroll, Jack. "And in this corner…" *Newsweek* February 10, 1997: 65.

_____. "Sunrise in South Africa." *Newsweek* April 5, 1993: 61.

Kruger, Loren. "'That Fluctuating Movement of National Consciousness': Protest, Publicity, and Post-Colonial Theatre in South Africa." *Imperialism and Theatre.* Ed. J. Ellen Gainor. New York: Routledge, 1995.

Lahr, John. "The Forest and the Trees." *New Yorker* April 12, 1993: 105–7.

Lane, Warren J., and Ann M. Lane. "The Politics of *Antigone.*" Euben 162–182.

Larlham, Peter. *Black Theatre, Dance, and Ritual in South Africa.* Ann Arbor: UMI Research, 1985.

_____. "Theatre in Transition: The Cultural Struggle in South Africa." *TDR* 35.1 (1991): 200–219.

Lefkowitz, Mary R. "Influential Women." *Images of Women in Antiquity.* Eds. A. Cameron and A. Kuhrt. Detroit: Wayne State UP, 1983.

_____. "Introduction." Lefkowitz and Rogers 1–11.

_____. *Not Out of Africa.* New York: New Republic, 1996.

_____. *Women in Greek Myth.* Baltimore: Johns Hopkins Press, 1986.

Lefkowitz, Mary R., and Guy MacLean Rogers, eds. *Black Athena Revisited.* Chapel Hill: U North Carolina P, 1996.

Leis, Philip E. *Enculturation and Socialization in an Ijaw Village.* New York: Holt, Rinehart, and Winston, 1972.

Leshoai, Thasbo. "Modern Twist to a Legendary Theme." *City Press* 22 July 1990: 12.

Lindfors, Bernth, ed. *Dem-Say: Interviews with Eight Nigerian Writers.* Austin: African and Afro-American Studies and Research Center, 1974.

Loraux, Nicole. *Tragic Ways of Killing a Woman.* Trans. Anthony Forster. Cambridge: Harvard UP, 1987.

Mackay, E.A. "Antigone and Orestes in the Works of Athol Fugard." *Theoria* 74 (October 1989): 31–2.

Maja-Pearce, Adewale. *Who's Afraid of Wole Soyinka?* Portsmouth: Heinemann, 1991.

Marriott, Michel. "Brother Against Brother." *Newsweek* May 22, 1995: 47.

Masland, Tom. "An African Big Man in Trouble." *Newsweek* December 15, 1997: 37–39.

Mathabane, Mark. *Kaffir Boy.* New York: Plume 1986.

"Maties update classic comedy in cabaret style." *Cape Argus: Tonight* 23 October 1996, 4.

Mattera, Don. "Xaba Shines in Masterly *Demea.*" *The Daily Mail* 31 July 1990: 8.

Mbiti, John S. *African Religions and Philosophy.* New York: Praeger, 1969.

_____. *Introduction to African Religion.* 2nd ed. Portsmouth: Heinemann, 1991.

McCormick, Joseph B., and Susan Fisher-Hoch. *Level 4: Virus Hunters of the C.D.C.* Atlanta: Turner, 1996.

McDonald, Marianne. *Ancient Sun, Modern Light.* New York: Columbia, 1992.

McMurtry, Mervyn. "'Greeks bearing gifts': Athol Fugard's *Orestes* Project and the Politics of Experience." *Modern Drama* 41 (1998): 105–118.

Mda, Zakes. *When People Play People.* Johannesburg: U Witwatersrand P, 1993.

Meer, Fatima. *The Trial of Andrew Zondo.* Johannesburg: Skotaville, 1987.

Michell, John. "Cruel Epic Remains Relevant." *Business Day* 31 July 1990: 8.

Mikalson, Jon D. *Honor Thy Gods.* Chapel Hill: U North Carolina P, 1991.

Moleko, Danny K. Interview with the author. 6 July 1998.

Mudimbe, V.Y. *The Idea of Africa*. Bloomington: Indiana UP, 1994.

Munk, Erika. "Preface." *Theatre and Politics*. New York: Ubu Repertory, 1990.

Ngugi wa Thiongo. *Decolonizing the Mind*. London: James Currey, 1986.

_____. *Moving the Center: The Struggle for Cultural Freedoms*. London: James Currey, 1993.

_____. *Writers in Politics*. London: Heinemann, 1981.

Njoku, John Eberegbulam. *Traditionalism versus Modernism at Death: Allegorical Tales of Africa*. Lewiston: Edwin Mellen, 1989.

Norval, Morgan. *Inside the ANC: The Evolution of a Terrorist Organization*. Washington: Selous Foundation, 1990.

Ober, Josiah, and Barry Strauss. "Drama, Political Rhetoric and the Discourse of Athenian Democracy." *Nothing to Do with Dionysus?* Eds. John J. Winkler and Froma I. Zeitlin. Princeton: Princeton UP, 1990.

Ogunba, Oyin. "Traditional African Festival Drama." Ogunba and Irele 3–26.

Ogunba, Oyin, and Abiola Irele, eds. *Theatre in Africa*. Ibadan: Ibadan UP, 1978.

Okafor, Chinyere G. "Ola Rotimi: The Man, the Playwright, and the Producer on the NigerianTheatre Scene. *World Literature Today* 64.1 (Winter 1990): 24–29.

Okpewho, Isidore. *The Epic in Africa*. New York: Columbia UP, 1979.

Olaniyan, Tejumola. *Scars of Conquest / Masks of Resistance*. Oxford: Oxford UP, 1995.

Olson, James S. *The Peoples of Africa: An Ethnohistorical Dictionary*. Westport: Greenwood, 1996.

Omodele, Oluremi. "Some African Leaders on Stage." *Madness in Drama*. Ed. James Redmond. New York: Cambridge UP, 1993.

Orkin, Martin. *Drama and the South African State*. Manchester: Manchester UP, 1991.

Osadebay, Chief Dennis. *Africa Sings*. London: Stockwell, 1952.

Osofisan, Femi. Letter to the author. 15 November 1994.

_____. "Ritual and the Revolutionary Ethos." *Okike* 22 (September 1982): 72–81.

_____. "Tegonni." Unpublished manuscript, 1994.

_____. "Tiger on Stage: Wole Soyinka and Nigerian Theatre." Ogunba and Irele 151–175.

Owusu, Martin. *Drama of the Gods: A Study of Seven African Plays*. Roxbury: Omenana, 1983.

Padel, Ruth. *Whom Gods Destroy: Elements of Greek and Tragic Madness*. Princeton: Princeton UP, 1995.

Palmer, Richard H. *Tragedy and Tragic Theory*. Westport: Greenwood, 1992.

Panger, Daniel. *Black Ulysseys*. Athens: Ohio UP, 1982.

Parker, Douglass. "*Lysistrata*: Introduction." *Four Plays by Aristophanes*. New York: Meridian, 1984: 341–347.

Peters, Julie Stone. "Intercultural Performance, Theatre Anthropology, and the Imperialist Critique." *Imperialism and Theatre*. Ed. J. Ellen Gainor. New York: Routledge, 1995.

Pindar. *The Odes of Pindar*. Trans. Richmond Lattimore. Chicago: U Chicago P, 1976.

Priebe, Richard K. *Myth, Realism, and the West African Writer*. Trenton: Africa World Press, 1988.

Quayson, Ato. *Strategic Transformations in Nigerian Writing*. Bloomington: Indiana UP, 1997.

Rabinowitz, Nancy Sorkin. *Anxiety Veiled: Euripides and the Traffic in Women*. Ithaca: Cornell, 1993.

Ramsey, F. Jeffress. *Global Studies: Africa*. 6th ed. Guilford: Brown & Benchmark, 1995.

Rehm, Rush. *Greek Tragic Theatre*. London: Routledge, 1994.

Richards, Sandra L. *Ancient Songs Set Ablaze: The Theatre of Femi Osofisan*. Washington, D.C.: Howard UP, 1996.

_____. "Under the 'Trickster's Sign': Toward a Reading of Ntozake Shange and Femi Osofisan." *Critical Theory and Performance*. Eds. Jannelle Reinelt and Joseph R. Roach. Ann Arbor: U Michigan P, 1992. 65–75.

Rogers, Guy MacLean. "Quo Vadis?" Lefkowitz and Rogers 447–453.

Ronge, Barry. "Exploring Roots of South Africa." *Sunday Times* August 5, 1990: 14.

Rotimi, Ola. *The Gods Are Not to Blame*. Oxford: Oxford UP, 1971.

_____. *Understanding The Gods Are Not to Blame*. Lagos: Kurunmi, 1984.

Said, Edward W. *Culture and Imperialism*. New York: Vintage 1993.

_____. *Orientalism*. New York: Vintage 1979.

Salhi, Kamal, ed. *African Theatre for Development*. Exeter: Intellect, 1998.

Segal, Charles. "*The Bacchae* as Metatragedy." *Directions in Euripidean Criticism*. Ed. Peter Burian. Durham: Duke UP, 1985. 156–174.

_____. *Greek Tragedy: Writing, Truth, and the Representation of the Self*. Chico: Scholar's Poem, 1984.

_____. *Interpreting Greek Tragedy*. Ithaca: Cornell UP, 1986.

Simon, John. "Not Quite Art; Not Quite Shaw." *New York Magazine* April 5, 1995: 84–5.

Simpson, Michael, ed. and trans. *Gods and Heroes of the Greeks: The Library of Apollodorus*. Amherst: U Massachusettes P, 1976.

Smith, Robert. *Kingdoms of the Yoruba*. 3rd ed. Madison: Wisconsin UP, 1988.

Snowden, Frank M., Jr., *Before Color Prejudice: The Ancient View of Blacks*. Cambridge: Harvard UP, 1983.

_____. "Bernal's 'Blacks' and the Afrocentrists." Lefkowitz and Rogers 112–128.

_____. *Blacks in Antiquity: Ethiopians in the Greco-Roman Experience*. Cambridge: Belknap, 1970.

Soyinka, Wole. *Art, Dialogue and Outrage*. Ibadan: New Horn Press, 1988.

_____. *The Bacchae of Euripides*. New York: W.W. Norton, 1973.

_____. *Myth, Literature, and the African World*. Cambridge: Cambridge UP, 1976.

_____. *The Open Sore of a Continent*. Oxford: Oxford UP, 1996.

Starr, Chester G. *A History of the Ancient World*. New York: Oxford UP, 1991.

Steiner, George. *Antigones*. New Haven: Yale UP, 1984.

_____. *The Death of Tragedy*. New York: Knopf, 1961.

Stone, Judy S.J. *Studies in West Indian Literature: Theatre*. London: Macmillan, 1994.

Sutherland, Efua T. *Edufa*. London: Longman, 1967.

Thompkins, Joanne. "'Spectacular Resistance': Metatheatre in Post-Colonial Drama." *Modern Drama* 38 (1995): 42–51.

Thompson, Leonard. *A History of South Africa*. New Haven: Yale UP, 1995.

Torrens, James S. "Review: *The Song of Jacob Zulu*." *America* June 19, 1993: 18.

Turner, Victor. *From Ritual to Theatre*. New York: PAJ, 1982.

———. *The Ritual Process*. New York: Aldine de Gruyter, 1969.

Tutuola, Amos. *The Palm Wine Drinkard*. Westport: Greenwood, 1970.

Tyrrell, William Blake, and Frieda S. Brown. *Athenian Myths and Institutions*. New York: Oxford UP, 1991.

Ukpokodu, I. Peter. *Socio-Political Theatre in Nigeria*. San Francisco: Mellen Research UP, 1992.

Utudjian, Eliane Saint-Andre. "Ghana and Nigeria." *Post-Colonial English Drama*. Ed. Bruce King. New York: St. Martin's, 1992: 186–199.

Vandenbroucke, Russell. *Truths the Hands Can Touch*. New York: TCG, 1985.

Vernant, Jean-Pierre. "Ambiguity and Reversal: On the Enigmatic Structure of *Oedipus Rex*." *Myth and Tragedy in Ancient Greece* Jean-Pierre Vernant and Pierre Vidal-Naquet. Trans. Janet Lloyd. New York: Zone Books, 1988: 113–140.

Walcot, Peter. *Greek Drama in Its Theatrical and Social Context*. Cardiff: U Wales P, 1976.

Walder, Dennis. *Athol Fugard*. New York: Grove, 1985.

Walton, J. Michael. *The Greek Sense of Theatre*. London: Methuen, 1984.

———. *Living Greek Theatre*. Westport: Greenwood, 1987.

Weber, Carl. "AC/TC: Currents of Theatrical Exchange." *Interculturalism and Performance*. Eds. Bonnie Marranca and Gautam Dasgupta. New York: PAJ, 1991: 27–37.

Wertheim, Albert. "Euripides in South Africa: *Medea* and *Demea*." *Comparative Drama* 29 (1995): 334–347.

———. "Political Acting and Political Action: Athol Fugard's *The Island*." *World Literature Written in English* 26 (1986): 245–252.

———. "The 1995 Grahamstown Festival." *South African Theatre Journal* 10:1 (1996): 94–100.

White, Jack E. "When Blacks Persecute Blacks." *Time* August 7, 1995: 39.

Williams, Raymond. *Modern Tragedy*. London: Chatto and Windus, 1969.

Willoughby, Guy. "One to Avoid." *Financial Mail* 10 August 1990: 74.

Winkler, Elizabeth Hale. "Three Recent Versions of *The Bacchae*." *Madness in Drama*. Ed. James Redmond. New York: Cambridge UP, 1993: 217–228.

Winkler, John J. "The Ephebos' Song: *Tragoidia* and *Polis*." *Nothing to Do with Dionysus?* Eds. John J. Winkler and Froma I. Zeitlin. Princeton: Princeton UP, 1990.

Wright, Derek. *Wole Soyinka Revisited*. New York: Twayne, 1993.

Wylie, Hal. "The Dancing Masks of Sylvain Bemba." *World Literature Today* 64.1 (1990): 20–24.

Yourgrau, Tug. *The Song of Jacob Zulu*. New York: Arcade, 1993.

Zuesse, Evan M. "Ritual." Eliade 12: 405–422.

INDEX

229